Team

Coach

Season

Personal Coaching Goals

Goal 1

Action Steps	Motivation for Goal
1.	
2.	
3.	
4.	
5.	

Goal 2

Action Steps	Motivation for Goal
1.	
2.	
3.	
4.	
5.	

Goal 3

Action Steps	Motivation for Goal
1.	
2.	
3.	
4.	
5.	

Team Goals

Goal 1	
Action Steps	**Motivation for Goal**
1.	
2.	
3.	
4.	
5.	

Goal 2	
Action Steps	**Motivation for Goal**
1.	
2.	
3.	
4.	
5.	

Goal 3	
Action Steps	**Motivation for Goal**
1.	
2.	
3.	
4.	
5.	

Date: Time Next Game/Opponent: Next Practice:

Target of the Day	Offensive Emphasis	Defensive Emphasis	Teams

Time Min	Drill/Activity	Focus/Emphasis

Notes/Reminders

Player Connections
Who are you connecting with 1-on-1? How?

1.

2.

3.

Player/Coach Challenges
Which players/coaches have challenges on/off the court that you can support and encourage?

1.

2.

3.

4 | Practice Plans

Practice Plans | 5

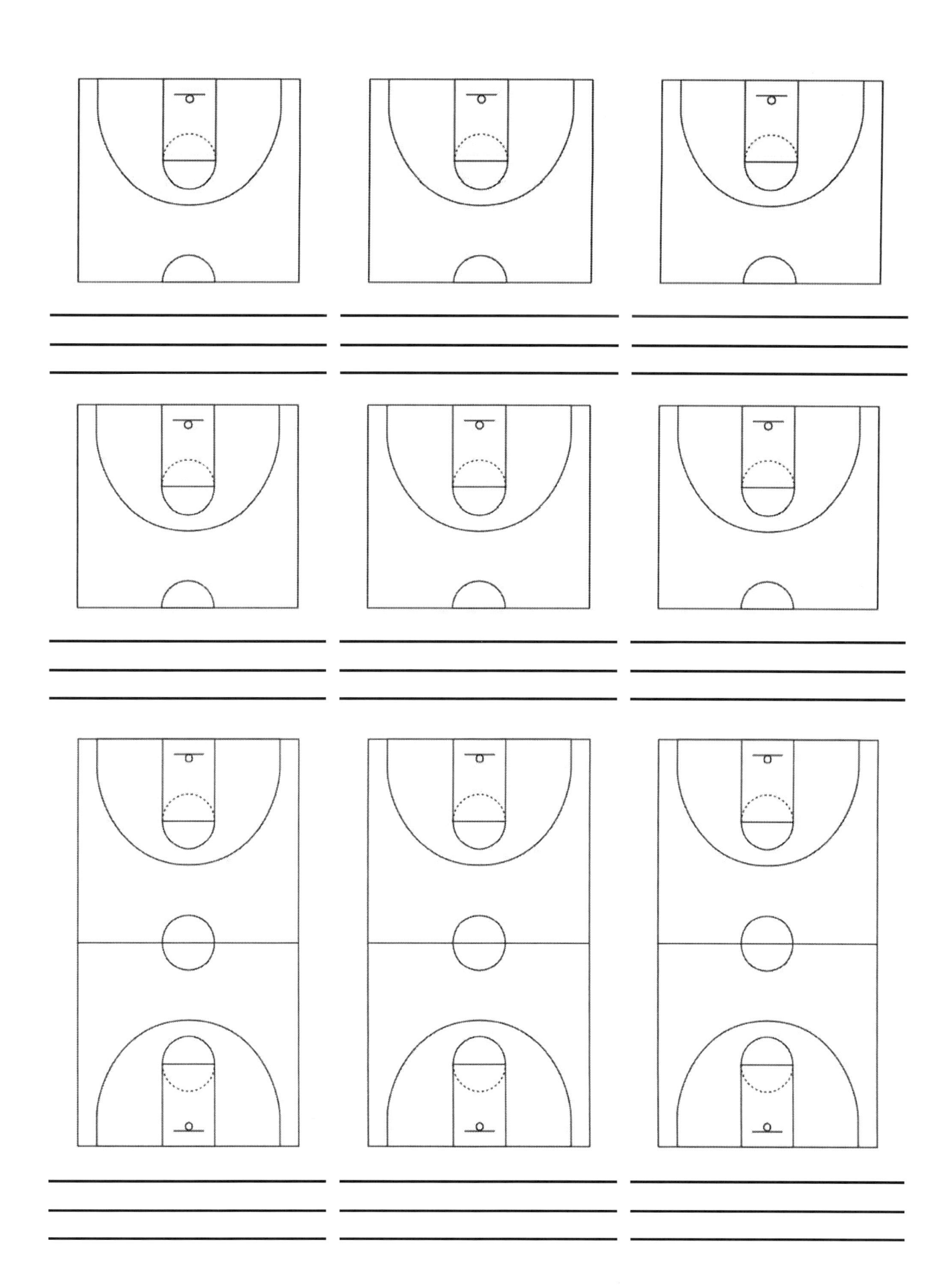

Date: Time   Next Game/Opponent: Next Practice:

Target of the Day	Offensive Emphasis	Defensive Emphasis	Teams

Time Min	Drill/Activity	Focus/Emphasis

Notes/Reminders

Player Connections
Who are you connecting with 1-on-1? How?

1.

2.

3.

Player/Coach Challenges
Which players/coaches have challenges on/off the court that you can support and encourage?

1.

2.

3.

6 | Practice Plans

Practice Plans | 7

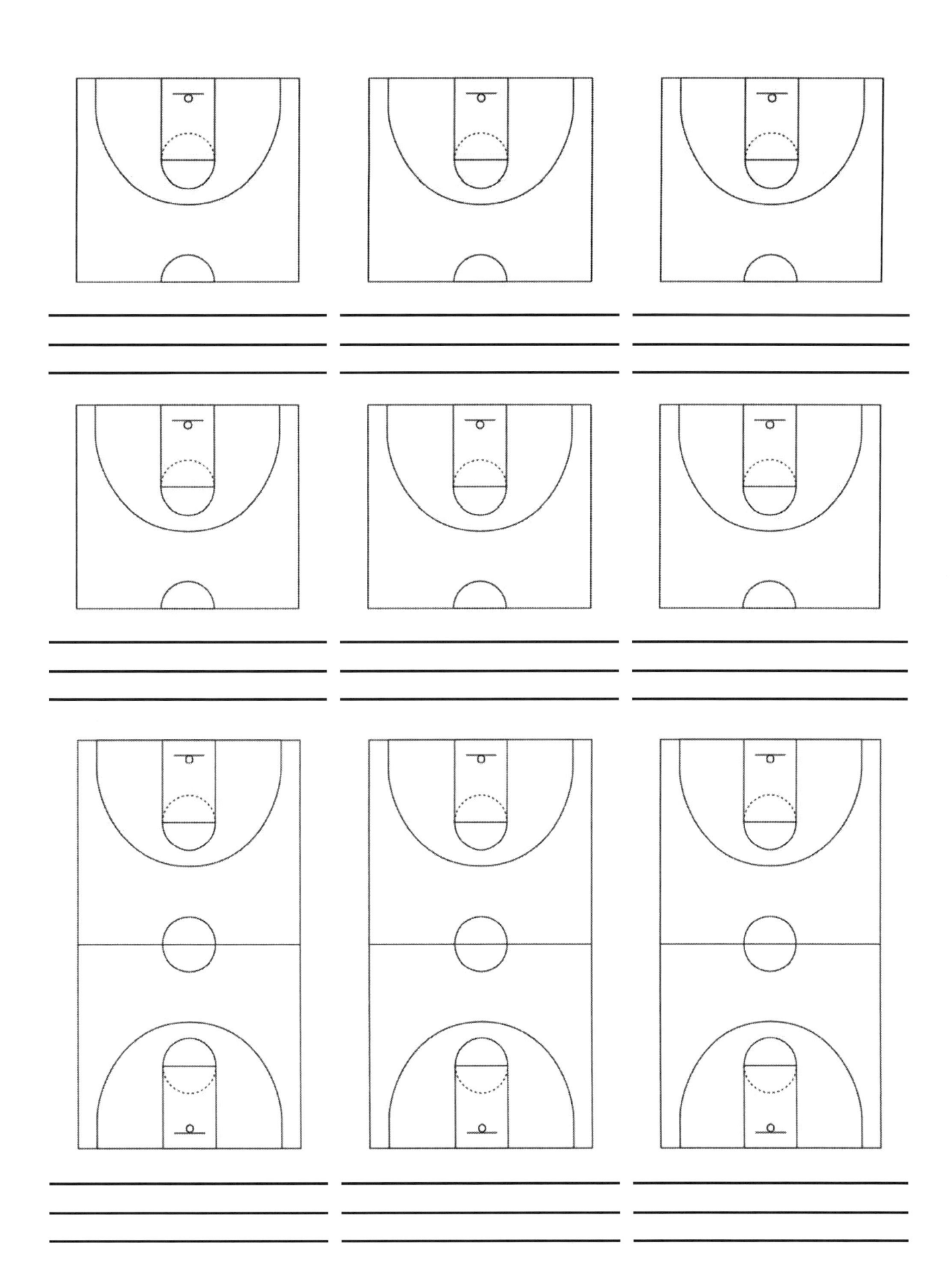

Date:　　　　　Time　　　　　Next Game/Opponent:　　　　　　　　　Next Practice:

Target of the Day	Offensive Emphasis	Defensive Emphasis	Teams

Time Min	Drill/Activity	Focus/Emphasis

Notes/Reminders

Player Connections
Who are you connecting with 1-on-1? How?

1.

2.

3.

Player/Coach Challenges
Which players/coaches have challenges on/off the court that you can support and encourage?

1.

2.

3.

8 | Practice Plans

Practice Plans | 9

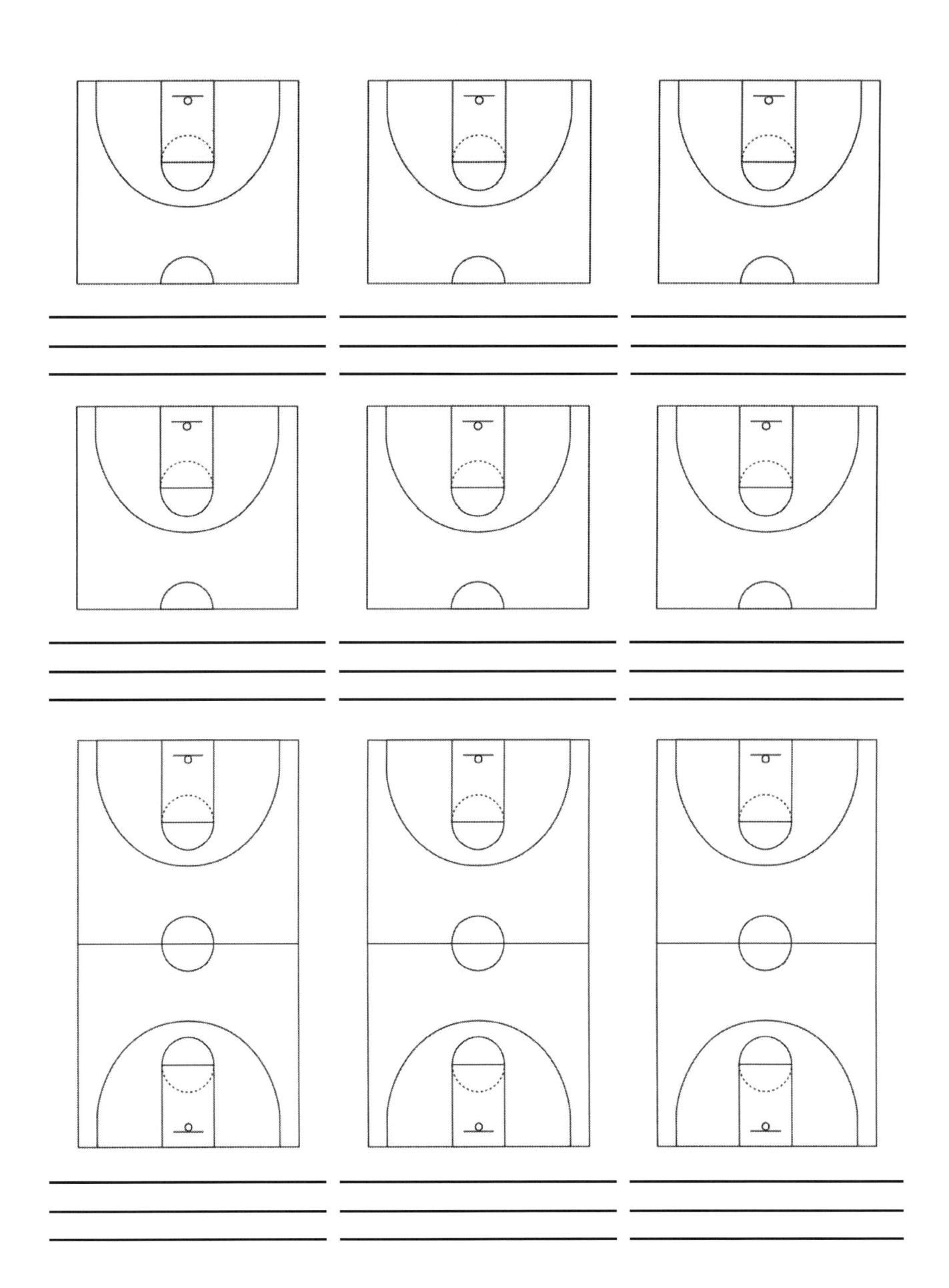

Date:　　　　　Time　　　　　Next Game/Opponent:　　　　　Next Practice:

Target of the Day	Offensive Emphasis	Defensive Emphasis	Teams

Time Min	Drill/Activity	Focus/Emphasis

Notes/Reminders

Player Connections
Who are you connecting with 1-on-1? How?

1.

2.

3.

Player/Coach Challenges
Which players/coaches have challenges on/off the court that you can support and encourage?

1.

2.

3.

10 | Practice Plans

Practice Plans | 11

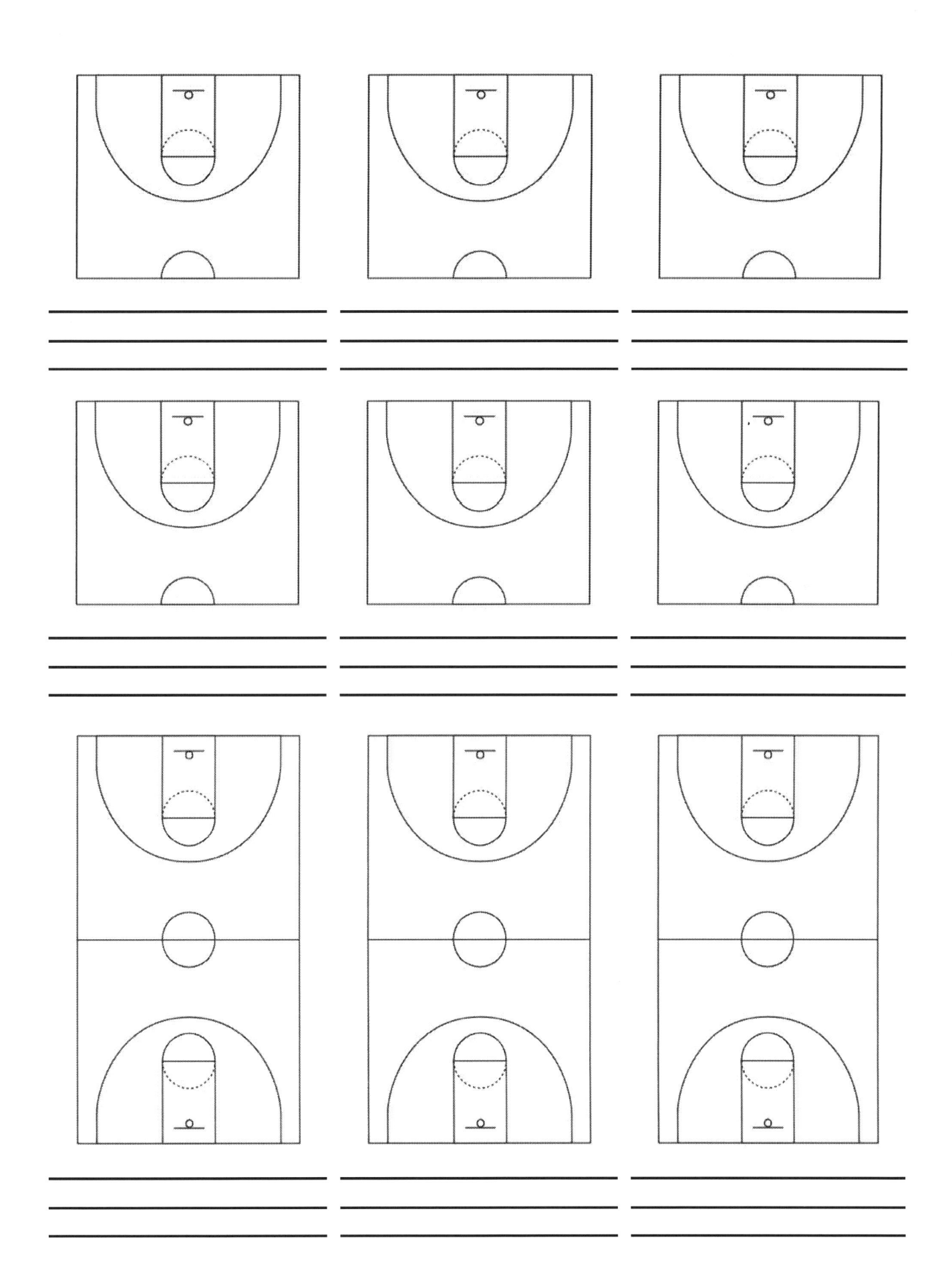

Date: Time   Next Game/Opponent: Next Practice:

Target of the Day	Offensive Emphasis	Defensive Emphasis	Teams

Time Min	Drill/Activity	Focus/Emphasis

Notes/Reminders

Player Connections
Who are you connecting with 1-on-1? How?

1.

2.

3.

Player/Coach Challenges
Which players/coaches have challenges on/off the court that you can support and encourage?

1.

2.

3.

Practice Plans | 13

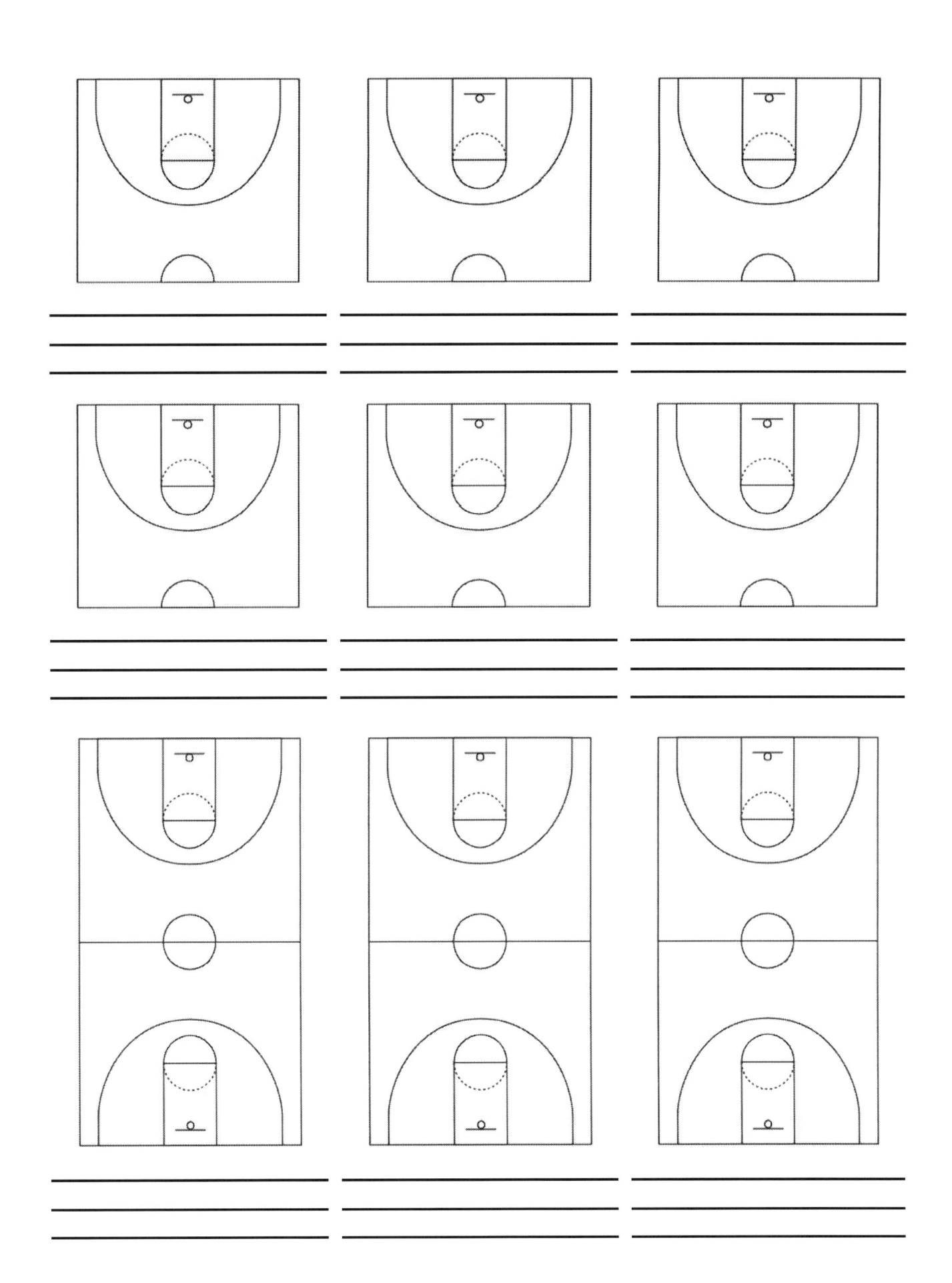

Date: Time: Next Game/Opponent: Next Practice:

Target of the Day	Offensive Emphasis	Defensive Emphasis	Teams

Time Min	Drill/Activity	Focus/Emphasis

Notes/Reminders

Player Connections
Who are you connecting with 1-on-1? How?

1.

2.

3.

Player/Coach Challenges
Which players/coaches have challenges on/off the court that you can support and encourage?

1.

2.

3.

14 | Practice Plans

Practice Plans | 15

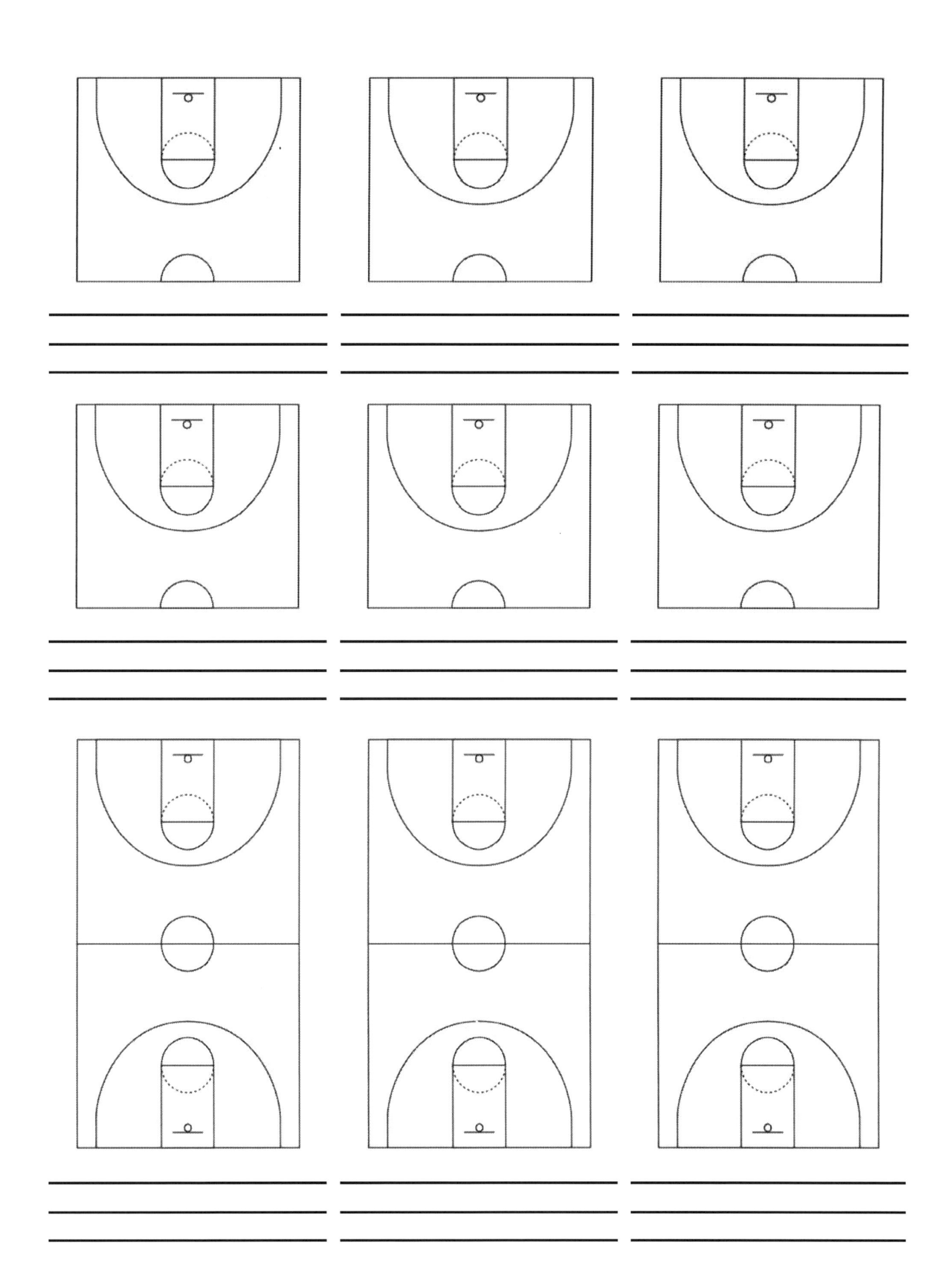

Date: Time   Next Game/Opponent: Next Practice:

Target of the Day	Offensive Emphasis	Defensive Emphasis	Teams

Time Min	Drill/Activity	Focus/Emphasis

Notes/Reminders

Player Connections
Who are you connecting with 1-on-1? How?

1.

2.

3.

Player/Coach Challenges
Which players/coaches have challenges on/off the court that you can support and encourage?

1.

2.

3.

16 | Practice Plans

Practice Plans | 17

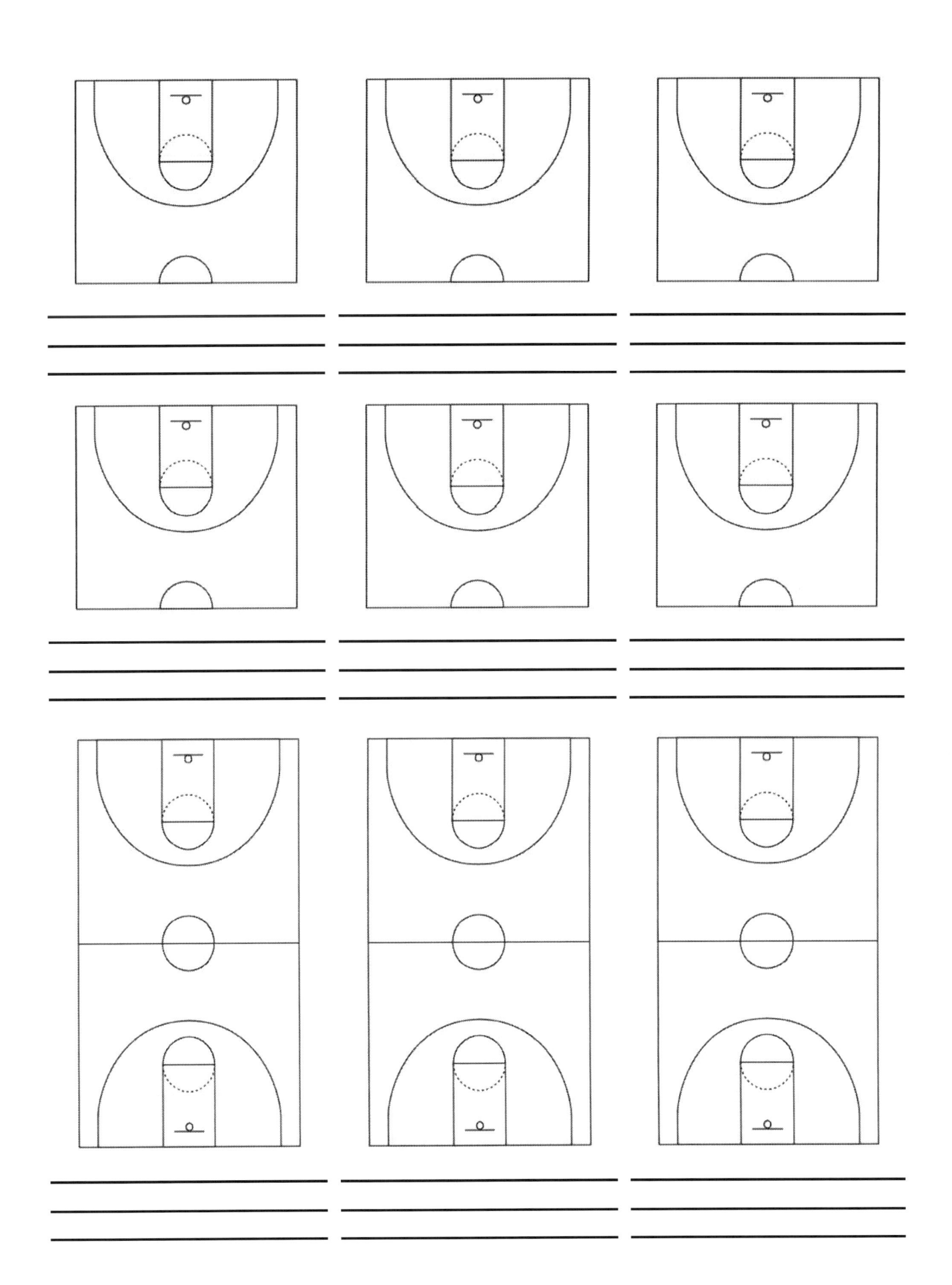

Date:		Time		Next Game/Opponent:		Next Practice:

Target of the Day	Offensive Emphasis	Defensive Emphasis	Teams

Time Min	Drill/Activity	Focus/Emphasis

Notes/Reminders

Player Connections
Who are you connecting with 1-on-1? How?

1.

2.

3.

Player/Coach Challenges
Which players/coaches have challenges on/off the court that you can support and encourage?

1.

2.

3.

Practice Plans | 19

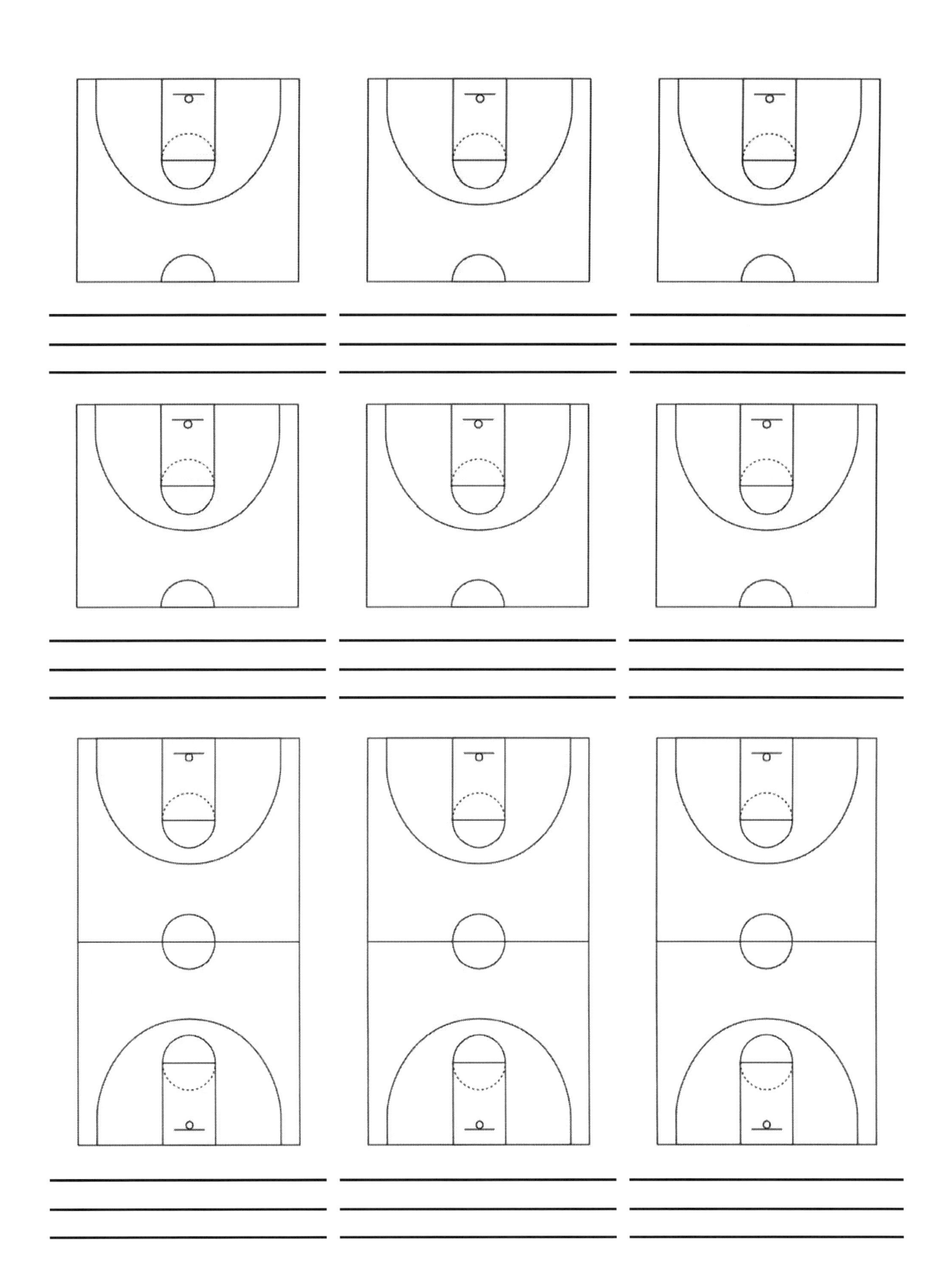

| Date: | Time | Next Game/Opponent: | Next Practice: |

Target of the Day	Offensive Emphasis	Defensive Emphasis	Teams

Time Min	Drill/Activity	Focus/Emphasis

Notes/Reminders

Player Connections
Who are you connecting with 1-on-1? How?

1.

2.

3.

Player/Coach Challenges
Which players/coaches have challenges on/off the court that you can support and encourage?

1.

2.

3.

20 | Practice Plans

Practice Plans | 21

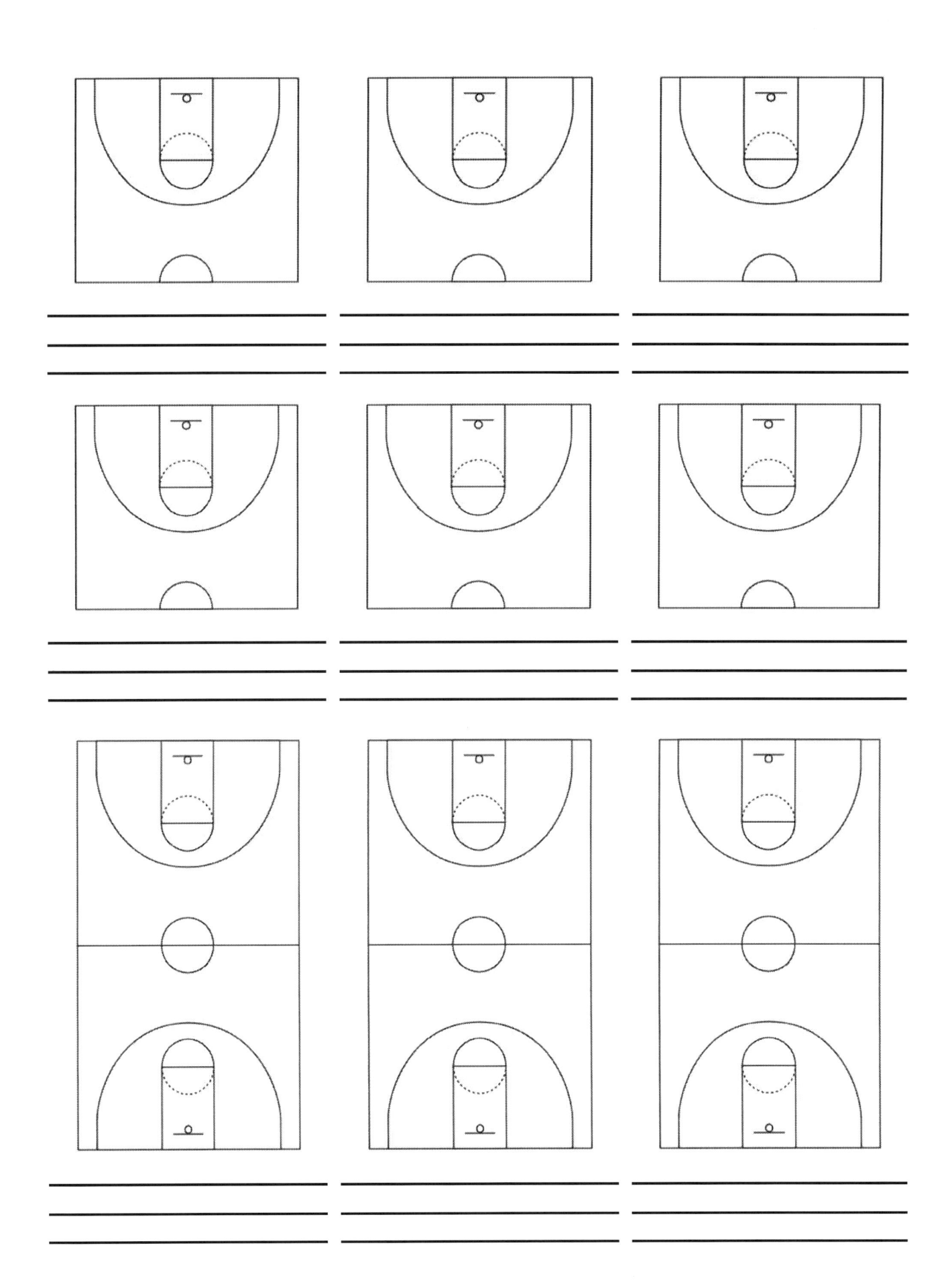

Date: Time   Next Game/Opponent: Next Practice:

Target of the Day	Offensive Emphasis	Defensive Emphasis	Teams

Time Min	Drill/Activity	Focus/Emphasis

Notes/Reminders

Player Connections
Who are you connecting with 1-on-1? How?

1.

2.

3.

Player/Coach Challenges
Which players/coaches have challenges on/off the court that you can support and encourage?

1.

2.

3.

22 | Practice Plans

Practice Plans | 23

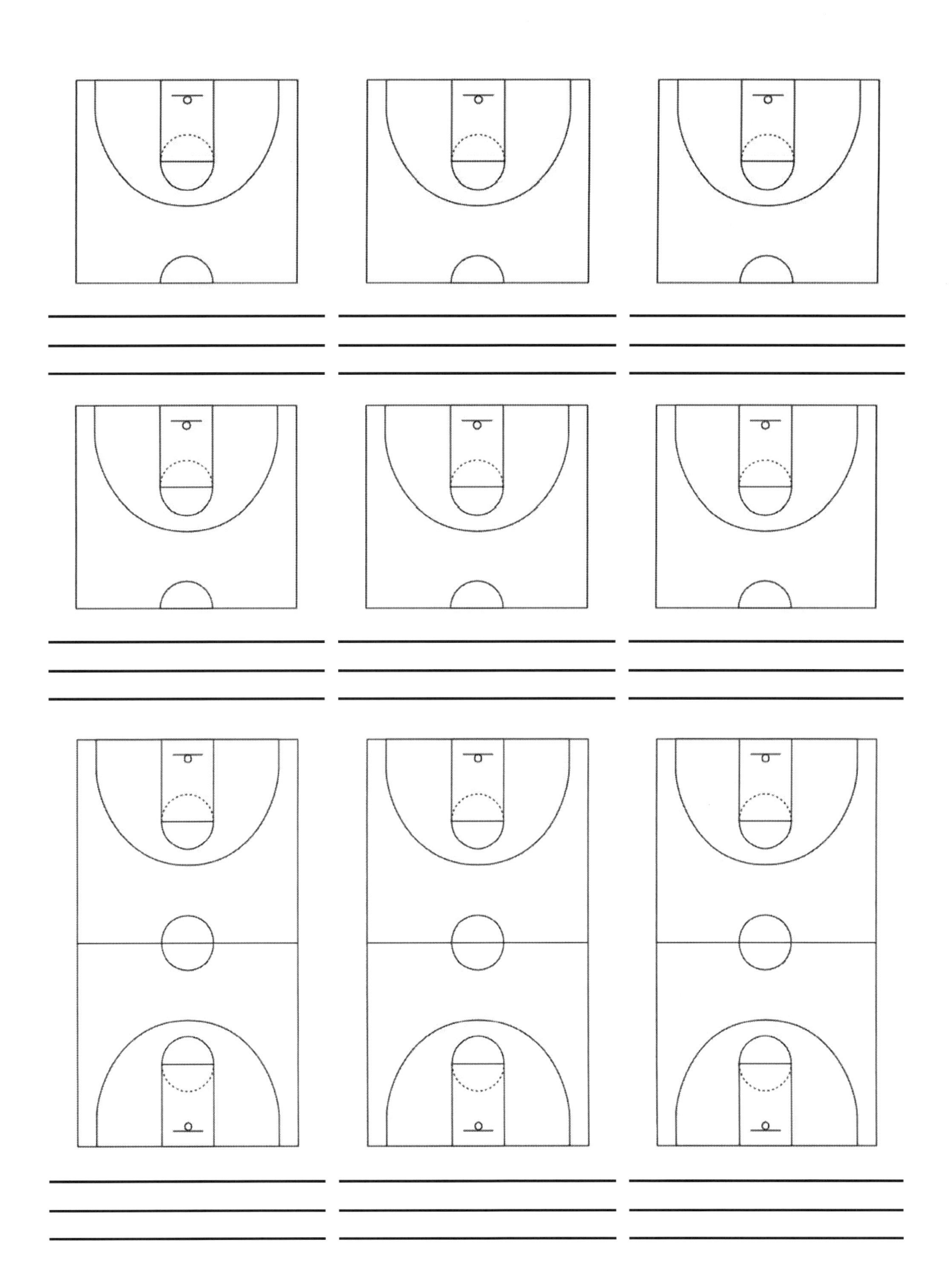

Date: Time   Next Game/Opponent: Next Practice:

Target of the Day	Offensive Emphasis	Defensive Emphasis	Teams

Time Min	Drill/Activity	Focus/Emphasis

Notes/Reminders

Player Connections
Who are you connecting with 1-on-1? How?

1.

2.

3.

Player/Coach Challenges
Which players/coaches have challenges on/off the court that you can support and encourage?

1.

2.

3.

Practice Plans | 25

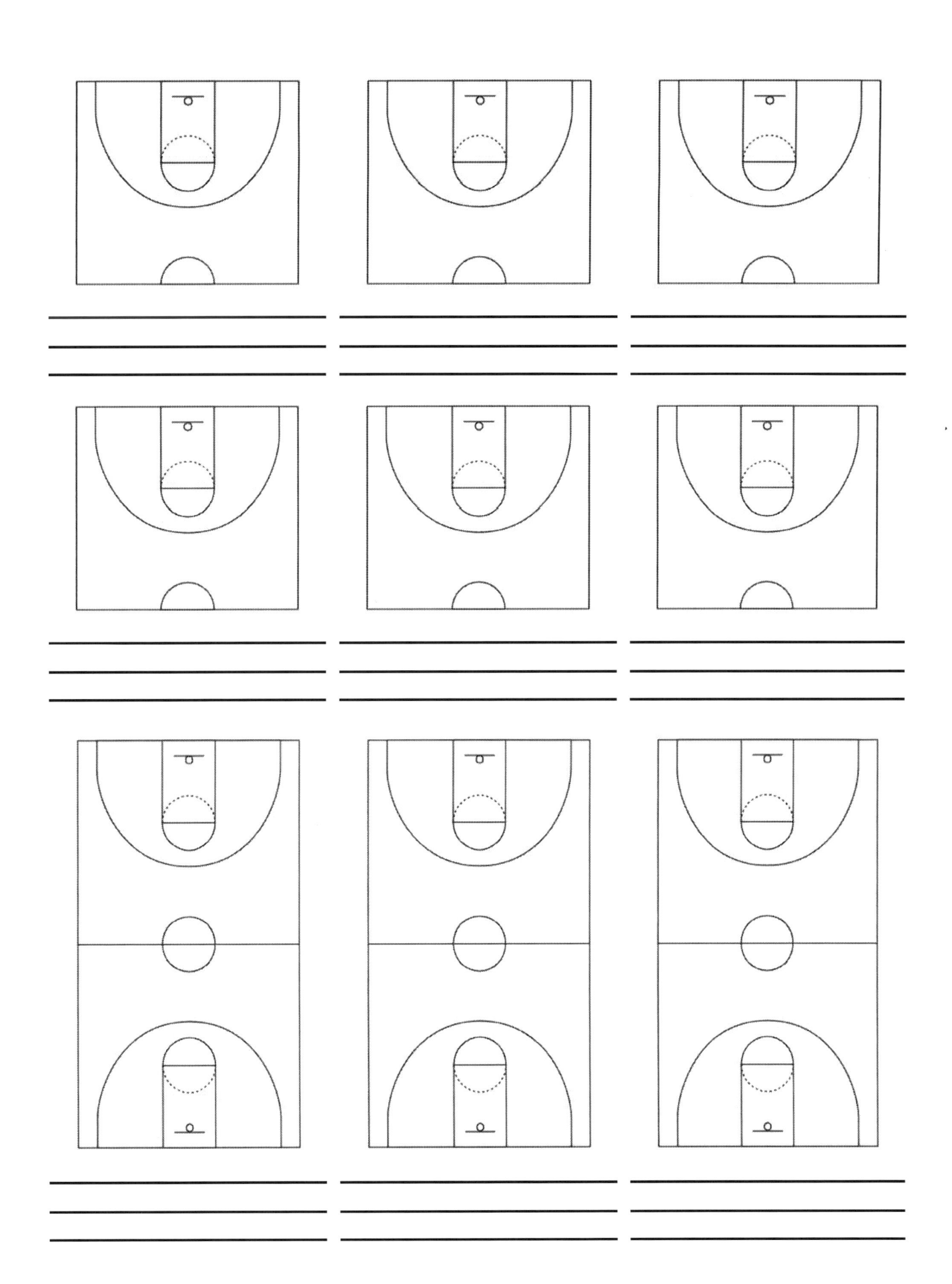

Date: Time   Next Game/Opponent: Next Practice:

Target of the Day	Offensive Emphasis	Defensive Emphasis	Teams

Time Min	Drill/Activity	Focus/Emphasis

Notes/Reminders

Player Connections
Who are you connecting with 1-on-1? How?

1.

2.

3.

Player/Coach Challenges
Which players/coaches have challenges on/off the court that you can support and encourage?

1.

2.

3.

26 | Practice Plans

Practice Plans | 27

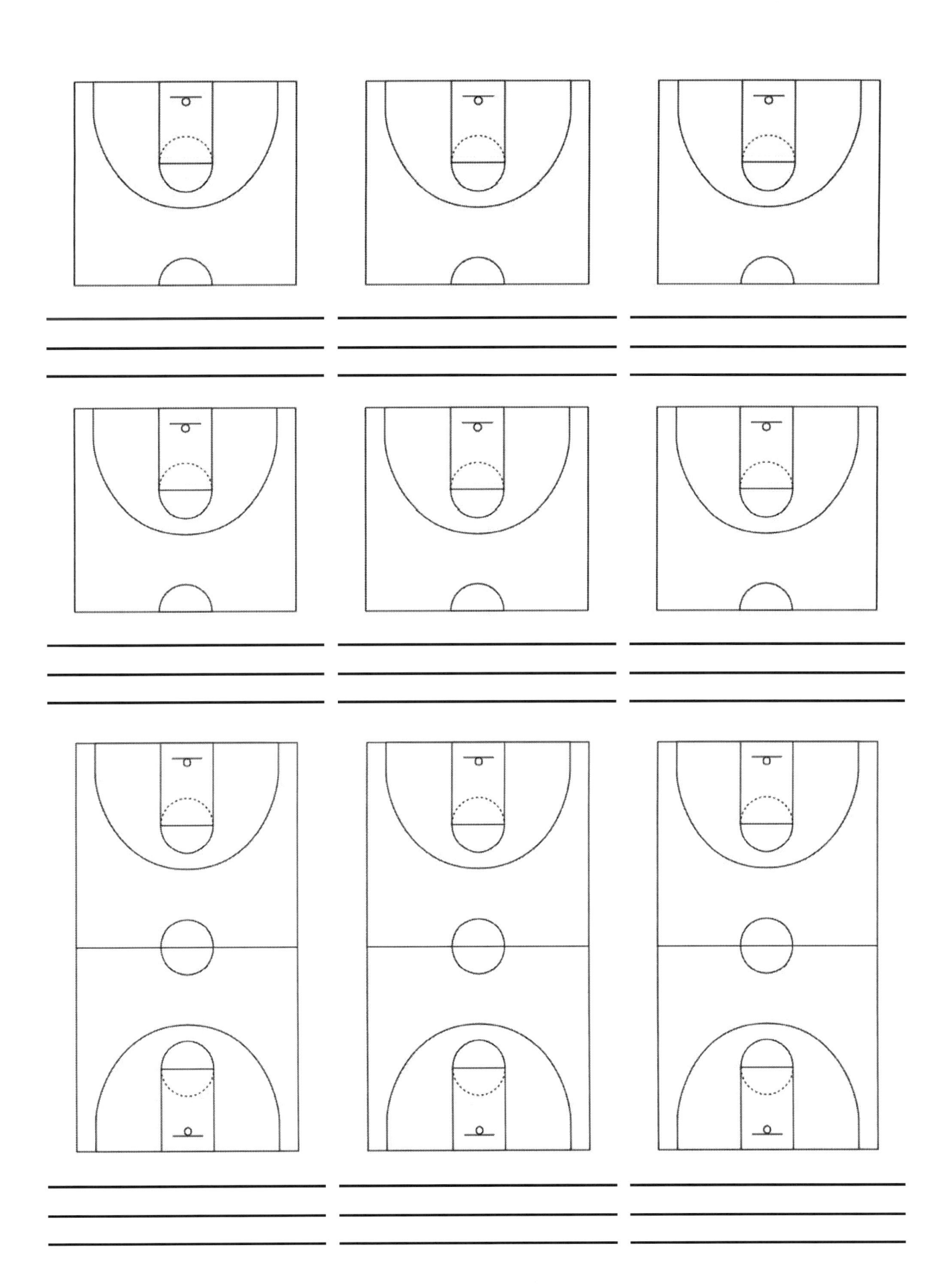

| Date: | Time | Next Game/Opponent: | | Next Practice: |

Target of the Day	Offensive Emphasis	Defensive Emphasis	Teams

Time Min	Drill/Activity	Focus/Emphasis

Notes/Reminders

Player Connections
Who are you connecting with 1-on-1? How?

1.

2.

3.

Player/Coach Challenges
Which players/coaches have challenges on/off the court that you can support and encourage?

1.

2.

3.

Practice Plans | 29

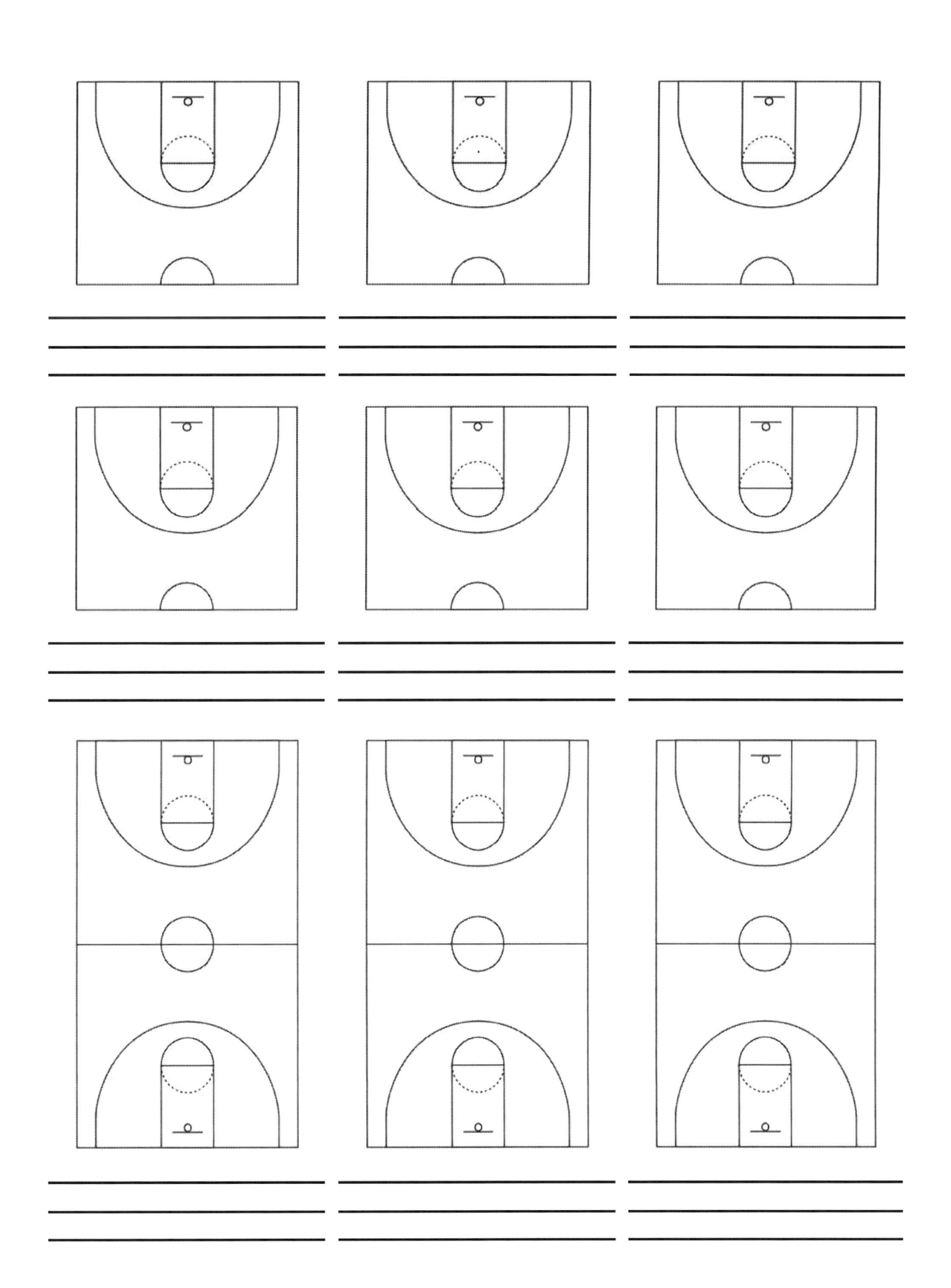

Date: Time   Next Game/Opponent: Next Practice:

Target of the Day	Offensive Emphasis	Defensive Emphasis	Teams

Time Min	Drill/Activity	Focus/Emphasis

Notes/Reminders

Player Connections
Who are you connecting with 1-on-1? How?

1.

2.

3.

Player/Coach Challenges
Which players/coaches have challenges on/off the court that you can support and encourage?

1.

2.

3.

Practice Plans | 31

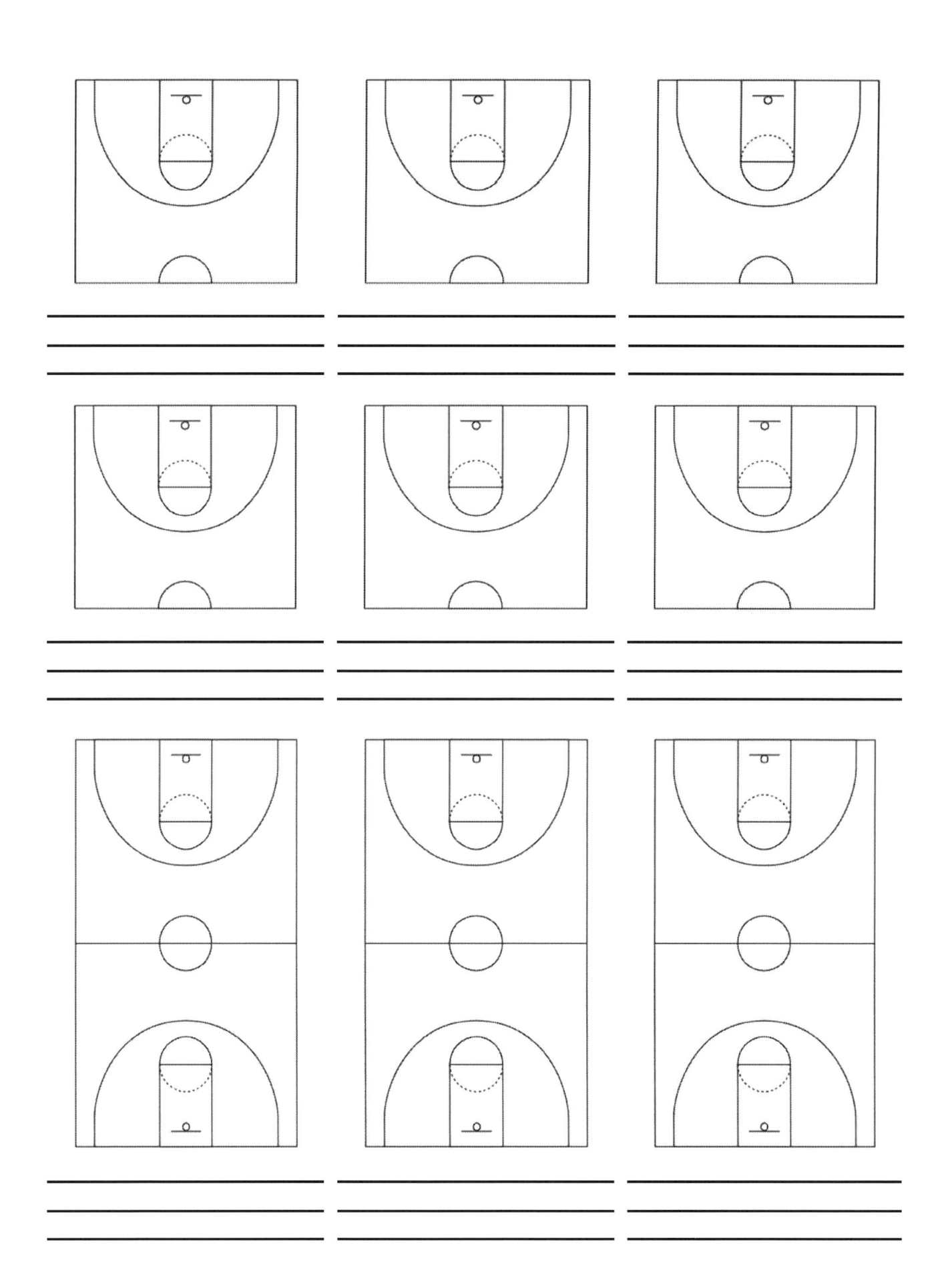

Date: Time Next Game/Opponent: Next Practice:

Target of the Day	Offensive Emphasis	Defensive Emphasis	Teams

Time Min	Drill/Activity	Focus/Emphasis

Notes/Reminders

Player Connections
Who are you connecting with 1-on-1? How?

1.

2.

3.

Player/Coach Challenges
Which players/coaches have challenges on/off the court that you can support and encourage?

1.

2.

3.

32 | Practice Plans

Practice Plans | 33

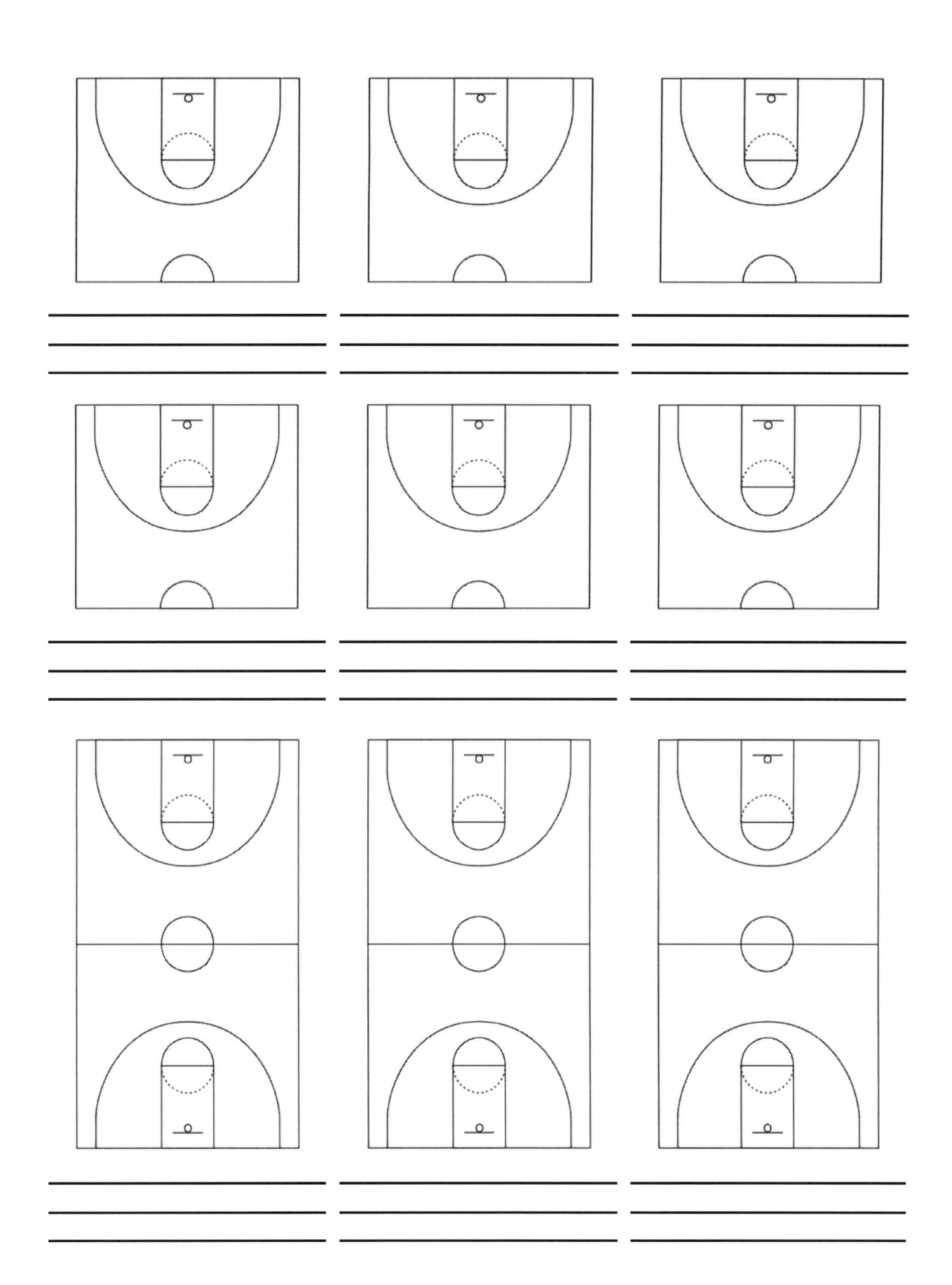

Date: Time Next Game/Opponent: Next Practice:

Target of the Day	Offensive Emphasis	Defensive Emphasis	Teams

Time Min	Drill/Activity	Focus/Emphasis

Notes/Reminders

Player Connections
Who are you connecting with 1-on-1? How?

1.

2.

3.

Player/Coach Challenges
Which players/coaches have challenges on/off the court that you can support and encourage?

1.

2.

3.

Practice Plans | 35

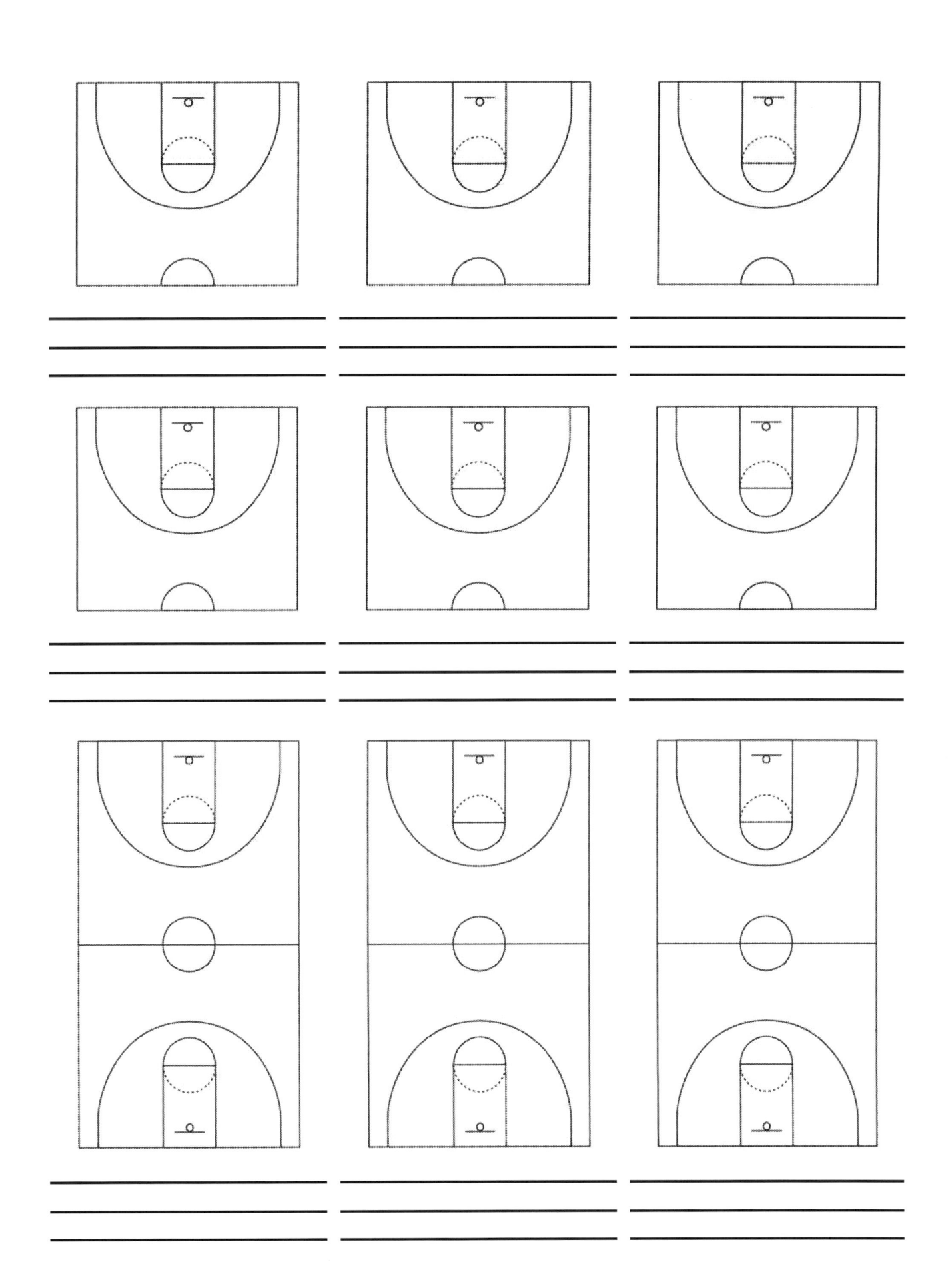

Date: Time: Next Game/Opponent: Next Practice:

Target of the Day	Offensive Emphasis	Defensive Emphasis	Teams

Time Min	Drill/Activity	Focus/Emphasis

Notes/Reminders

Player Connections
Who are you connecting with 1-on-1? How?

1.

2.

3.

Player/Coach Challenges
Which players/coaches have challenges on/off the court that you can support and encourage?

1.

2.

3.

Practice Plans | 37

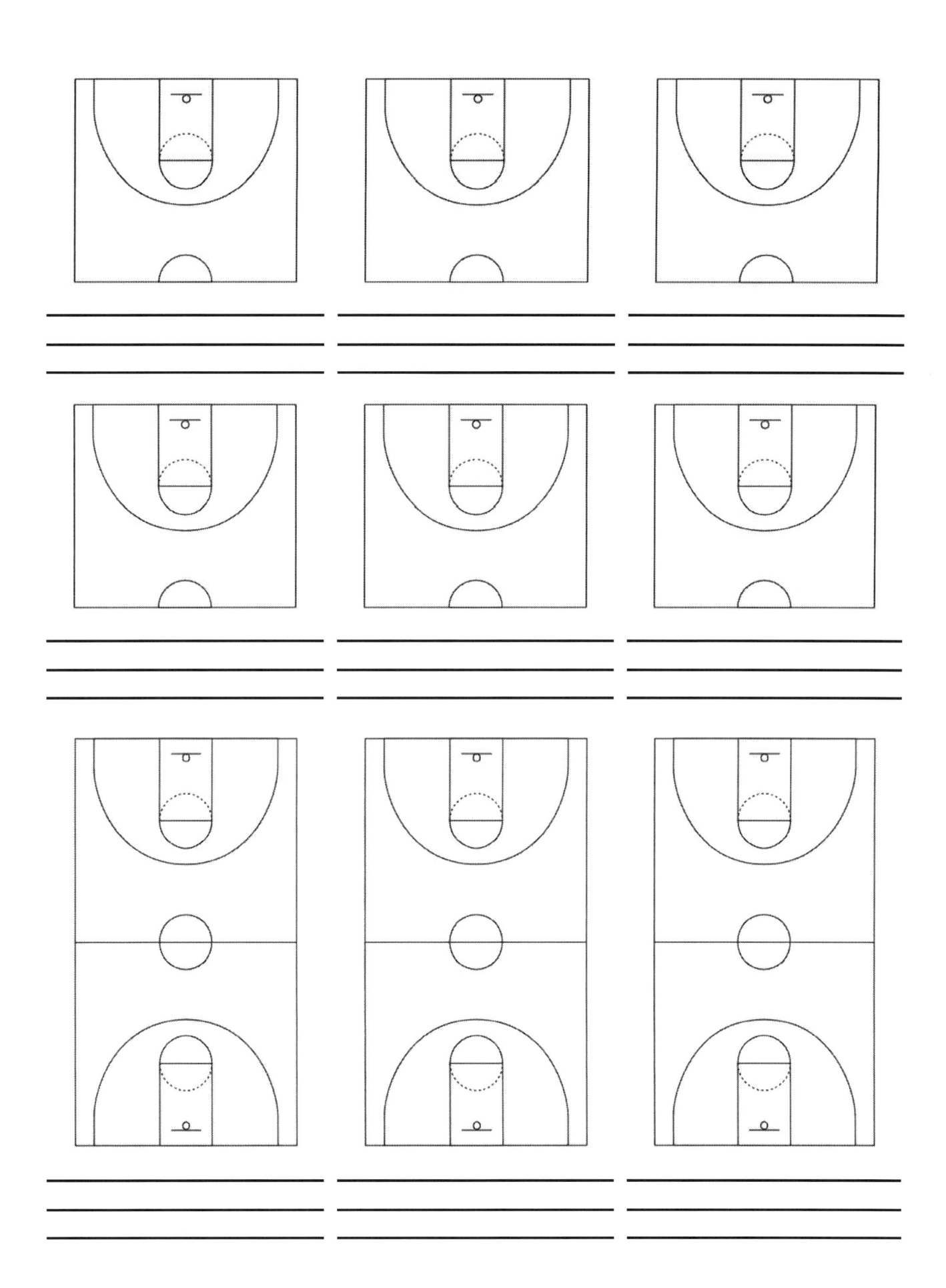

| Date: | Time | Next Game/Opponent: | | Next Practice: |

Target of the Day	Offensive Emphasis	Defensive Emphasis	Teams

Time Min	Drill/Activity	Focus/Emphasis

Notes/Reminders

Player Connections
Who are you connecting with 1-on-1? How?

1.

2.

3.

Player/Coach Challenges
Which players/coaches have challenges on/off the court that you can support and encourage?

1.

2.

3.

Practice Plans | 39

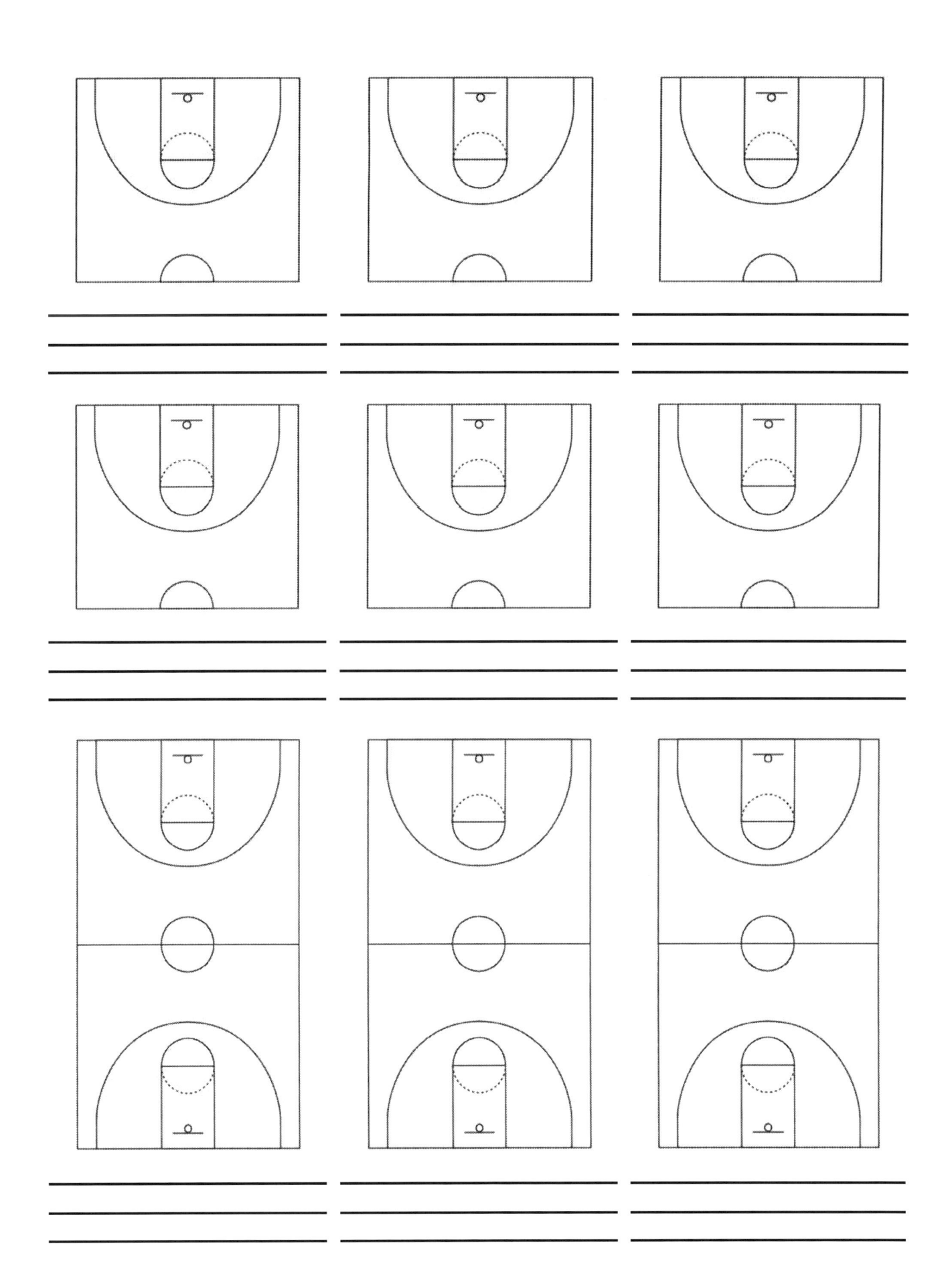

Date:　　　　　Time　　　　　Next Game/Opponent:　　　　　Next Practice:

Target of the Day	Offensive Emphasis	Defensive Emphasis	Teams

Time Min	Drill/Activity	Focus/Emphasis

Notes/Reminders

Player Connections
Who are you connecting with 1-on-1? How?

1.

2.

3.

Player/Coach Challenges
Which players/coaches have challenges on/off the court that you can support and encourage?

1.

2.

3.

40 | Practice Plans

Practice Plans | 41

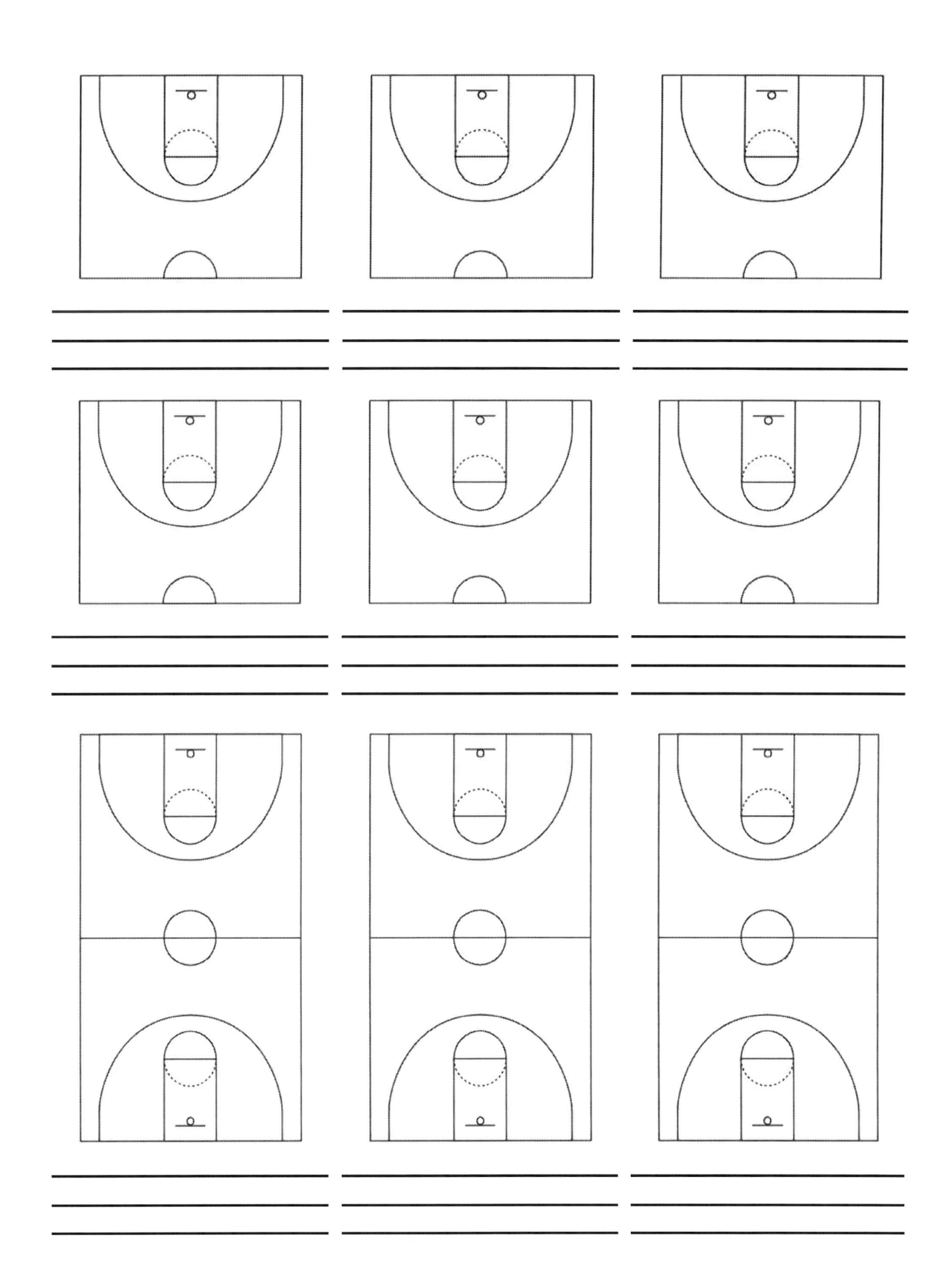

Date: Time   Next Game/Opponent: Next Practice:

Target of the Day	Offensive Emphasis	Defensive Emphasis	Teams

Time Min	Drill/Activity	Focus/Emphasis

Notes/Reminders

Player Connections
Who are you connecting with 1-on-1? How?

1.

2.

3.

Player/Coach Challenges
Which players/coaches have challenges on/off the court that you can support and encourage?

1.

2.

3.

Practice Plans | 43

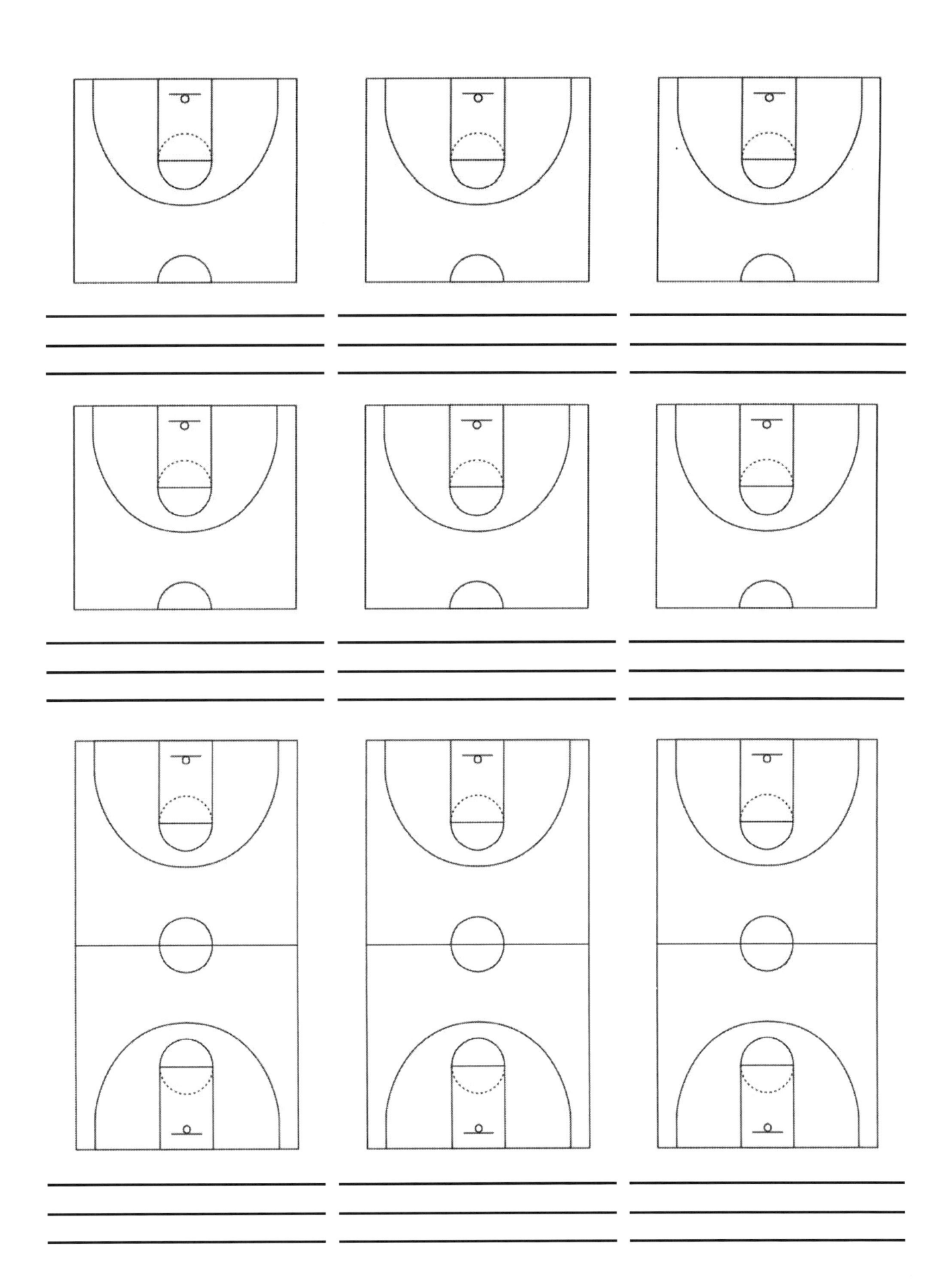

Date:	Time	Next Game/Opponent:	Next Practice:

Target of the Day	Offensive Emphasis	Defensive Emphasis	Teams

Time Min	Drill/Activity	Focus/Emphasis

Notes/Reminders

Player Connections
Who are you connecting with 1-on-1? How?

1.

2.

3.

Player/Coach Challenges
Which players/coaches have challenges on/off the court that you can support and encourage?

1.

2.

3.

Practice Plans | 45

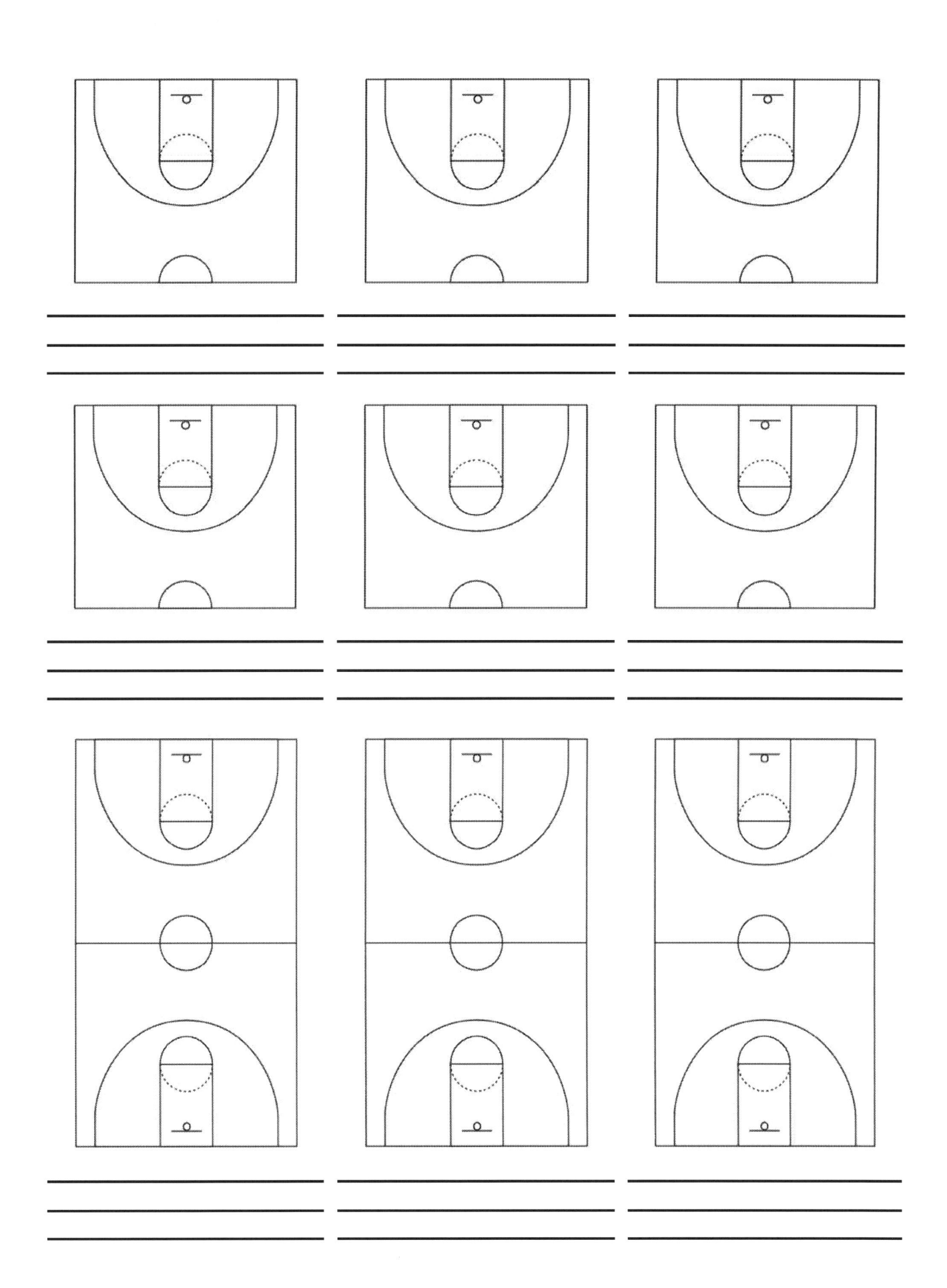

Date: Time Next Game/Opponent: Next Practice:

Target of the Day	Offensive Emphasis	Defensive Emphasis	Teams

Time Min	Drill/Activity	Focus/Emphasis

Notes/Reminders

Player Connections
Who are you connecting with 1-on-1? How?

1.

2.

3.

Player/Coach Challenges
Which players/coaches have challenges on/off the court that you can support and encourage?

1.

2.

3.

Practice Plans | 47

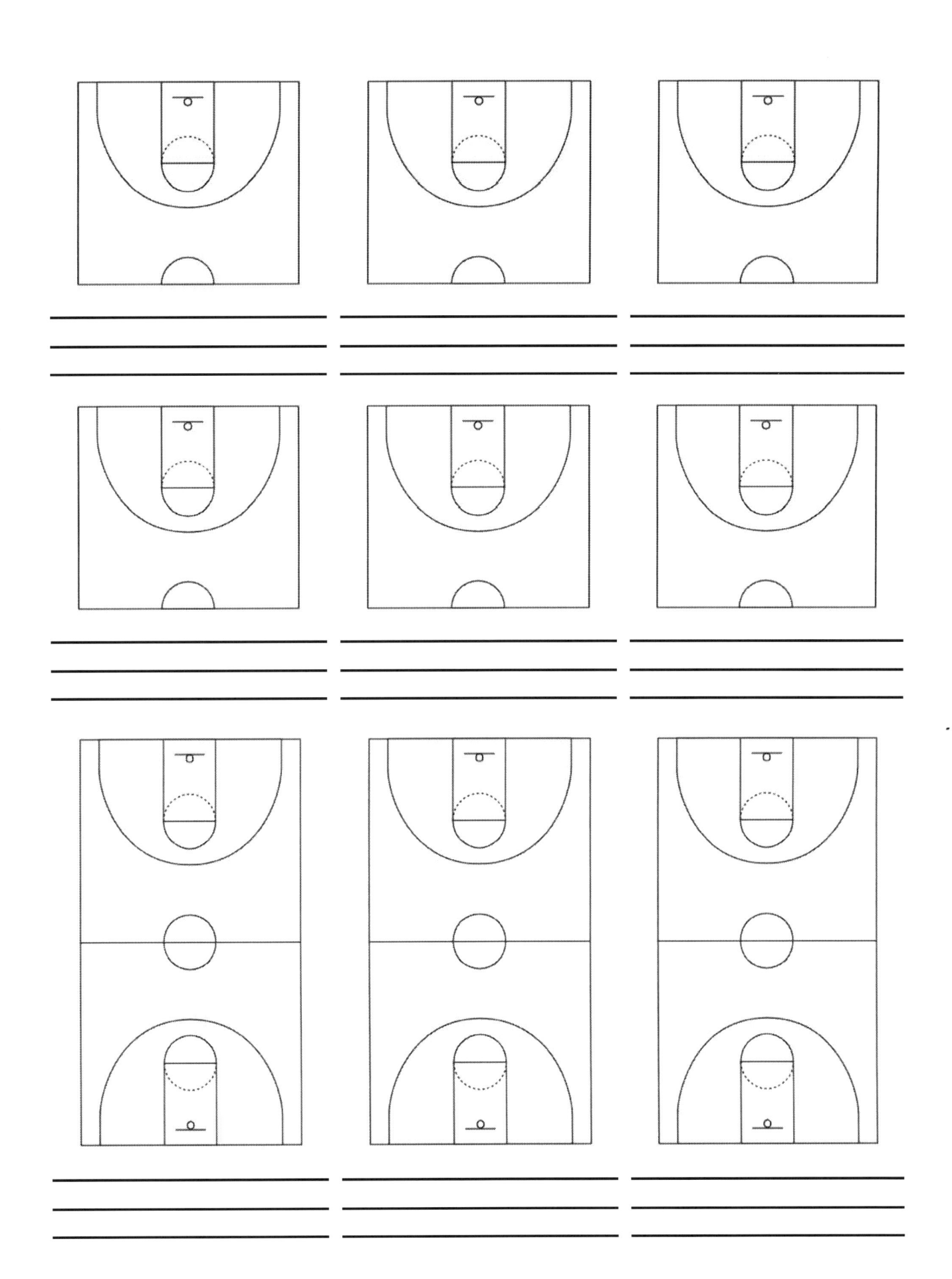

Date: Time   Next Game/Opponent: Next Practice:

Target of the Day	Offensive Emphasis	Defensive Emphasis	Teams

Time Min	Drill/Activity	Focus/Emphasis

Notes/Reminders

Player Connections
Who are you connecting with 1-on-1? How?

1.

2.

3.

Player/Coach Challenges
Which players/coaches have challenges on/off the court that you can support and encourage?

1.

2.

3.

Practice Plans | 49

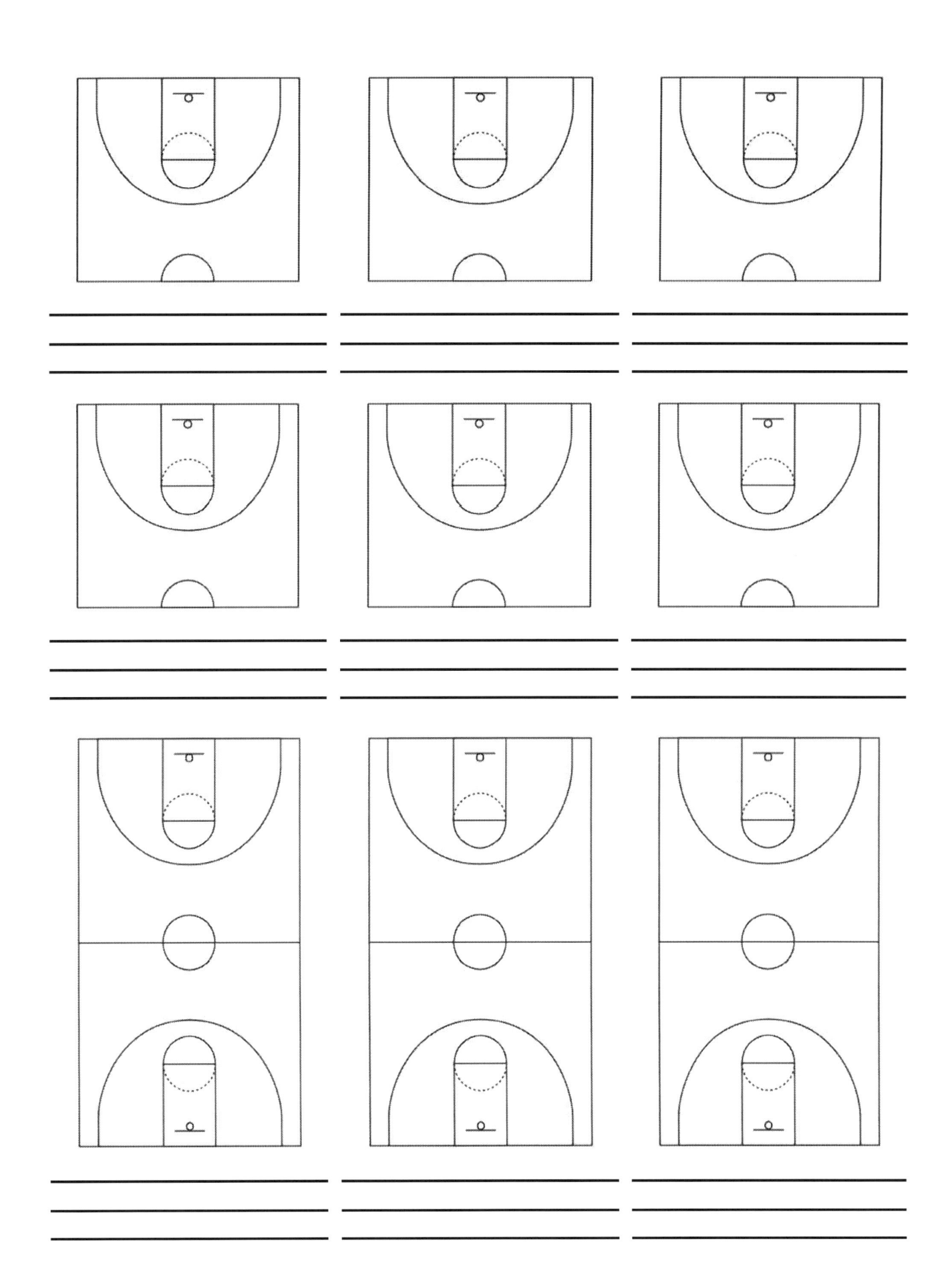

| Date: | Time | Next Game/Opponent: | | Next Practice: |

Target of the Day	Offensive Emphasis	Defensive Emphasis	Teams

Time Min	Drill/Activity	Focus/Emphasis

Notes/Reminders

Player Connections
Who are you connecting with 1-on-1? How?

1.

2.

3.

Player/Coach Challenges
Which players/coaches have challenges on/off the court that you can support and encourage?

1.

2.

3.

Practice Plans | 51

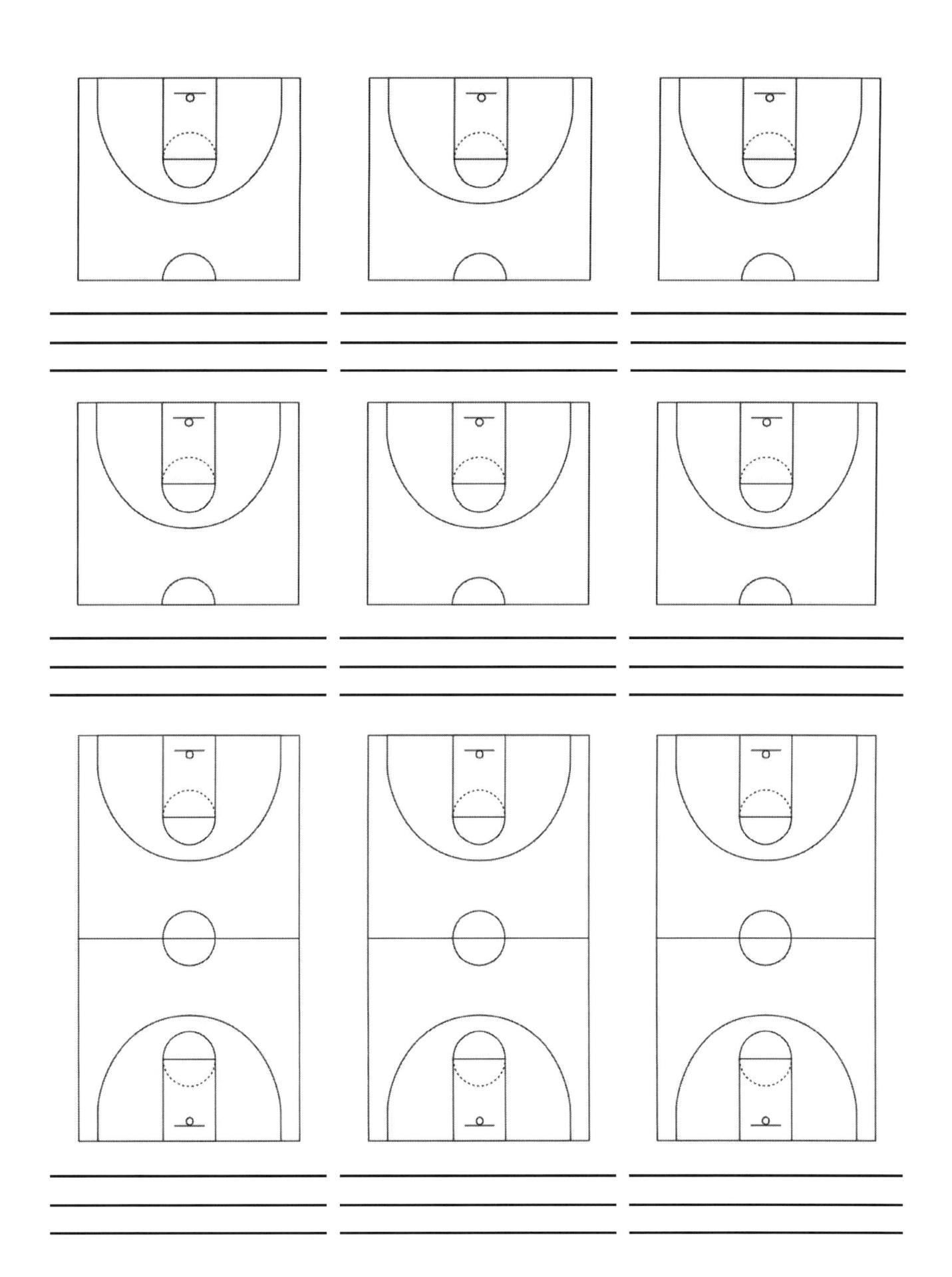

Date: Time: Next Game/Opponent: Next Practice:

Target of the Day	Offensive Emphasis	Defensive Emphasis	Teams

Time Min	Drill/Activity	Focus/Emphasis

Notes/Reminders

Player Connections
Who are you connecting with 1-on-1? How?

1.

2.

3.

Player/Coach Challenges
Which players/coaches have challenges on/off the court that you can support and encourage?

1.

2.

3.

Practice Plans | 53

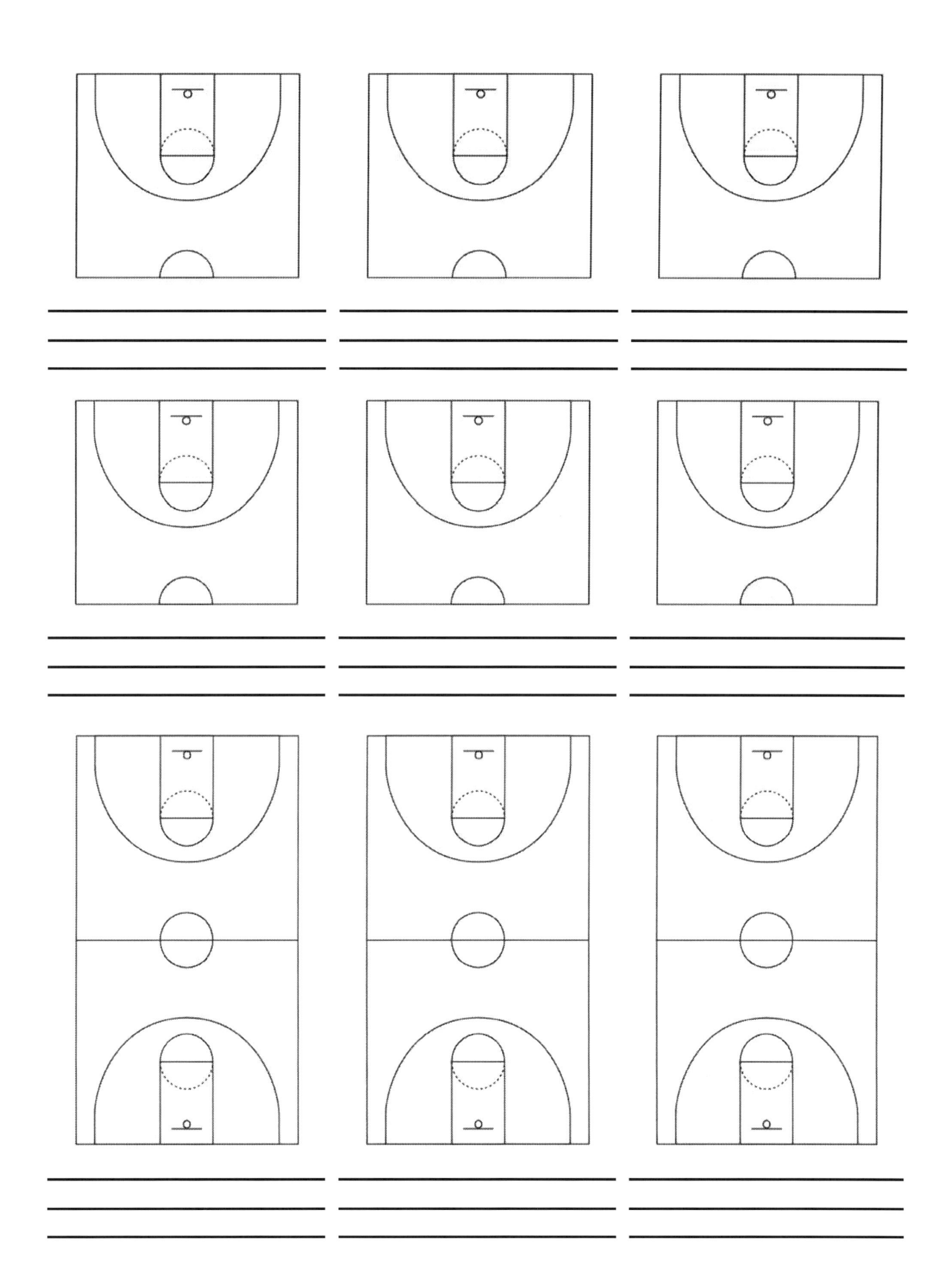

Date: Time   Next Game/Opponent: Next Practice:

Target of the Day	Offensive Emphasis	Defensive Emphasis	Teams

Time Min	Drill/Activity	Focus/Emphasis

Notes/Reminders

Player Connections
Who are you connecting with 1-on-1? How?

1.

2.

3.

Player/Coach Challenges
Which players/coaches have challenges on/off the court that you can support and encourage?

1.

2.

3.

54 | Practice Plans

Practice Plans | 55

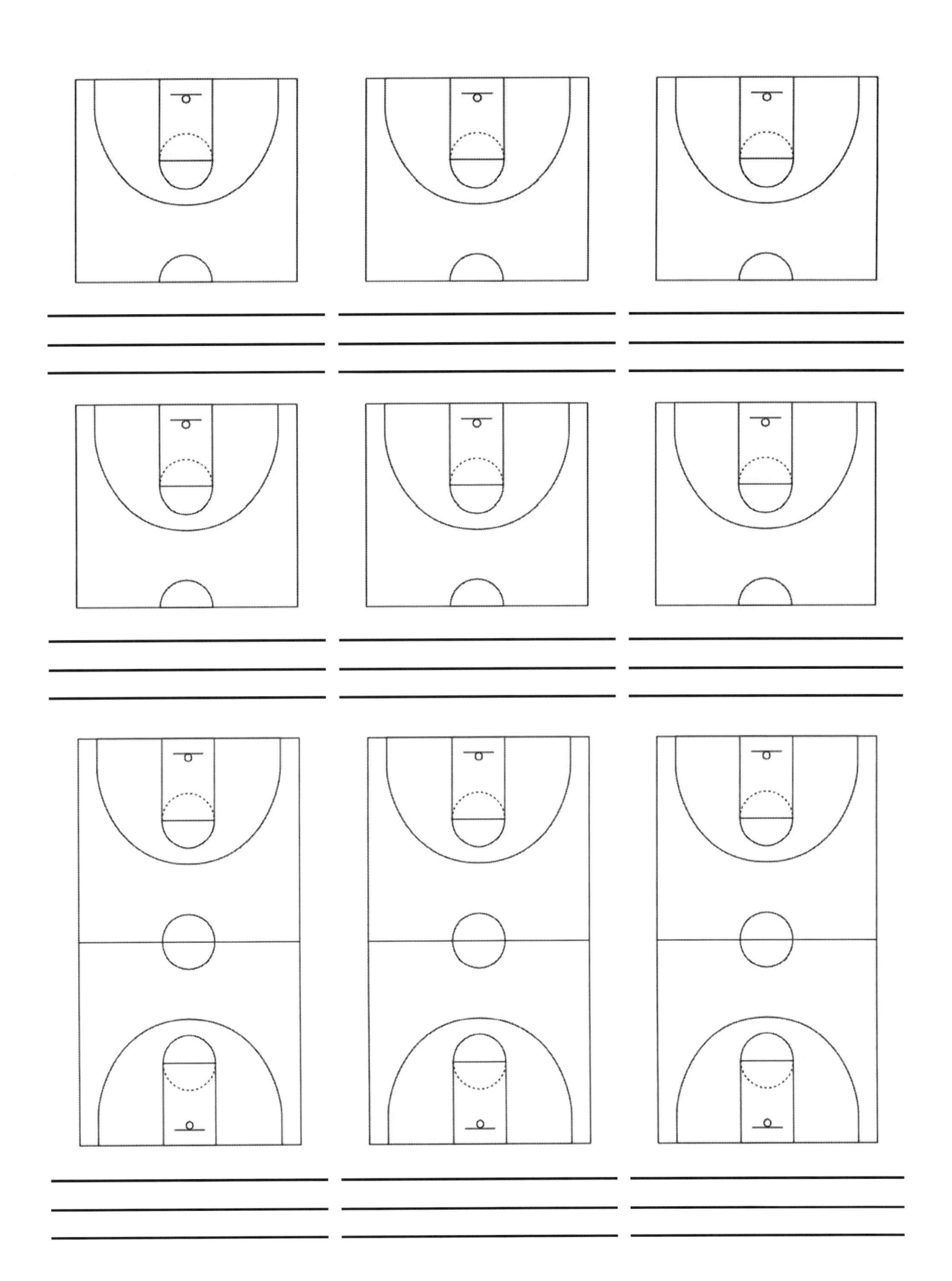

Date: Time Next Game/Opponent: Next Practice:

Target of the Day	Offensive Emphasis	Defensive Emphasis	Teams

Time Min	Drill/Activity	Focus/Emphasis

Notes/Reminders

Player Connections
Who are you connecting with 1-on-1? How?

1.

2.

3.

Player/Coach Challenges
Which players/coaches have challenges on/off the court that you can support and encourage?

1.

2.

3.

Practice Plans | 57

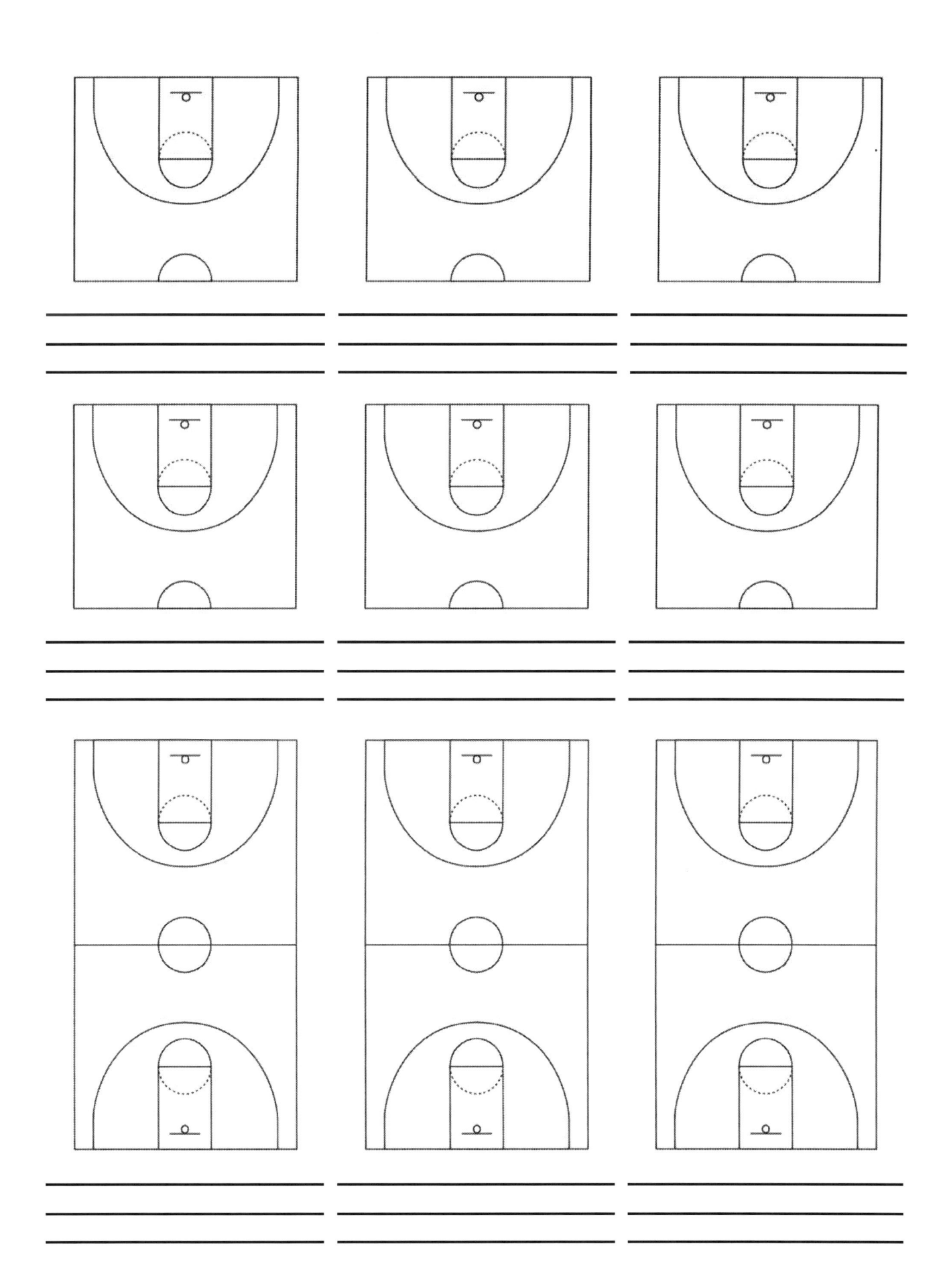

Date: Time Next Game/Opponent: Next Practice:

Target of the Day	Offensive Emphasis	Defensive Emphasis	Teams

Time Min	Drill/Activity	Focus/Emphasis

Notes/Reminders

Player Connections
Who are you connecting with 1-on-1? How?

1.

2.

3.

Player/Coach Challenges
Which players/coaches have challenges on/off the court that you can support and encourage?

1.

2.

3.

Practice Plans | 59

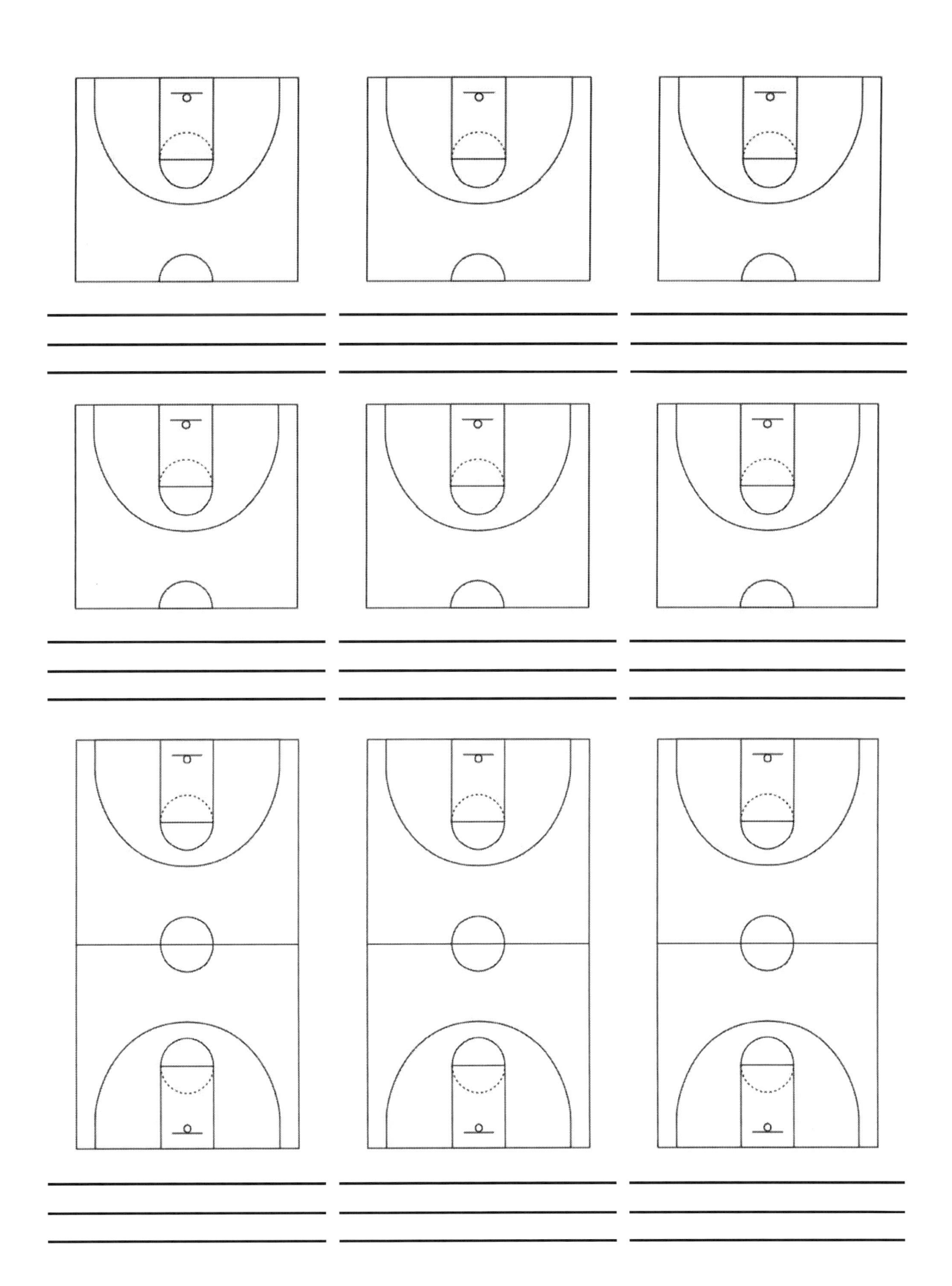

| Date: | Time | Next Game/Opponent: | | Next Practice: |

Target of the Day	Offensive Emphasis	Defensive Emphasis	Teams

Time Min	Drill/Activity	Focus/Emphasis

Notes/Reminders

Player Connections
Who are you connecting with 1-on-1? How?

1.

2.

3.

Player/Coach Challenges
Which players/coaches have challenges on/off the court that you can support and encourage?

1.

2.

3.

Practice Plans | 61

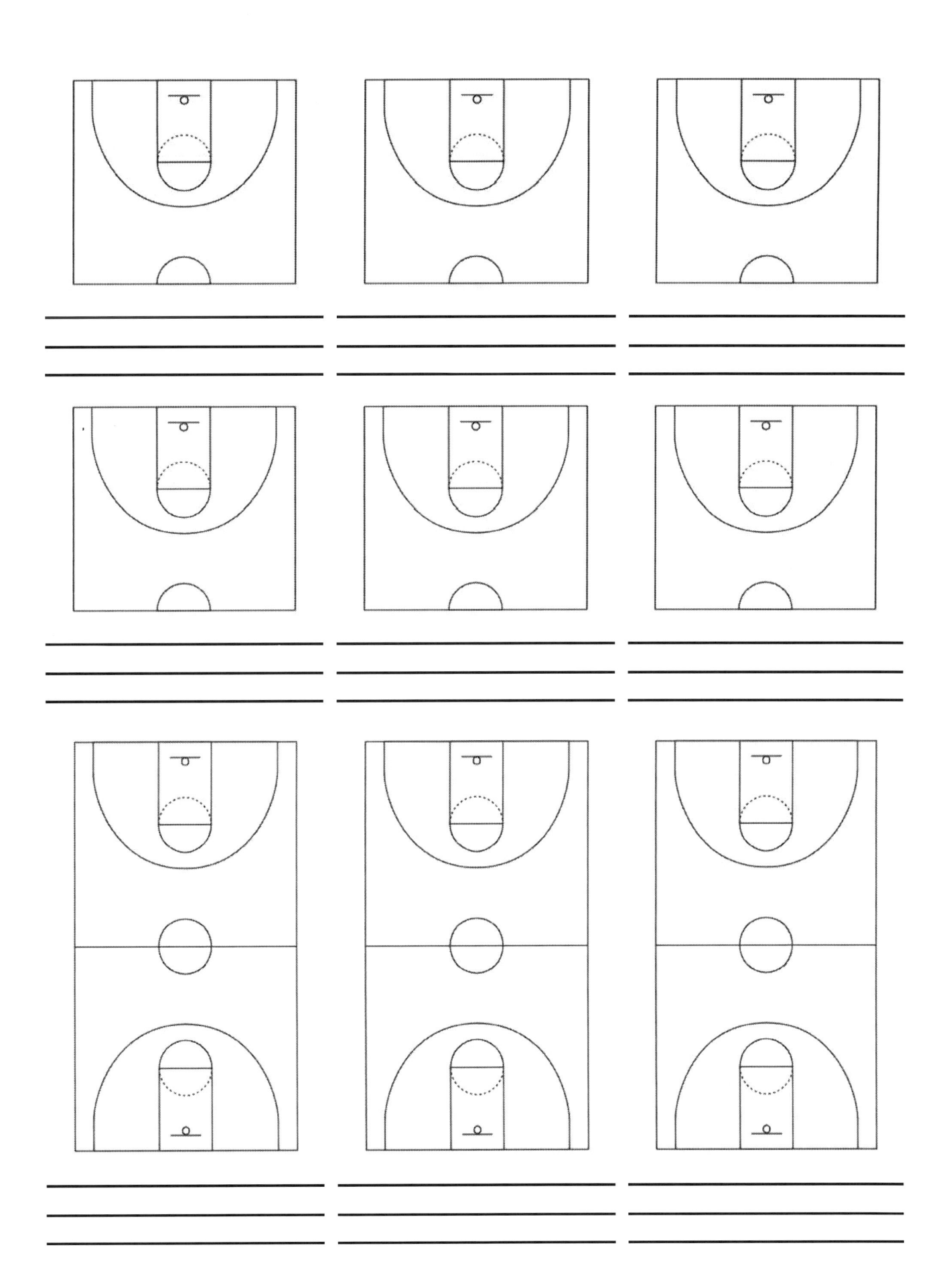

Date: Time   Next Game/Opponent: Next Practice:

Target of the Day	Offensive Emphasis	Defensive Emphasis	Teams

Time Min	Drill/Activity	Focus/Emphasis

Notes/Reminders

Player Connections
Who are you connecting with 1-on-1? How?

1.

2.

3.

Player/Coach Challenges
Which players/coaches have challenges on/off the court that you can support and encourage?

1.

2.

3.

Practice Plans | 63

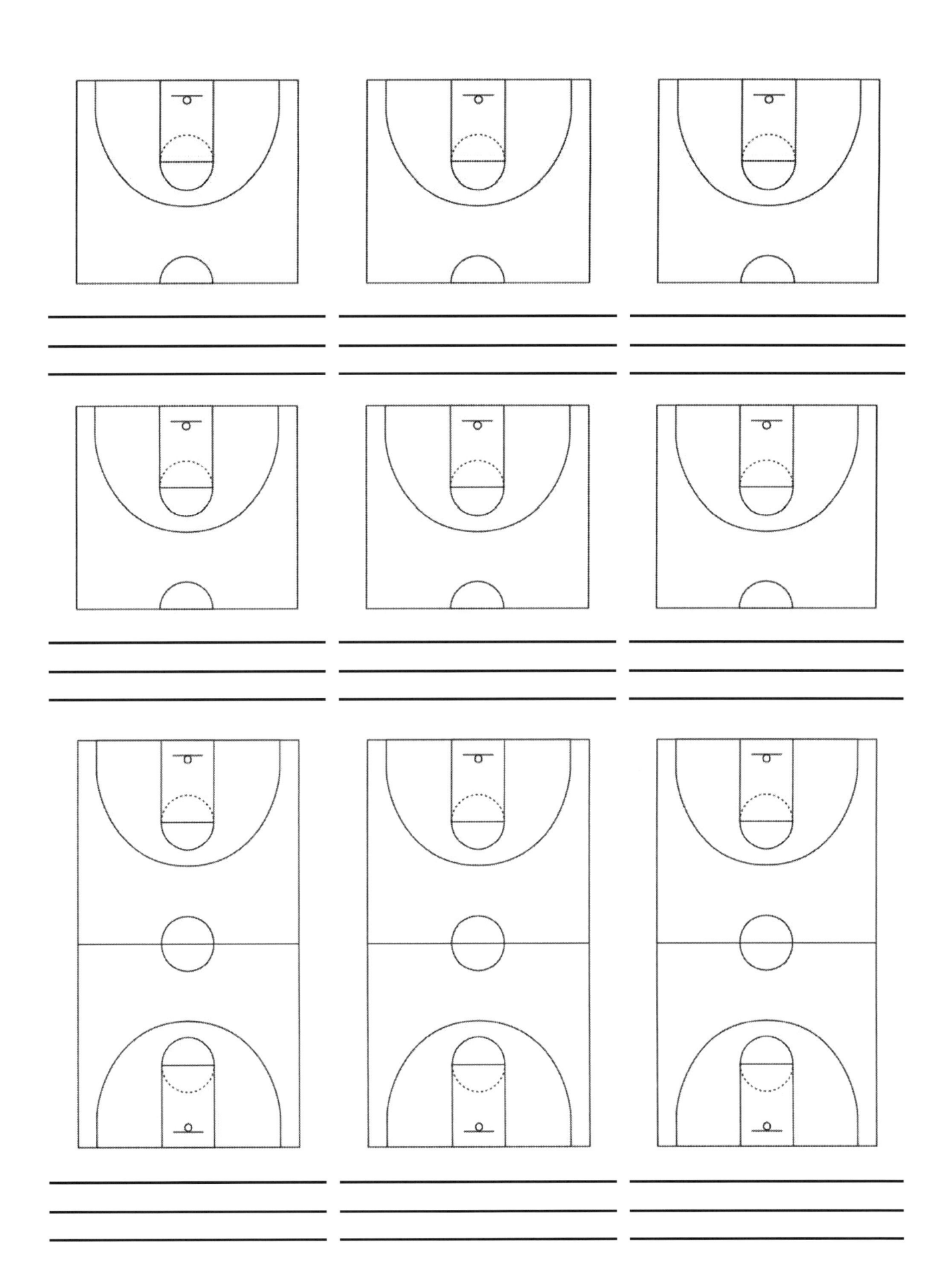

Date: Time   Next Game/Opponent: Next Practice:

Target of the Day	Offensive Emphasis	Defensive Emphasis	Teams

Time Min	Drill/Activity	Focus/Emphasis

Notes/Reminders

Player Connections
Who are you connecting with 1-on-1? How?

1.

2.

3.

Player/Coach Challenges
Which players/coaches have challenges on/off the court that you can support and encourage?

1.

2.

3.

Practice Plans | 65

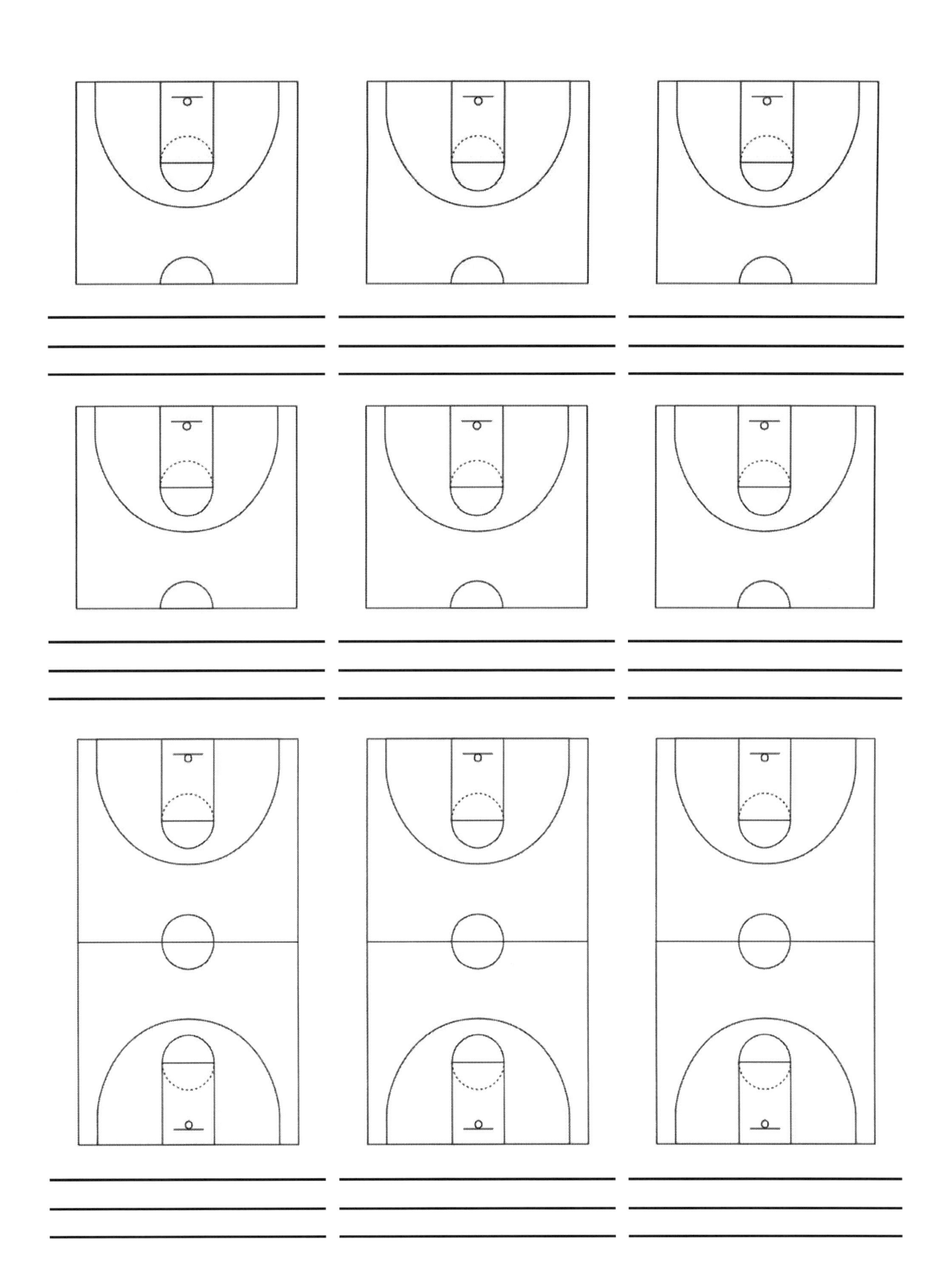

Date:　　　　　Time　　　　　Next Game/Opponent:　　　　　Next Practice:

Target of the Day	Offensive Emphasis	Defensive Emphasis	Teams

Time Min	Drill/Activity	Focus/Emphasis

Notes/Reminders

Player Connections
Who are you connecting with 1-on-1? How?

1.

2.

3.

Player/Coach Challenges
Which players/coaches have challenges on/off the court that you can support and encourage?

1.

2.

3.

Practice Plans | 67

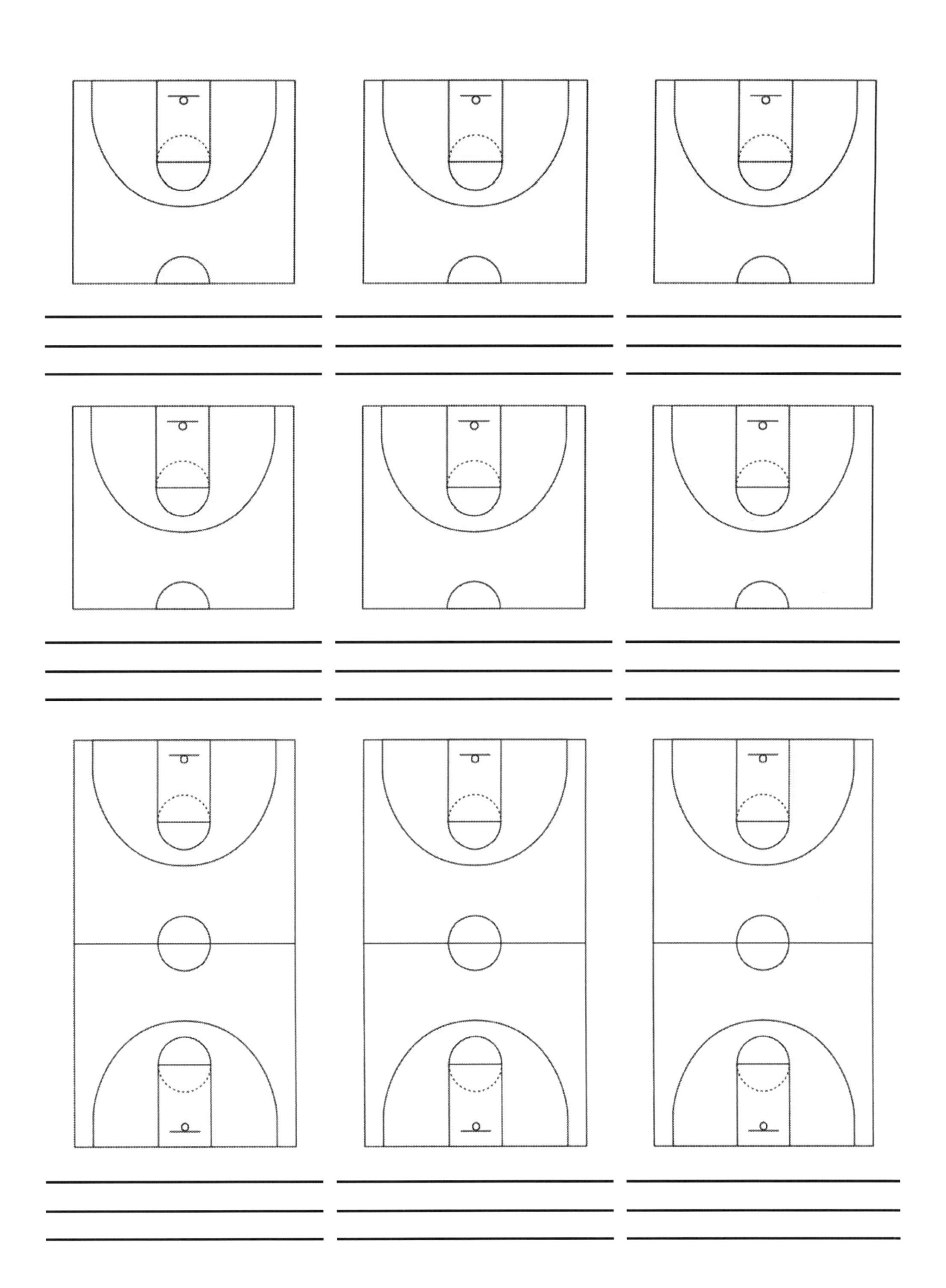

Date: Time Next Game/Opponent: Next Practice:

Target of the Day	Offensive Emphasis	Defensive Emphasis	Teams

Time Min	Drill/Activity	Focus/Emphasis

Notes/Reminders

Player Connections
Who are you connecting with 1-on-1? How?

1.

2.

3.

Player/Coach Challenges
Which players/coaches have challenges on/off the court that you can support and encourage?

1.

2.

3.

Practice Plans | 69

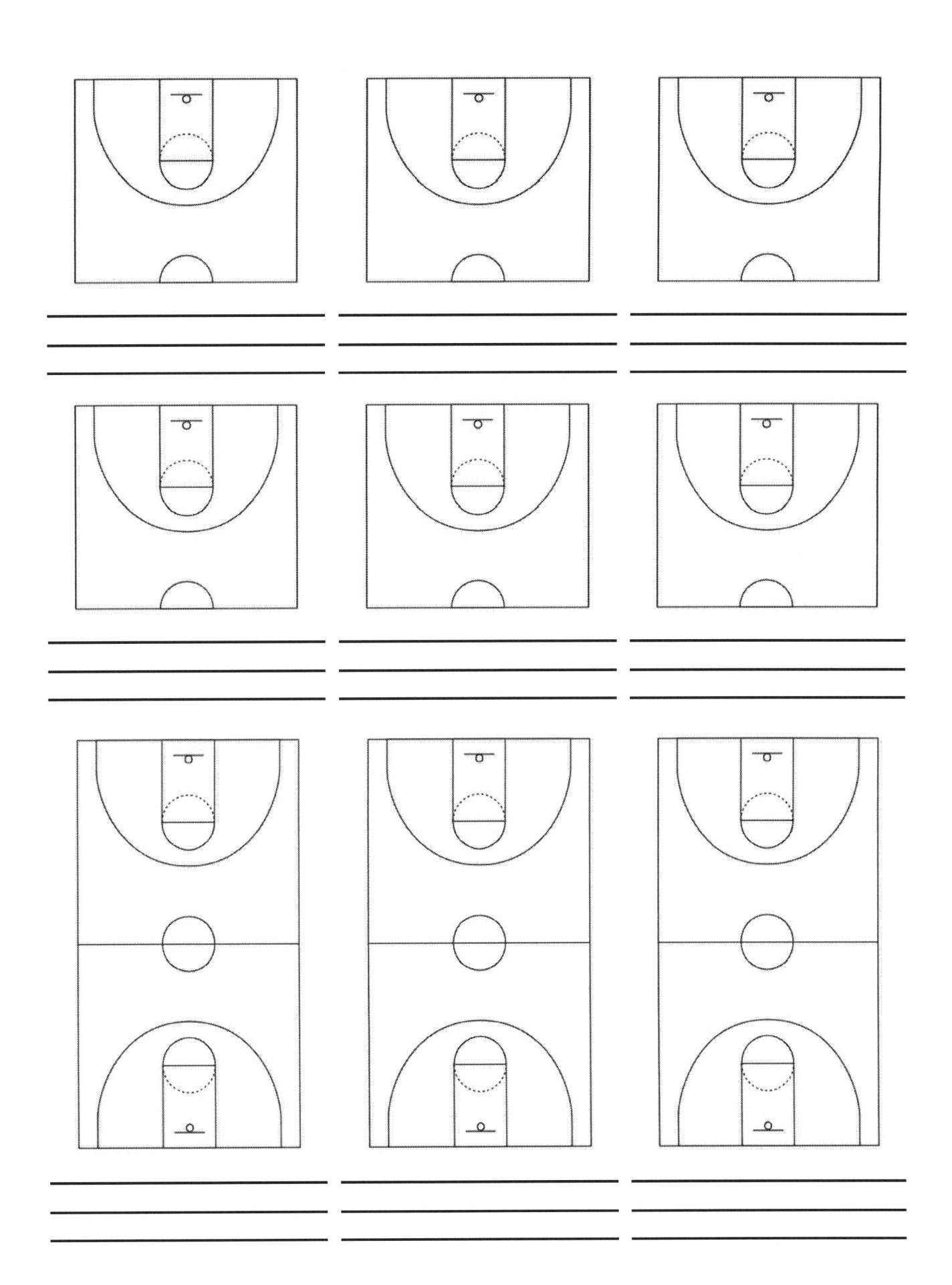

Date:　　　　　Time　　　　　Next Game/Opponent:　　　　　　　　　Next Practice:

Target of the Day	Offensive Emphasis	Defensive Emphasis	Teams

Time Min	Drill/Activity	Focus/Emphasis

Notes/Reminders

Player Connections
Who are you connecting with 1-on-1? How?

1.

2.

3.

Player/Coach Challenges
Which players/coaches have challenges on/off the court that you can support and encourage?

1.

2.

3.

Practice Plans | 71

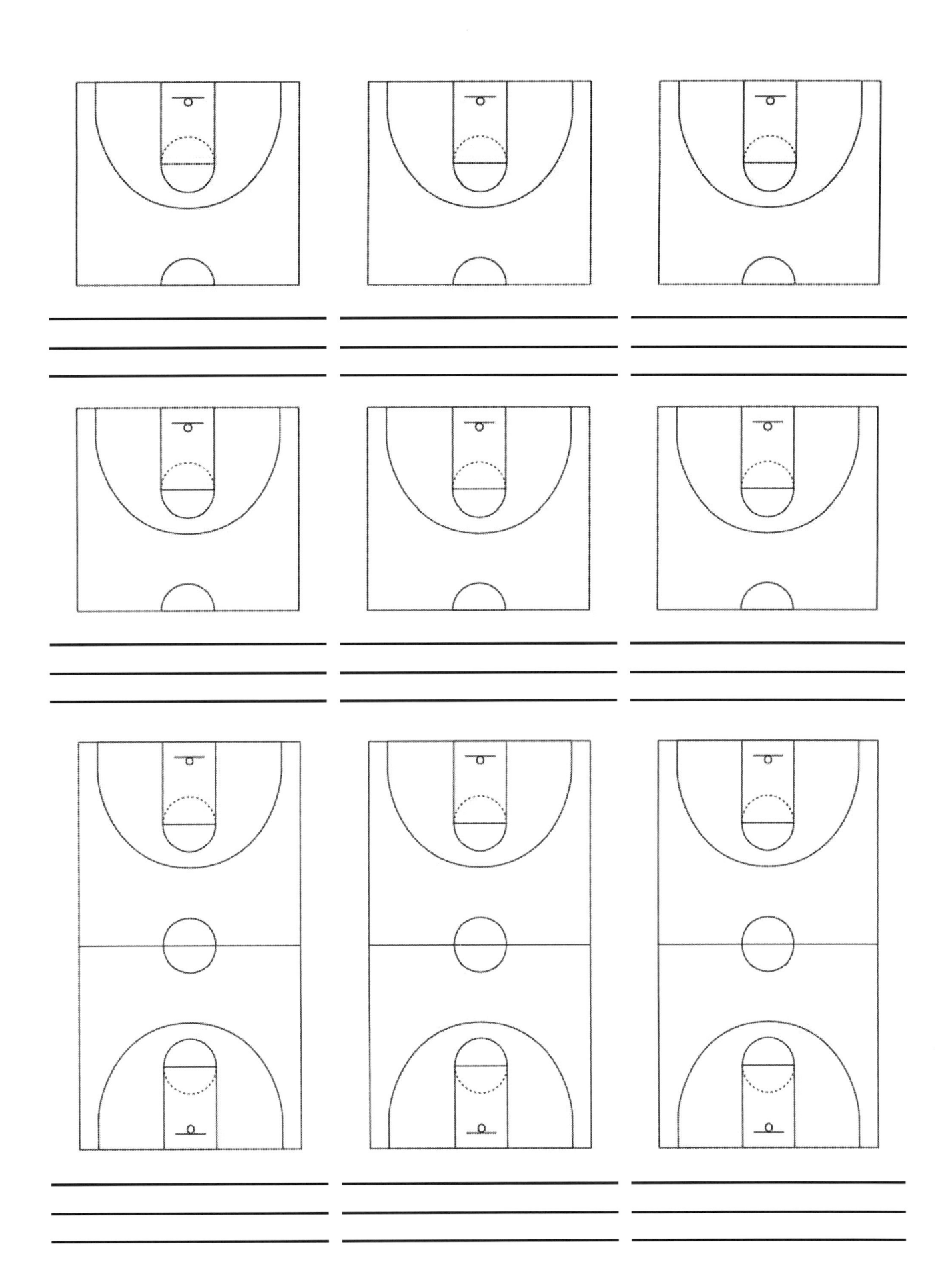

Date: Time   Next Game/Opponent: Next Practice:

Target of the Day	Offensive Emphasis	Defensive Emphasis	Teams

Time Min	Drill/Activity	Focus/Emphasis

Notes/Reminders

Player Connections
Who are you connecting with 1-on-1? How?

1.

2.

3.

Player/Coach Challenges
Which players/coaches have challenges on/off the court that you can support and encourage?

1.

2.

3.

Practice Plans | 73

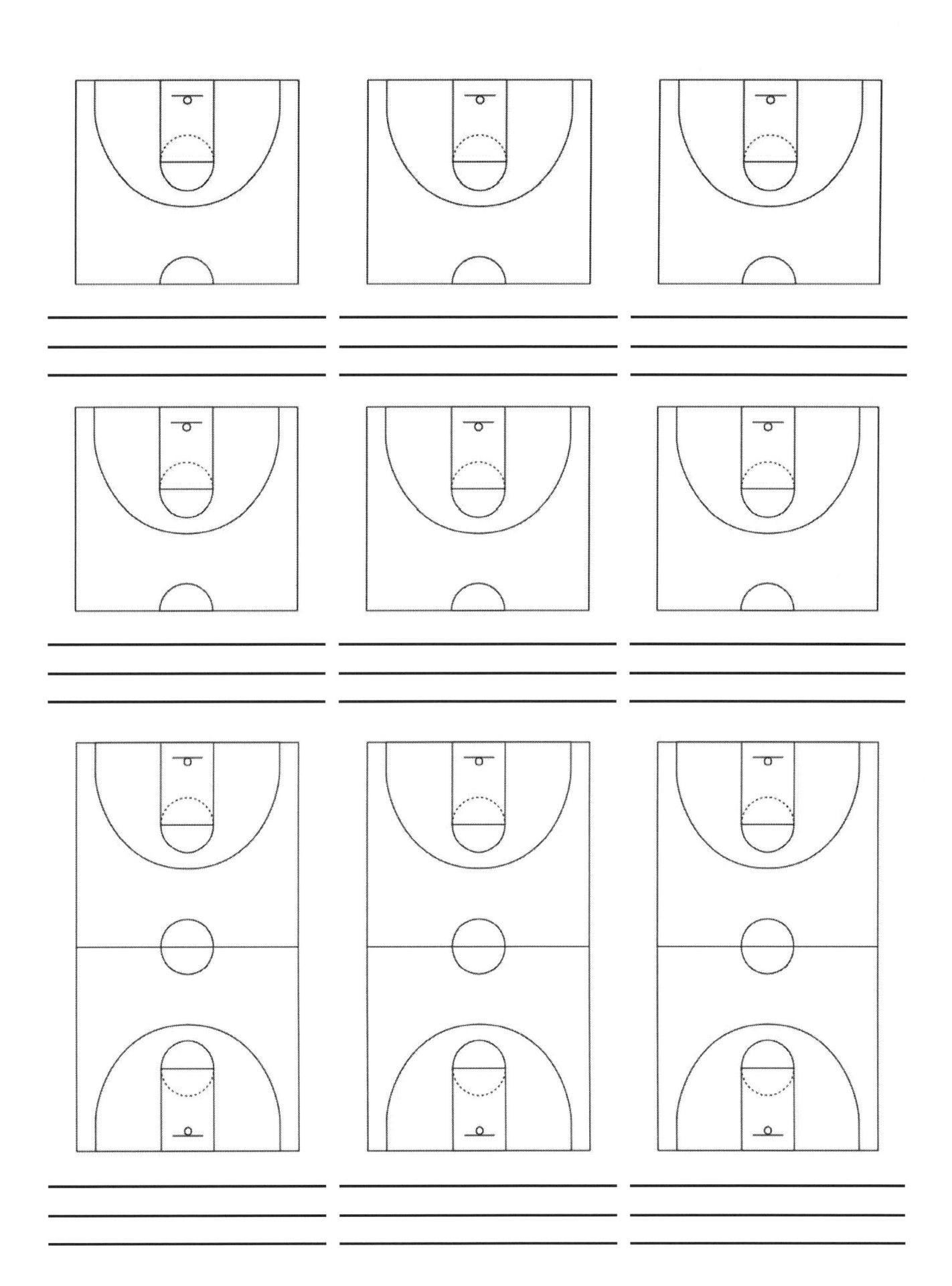

Date: Time   Next Game/Opponent: Next Practice:

Target of the Day	Offensive Emphasis	Defensive Emphasis	Teams

Time Min	Drill/Activity	Focus/Emphasis

Notes/Reminders

Player Connections
Who are you connecting with 1-on-1? How?

1.

2.

3.

Player/Coach Challenges
Which players/coaches have challenges on/off the court that you can support and encourage?

1.

2.

3.

Practice Plans | 75

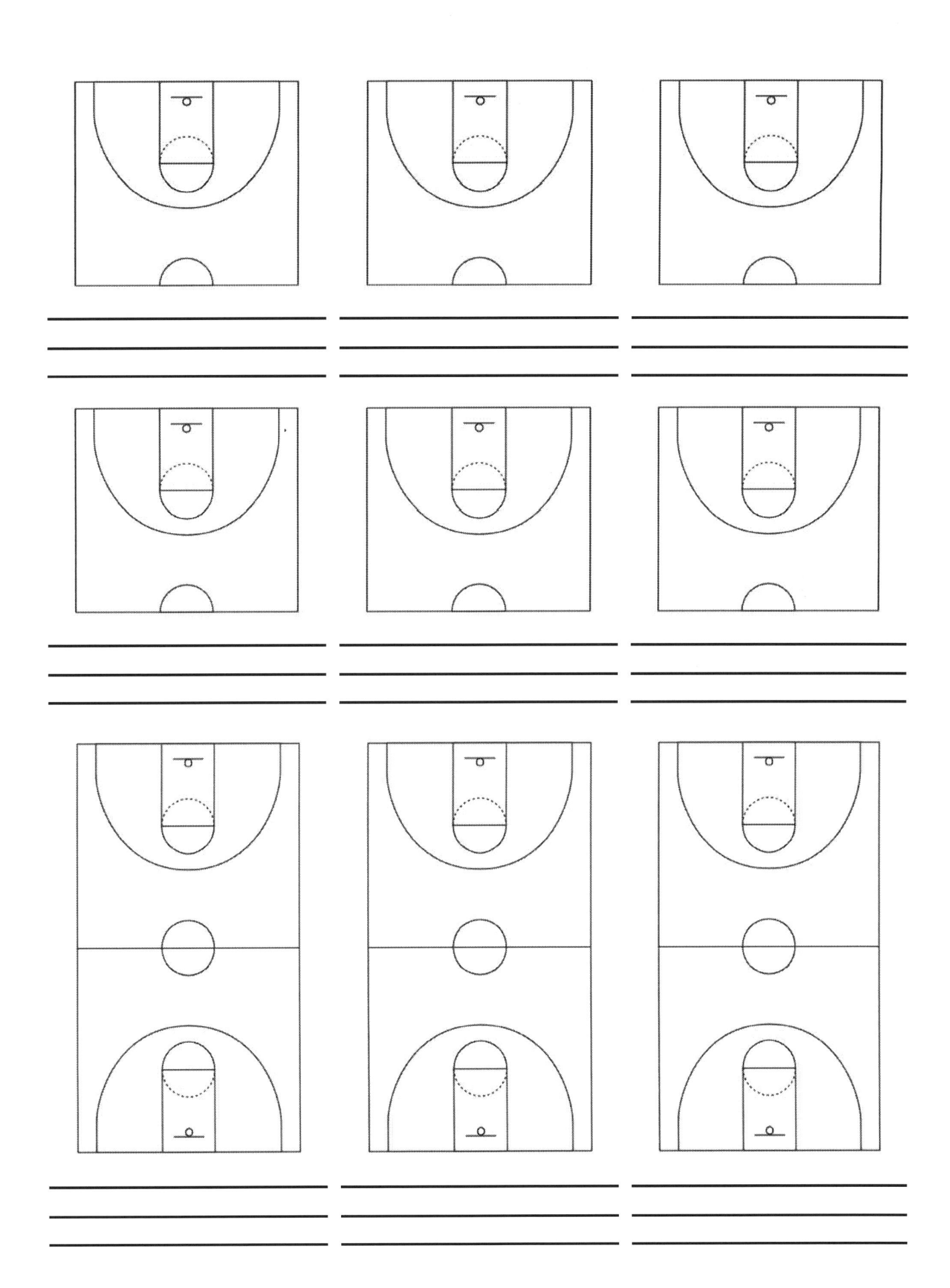

Date: Time Next Game/Opponent: Next Practice:

Target of the Day	Offensive Emphasis	Defensive Emphasis	Teams

Time Min	Drill/Activity	Focus/Emphasis

Notes/Reminders

Player Connections
Who are you connecting with 1-on-1? How?

1.

2.

3.

Player/Coach Challenges
Which players/coaches have challenges on/off the court that you can support and encourage?

1.

2.

3.

Practice Plans | 77

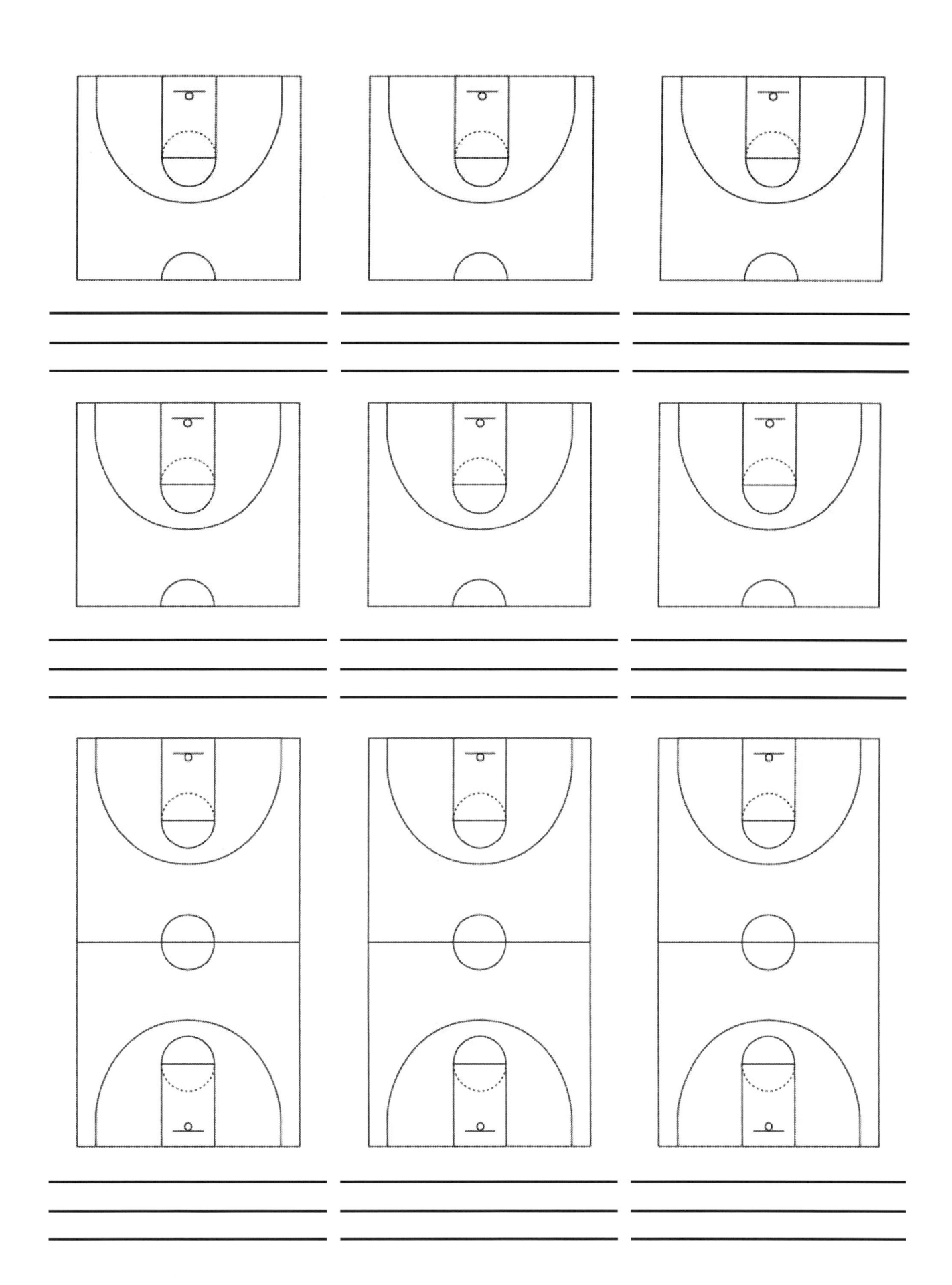

Date: Time   Next Game/Opponent: Next Practice:

Target of the Day	Offensive Emphasis	Defensive Emphasis	Teams

Time Min	Drill/Activity	Focus/Emphasis

Notes/Reminders

Player Connections
Who are you connecting with 1-on-1? How?

1.

2.

3.

Player/Coach Challenges
Which players/coaches have challenges on/off the court that you can support and encourage?

1.

2.

3.

78 | Practice Plans

Practice Plans | 79

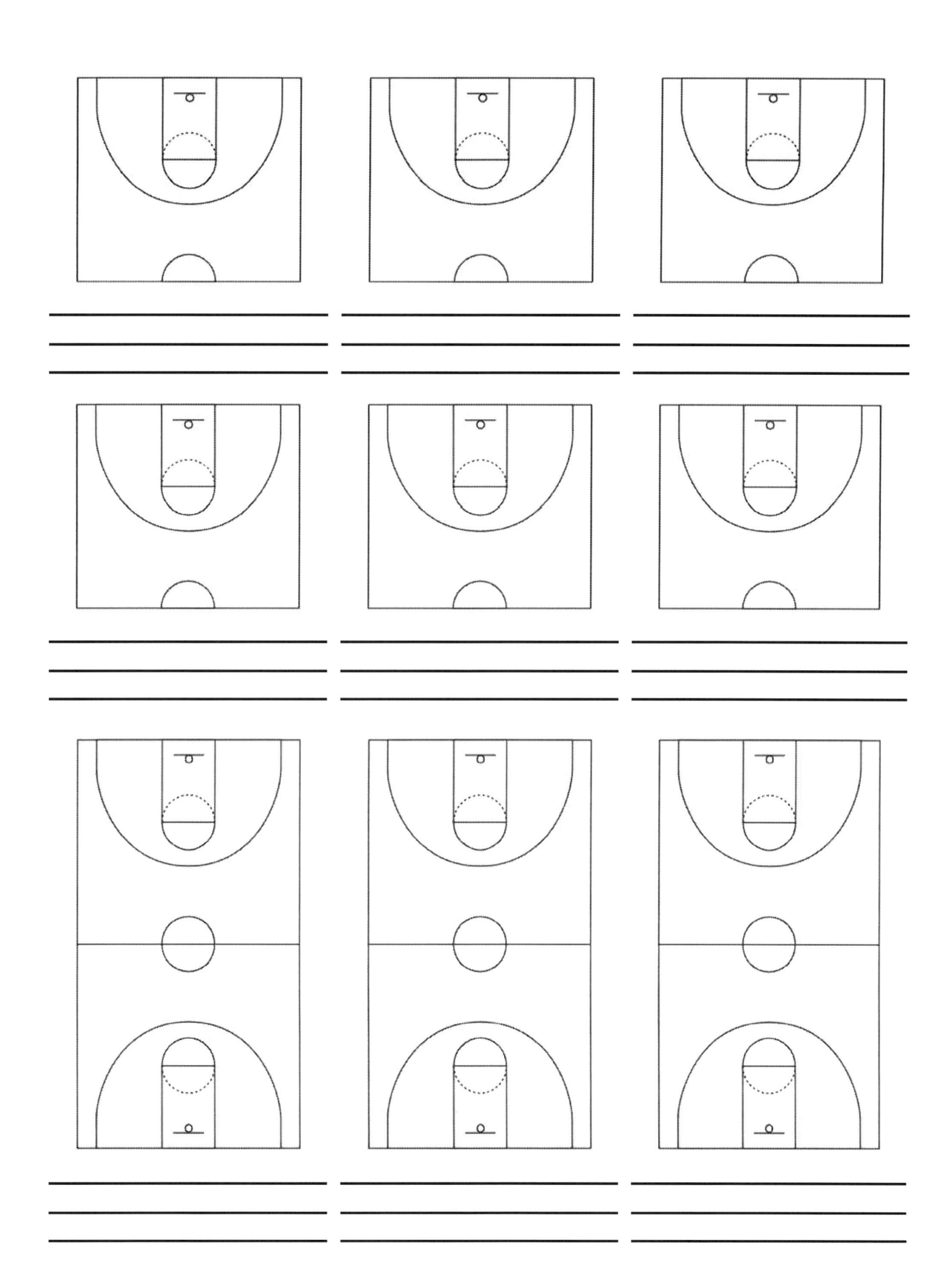

Date:　　　　　Time　　　　　Next Game/Opponent:　　　　　Next Practice:

Target of the Day	Offensive Emphasis	Defensive Emphasis	Teams

Time Min	Drill/Activity	Focus/Emphasis

Notes/Reminders

Player Connections
Who are you connecting with 1-on-1? How?

1.

2.

3.

Player/Coach Challenges
Which players/coaches have challenges on/off the court that you can support and encourage?

1.

2.

3.

Practice Plans | 81

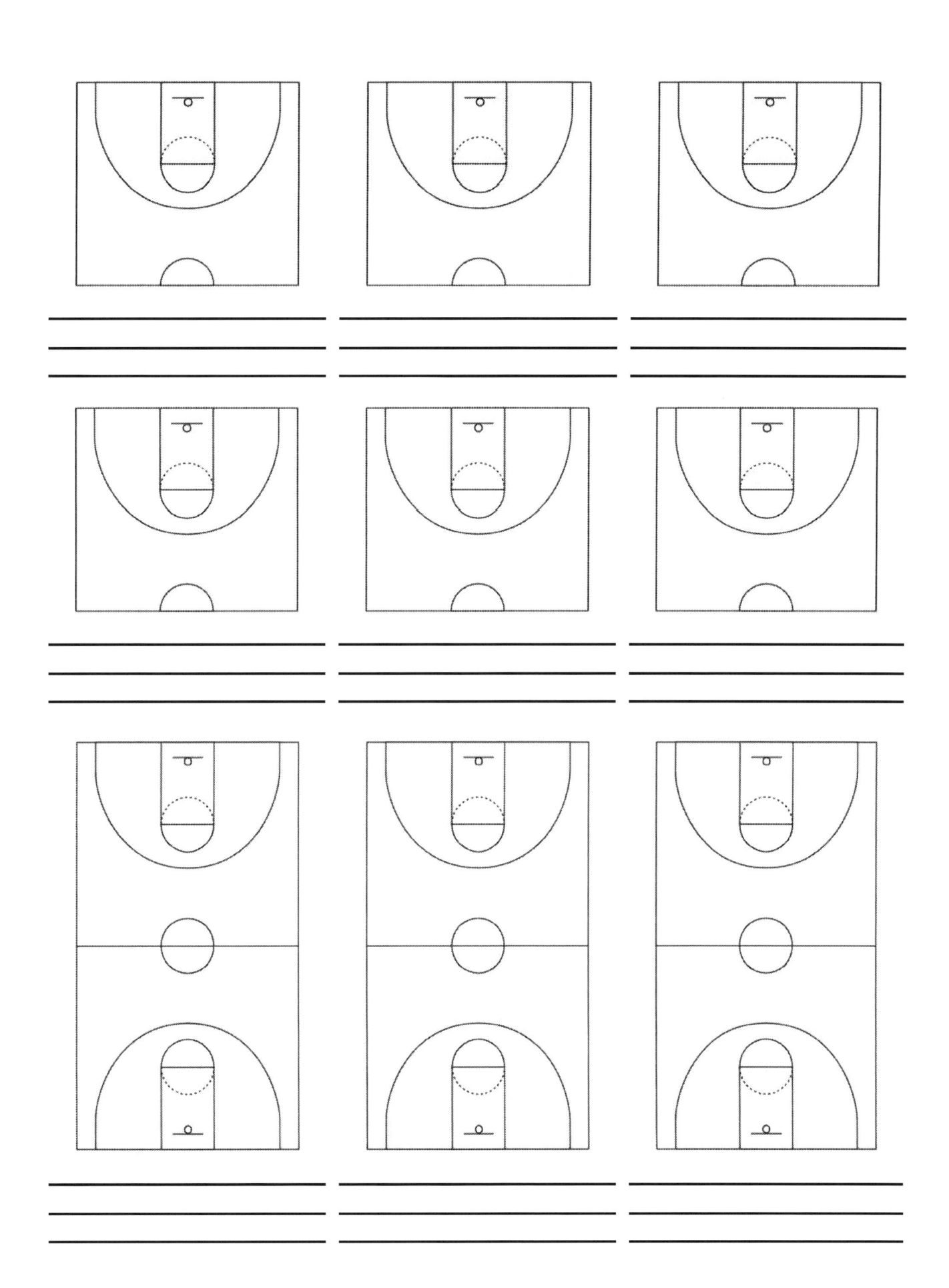

Date:　　　　　Time　　　　　Next Game/Opponent:　　　　　Next Practice:

Target of the Day	Offensive Emphasis	Defensive Emphasis	Teams

Time Min	Drill/Activity	Focus/Emphasis

Notes/Reminders

Player Connections
Who are you connecting with 1-on-1? How?

1.

2.

3.

Player/Coach Challenges
Which players/coaches have challenges on/off the court that you can support and encourage?

1.

2.

3.

82 | Practice Plans

Practice Plans | 83

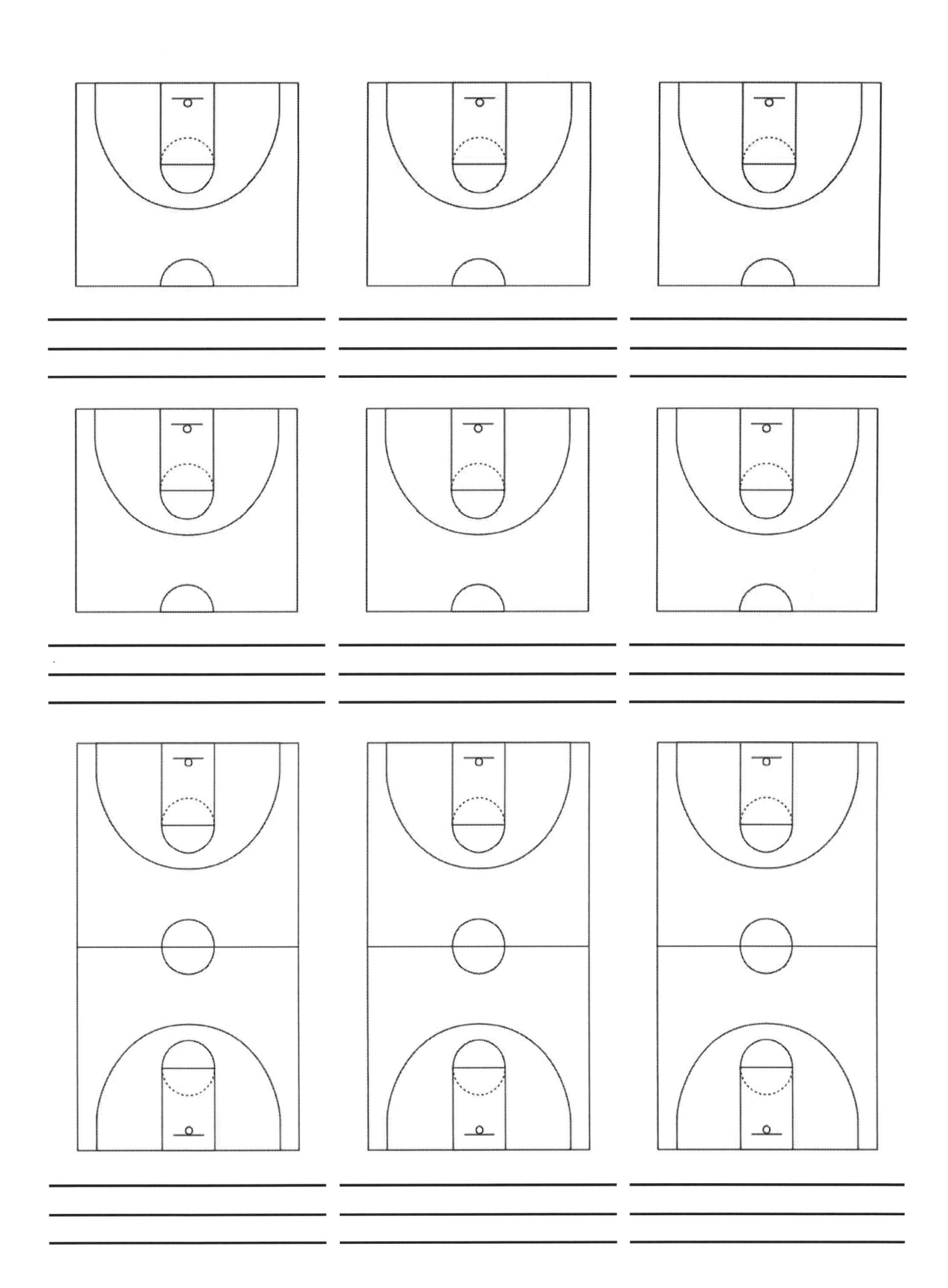

Date: Time Next Game/Opponent: Next Practice:

Target of the Day	Offensive Emphasis	Defensive Emphasis	Teams

Time Min	Drill/Activity	Focus/Emphasis

Notes/Reminders

Player Connections
Who are you connecting with 1-on-1? How?

1.

2.

3.

Player/Coach Challenges
Which players/coaches have challenges on/off the court that you can support and encourage?

1.

2.

3.

Practice Plans | 85

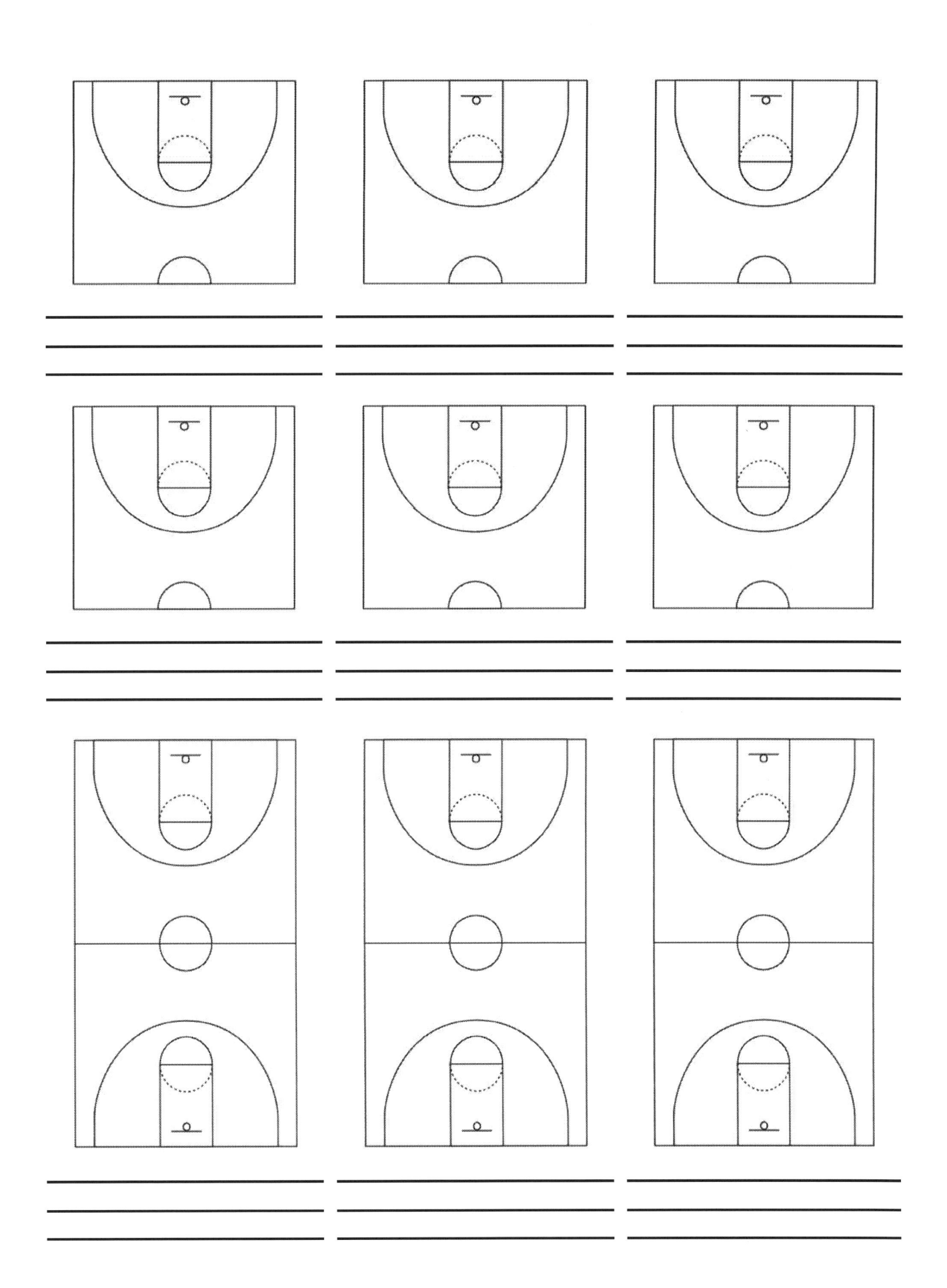

Date: Time   Next Game/Opponent: Next Practice:

Target of the Day	Offensive Emphasis	Defensive Emphasis	Teams

Time Min	Drill/Activity	Focus/Emphasis

Notes/Reminders

Player Connections
Who are you connecting with 1-on-1? How?

1.

2.

3.

Player/Coach Challenges
Which players/coaches have challenges on/off the court that you can support and encourage?

1.

2.

3.

Practice Plans | 87

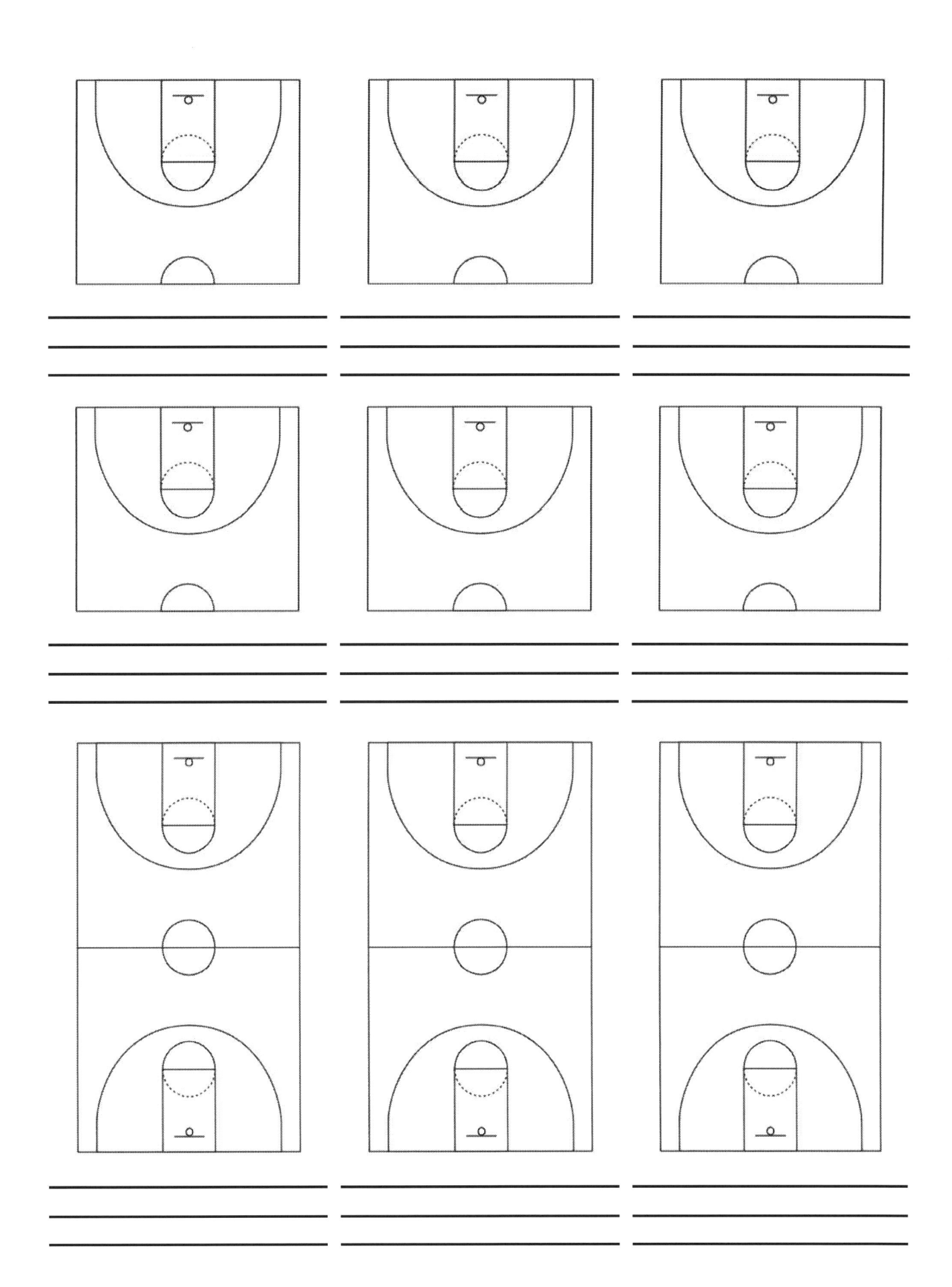

Date:　　　　Time　　　　　　Next Game/Opponent:　　　　　　　　　Next Practice:

Target of the Day	Offensive Emphasis	Defensive Emphasis	Teams

Time Min	Drill/Activity	Focus/Emphasis

Notes/Reminders

Player Connections
Who are you connecting with 1-on-1? How?

1.

2.

3.

Player/Coach Challenges
Which players/coaches have challenges on/off the court that you can support and encourage?

1.

2.

3.

88 | Practice Plans

Practice Plans | 89

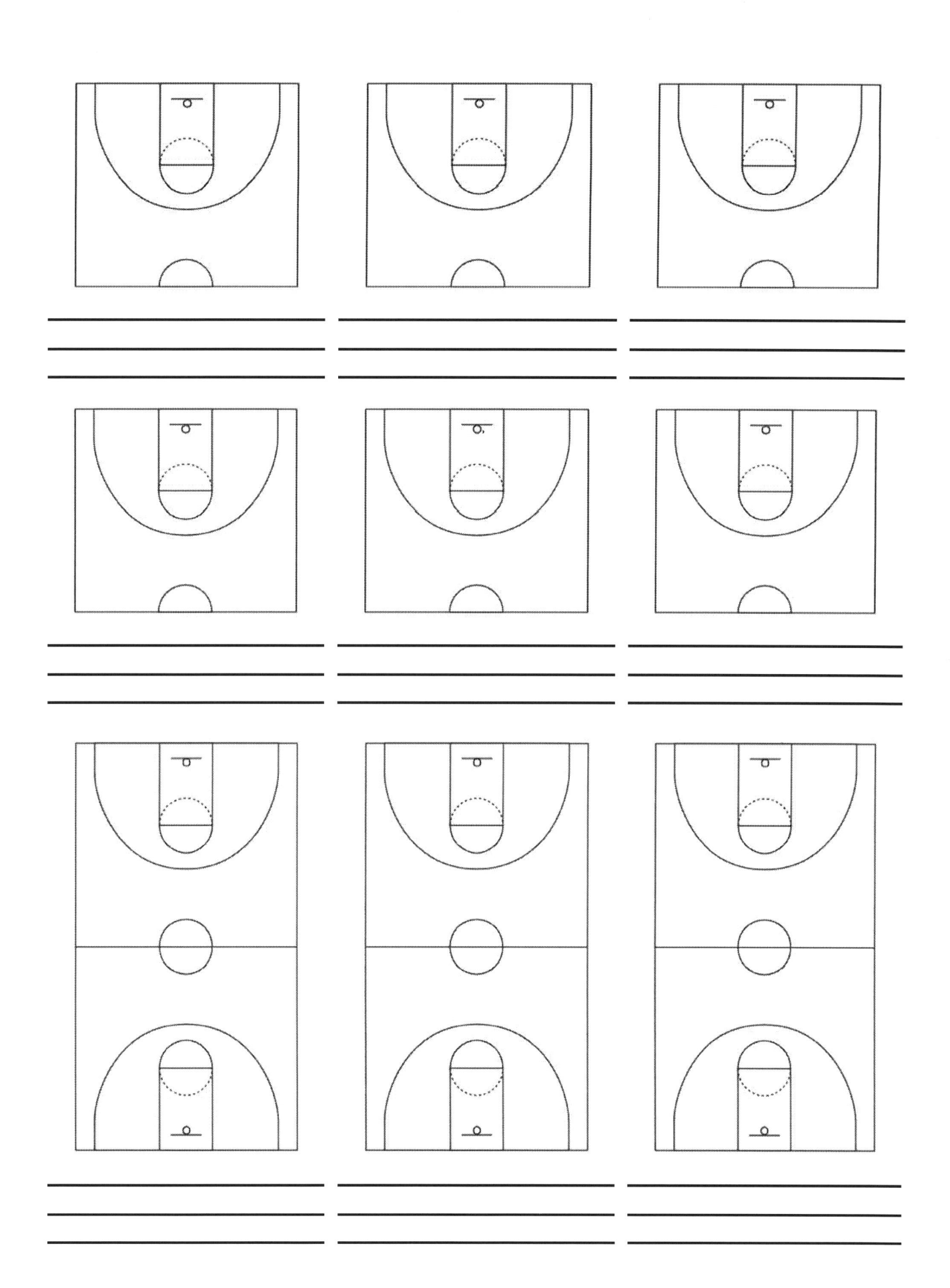

Date: Time Next Game/Opponent: Next Practice:

Target of the Day	Offensive Emphasis	Defensive Emphasis	Teams

Time Min	Drill/Activity	Focus/Emphasis

Notes/Reminders

Player Connections
Who are you connecting with 1-on-1? How?

1.

2.

3.

Player/Coach Challenges
Which players/coaches have challenges on/off the court that you can support and encourage?

1.

2.

3.

Practice Plans | 91

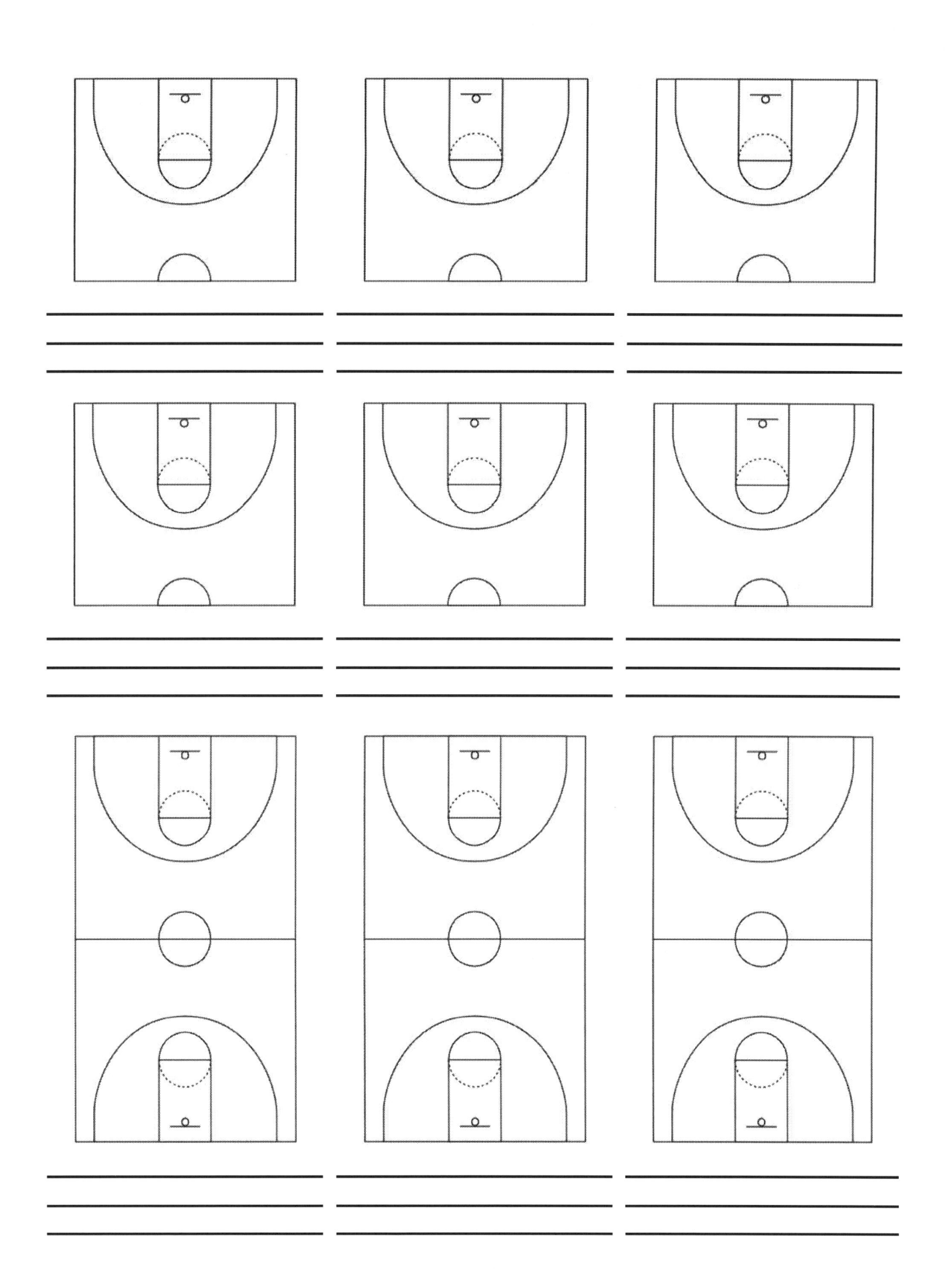

Date: Time   Next Game/Opponent: Next Practice:

Target of the Day	Offensive Emphasis	Defensive Emphasis	Teams

Time Min	Drill/Activity	Focus/Emphasis

Notes/Reminders

Player Connections
Who are you connecting with 1-on-1? How?

1.

2.

3.

Player/Coach Challenges
Which players/coaches have challenges on/off the court that you can support and encourage?

1.

2.

3.

Practice Plans | 93

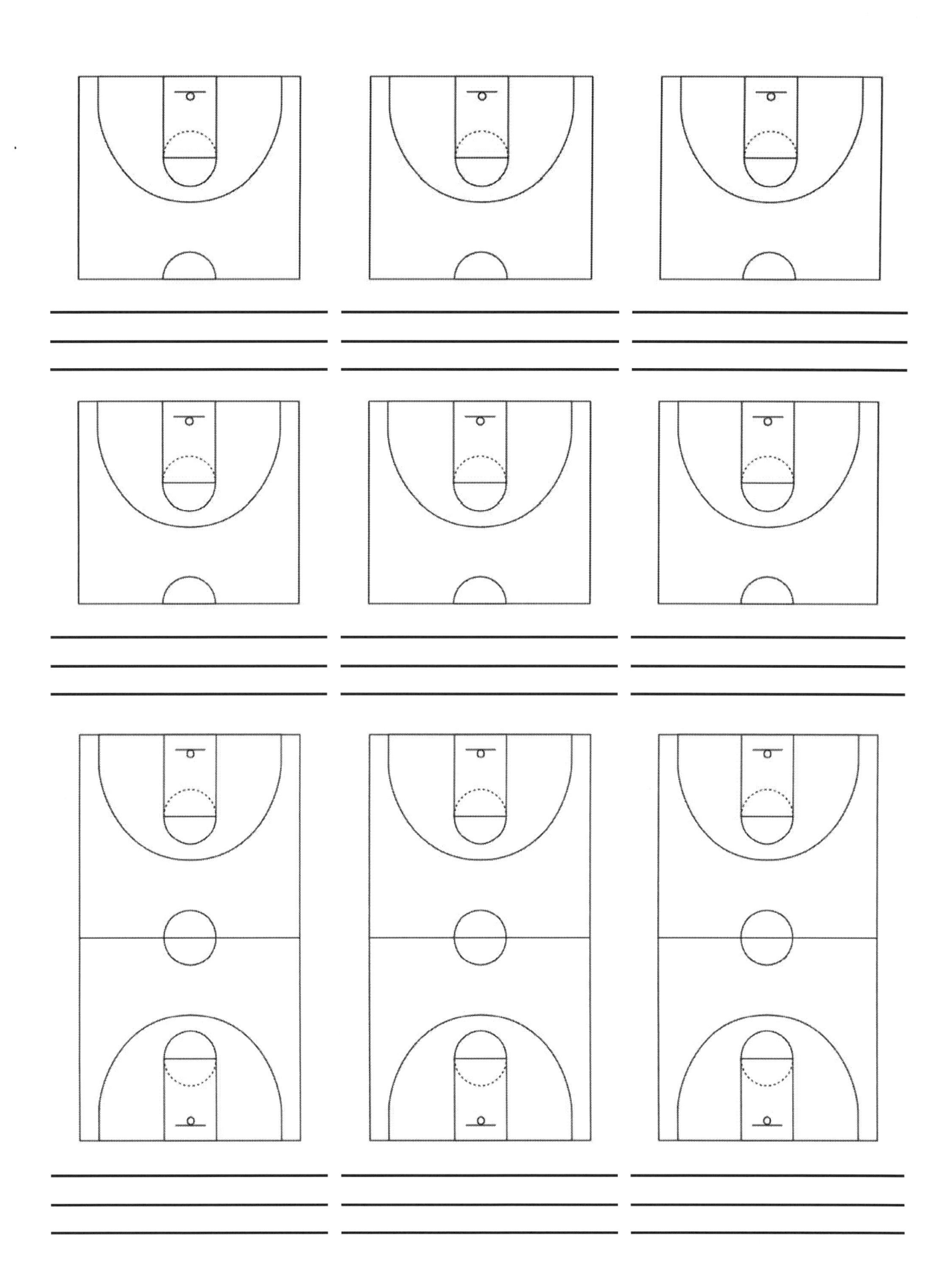

Date: Time   Next Game/Opponent: Next Practice:

Target of the Day	Offensive Emphasis	Defensive Emphasis	Teams

Time Min	Drill/Activity	Focus/Emphasis

Notes/Reminders

Player Connections
Who are you connecting with 1-on-1? How?

1.

2.

3.

Player/Coach Challenges
Which players/coaches have challenges on/off the court that you can support and encourage?

1.

2.

3.

Practice Plans | 95

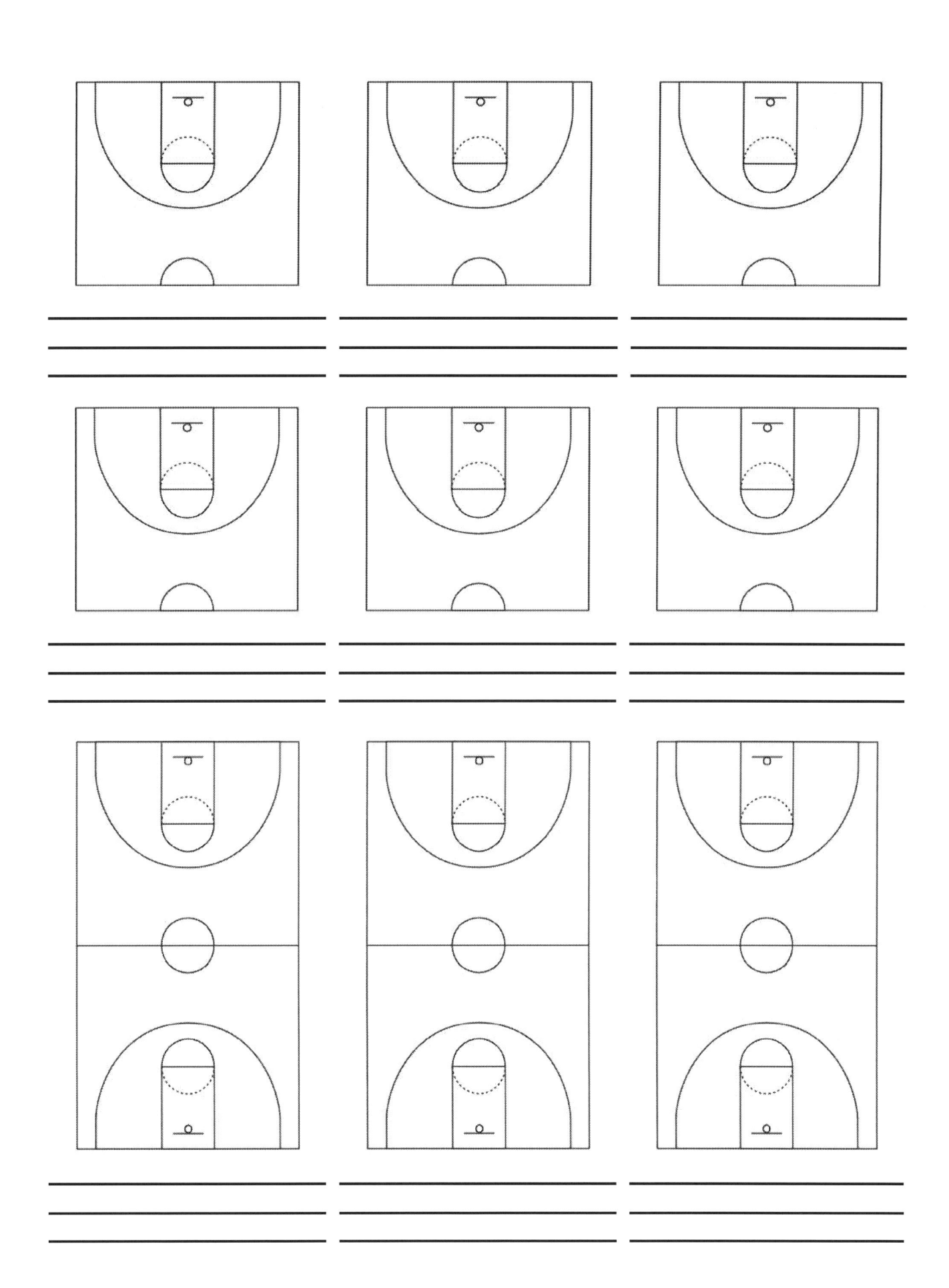

Date:　　　　　　Time　　　　　　Next Game/Opponent:　　　　　　　　Next Practice:

Target of the Day	Offensive Emphasis	Defensive Emphasis	Teams

Time Min	Drill/Activity	Focus/Emphasis

Notes/Reminders

Player Connections
Who are you connecting with 1-on-1? How?

1.

2.

3.

Player/Coach Challenges
Which players/coaches have challenges on/off the court that you can support and encourage?

1.

2.

3.

Practice Plans | 97

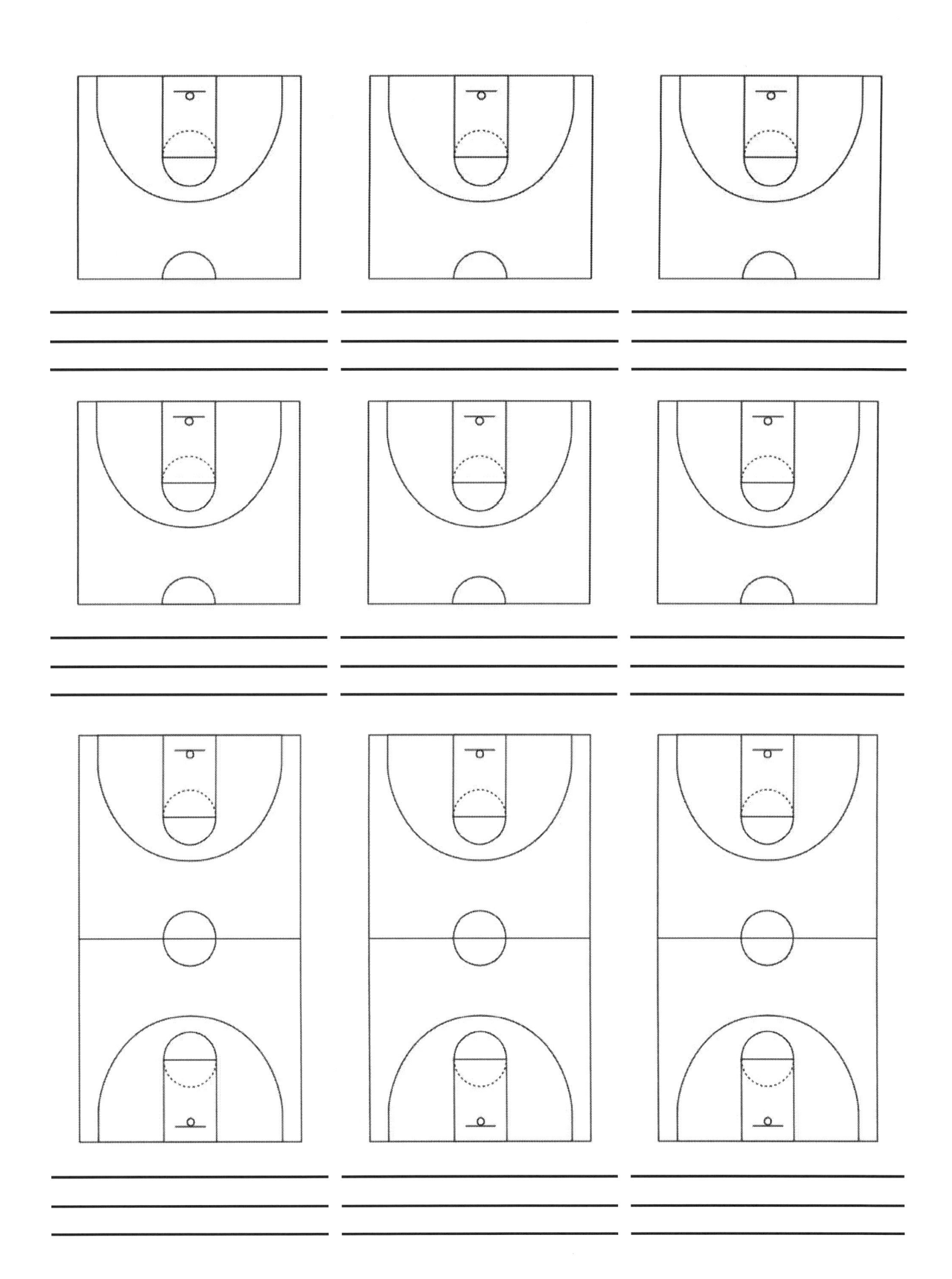

Date: Time   Next Game/Opponent: Next Practice:

Target of the Day	Offensive Emphasis	Defensive Emphasis	Teams

Time Min	Drill/Activity	Focus/Emphasis

Notes/Reminders

Player Connections
Who are you connecting with 1-on-1? How?

1.

2.

3.

Player/Coach Challenges
Which players/coaches have challenges on/off the court that you can support and encourage?

1.

2.

3.

Practice Plans | 99

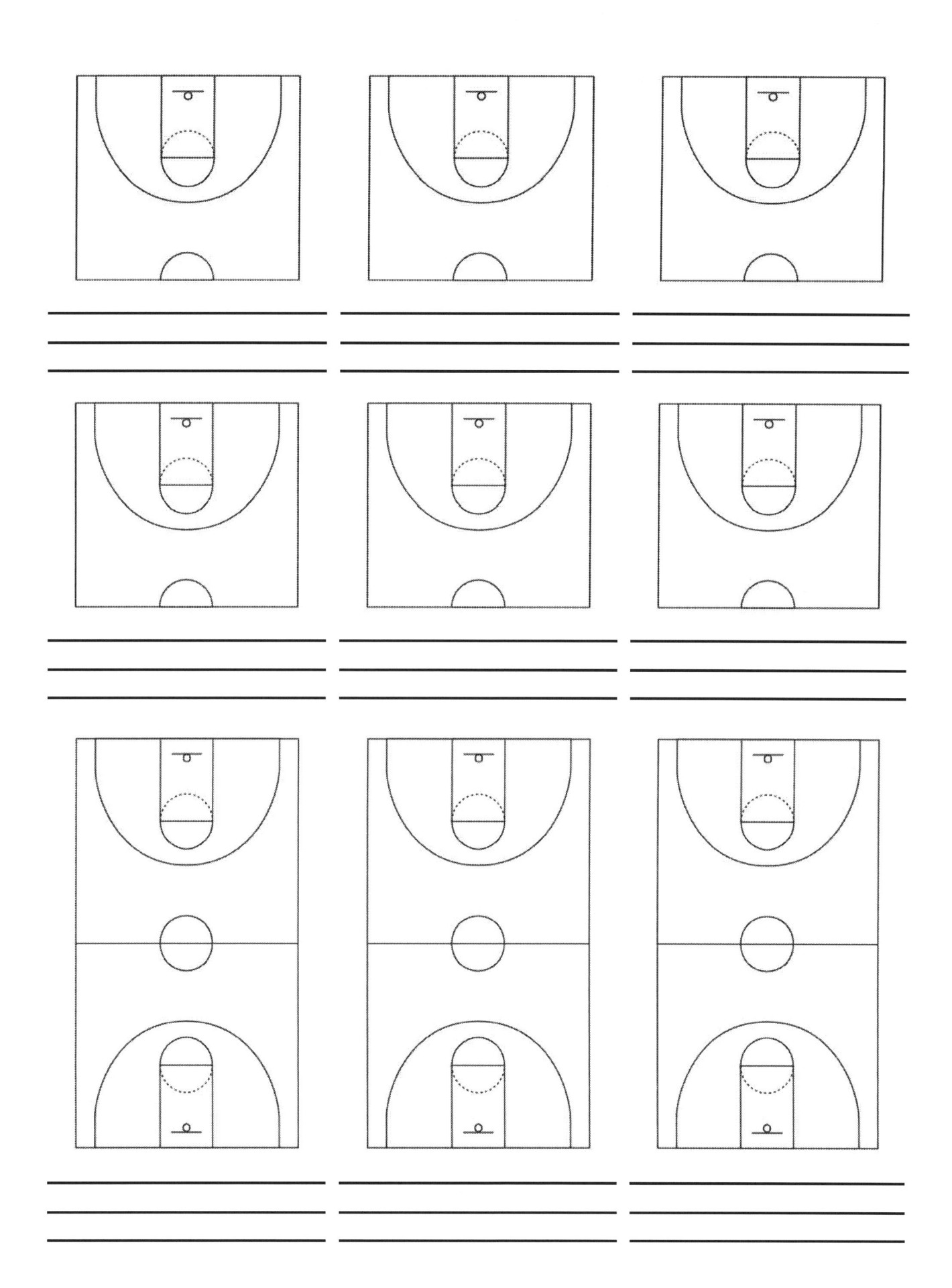

Date: Time   Next Game/Opponent: Next Practice:

Target of the Day	Offensive Emphasis	Defensive Emphasis	Teams

Time Min	Drill/Activity	Focus/Emphasis

Notes/Reminders

Player Connections
Who are you connecting with 1-on-1? How?

1.

2.

3.

Player/Coach Challenges
Which players/coaches have challenges on/off the court that you can support and encourage?

1.

2.

3.

100 | Practice Plans

Practice Plans | 101

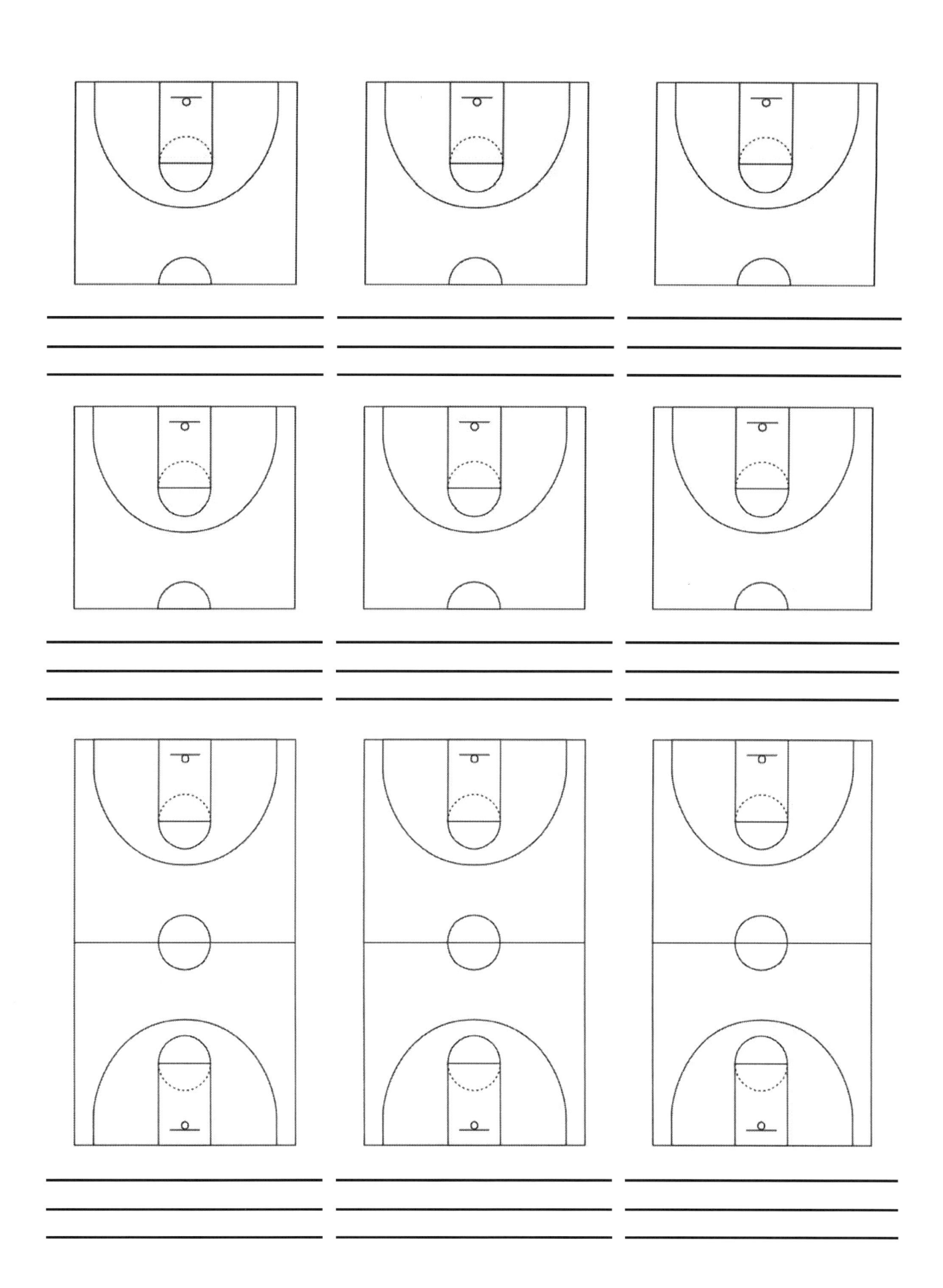

| Date: | Time | Next Game/Opponent: | Next Practice: |

Target of the Day	Offensive Emphasis	Defensive Emphasis	Teams

Time Min	Drill/Activity	Focus/Emphasis

Notes/Reminders

Player Connections
Who are you connecting with 1-on-1? How?

1.

2.

3.

Player/Coach Challenges
Which players/coaches have challenges on/off the court that you can support and encourage?

1.

2.

3.

Practice Plans | 103

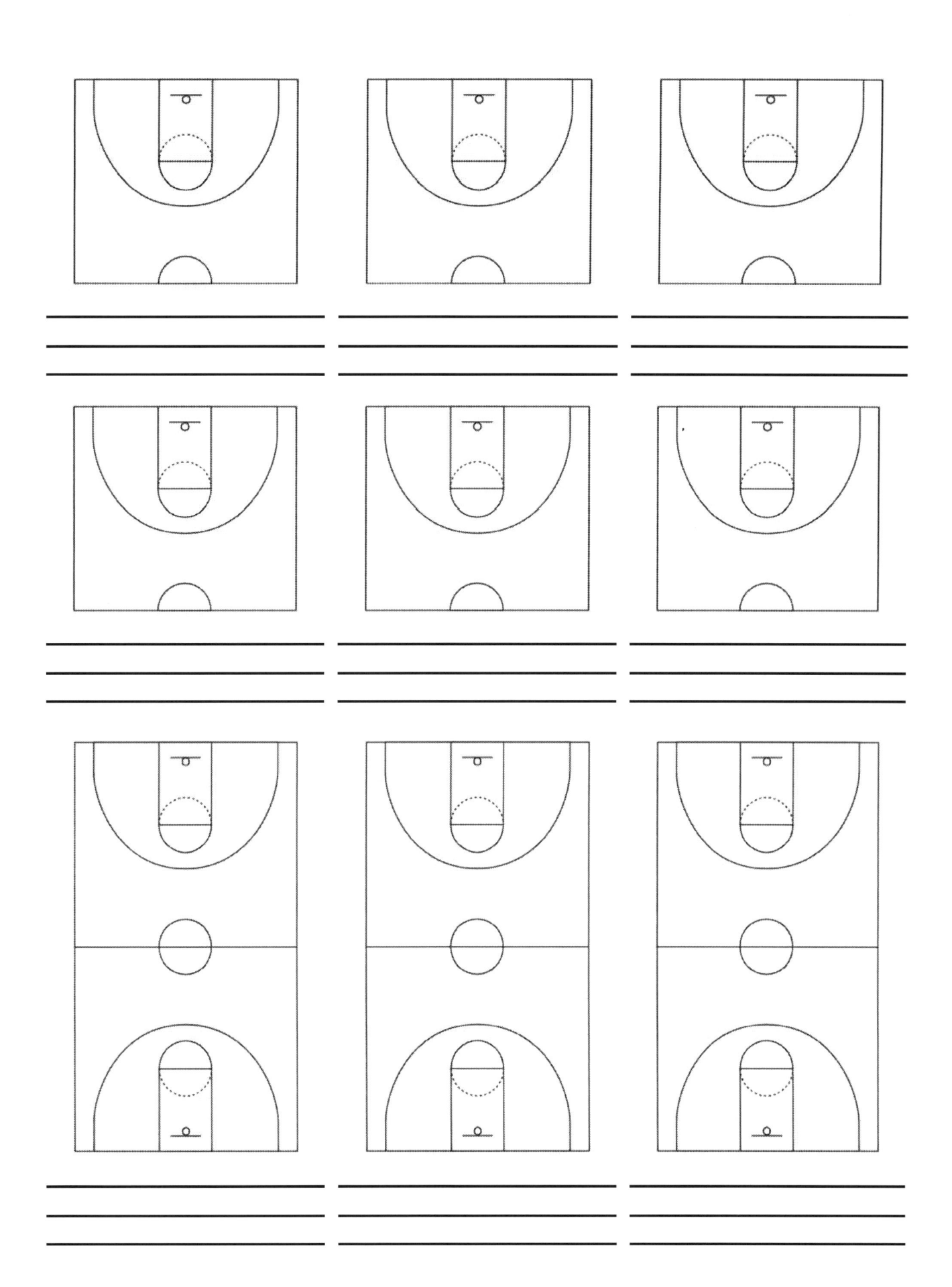

Date: Opponent: Location

Top 5 Keys	Starters	First Substitutions

Man Offense	Zone Offense	Defense	BLOB	SLOB

Line Ups

Scoring	Go Big	Go Small	Defensive	Pressing	End of Game

Other Notes

Post Game Reflection

Positives	Executed Well	Areas to Improve
Game Highlight	Player Experience	Plan for Improvement

Other Notes:

Date: Opponent: Location

Top 5 Keys	Starters	First Substitutions

Man Offense	Zone Offense	Defense	BLOB	SLOB

Line Ups					
Scoring	Go Big	Go Small	Defensive	Pressing	End of Game

Other Notes

Post Game Reflection

Positives	Executed Well	Areas to Improve
Game Highlight	Player Experience	Plan for Improvement

Other Notes:

Date: Opponent: Location

Top 5 Keys	Starters	First Substitutions

Man Offense	Zone Offense	Defense	BLOB	SLOB

Line Ups					
Scoring	Go Big	Go Small	Defensive	Pressing	End of Game

Other Notes

108 | Game Plans

Post Game Reflection

Positives	Executed Well	Areas to Improve
Game Highlight	Player Experience	Plan for Improvement

Other Notes:

Date: Opponent: Location

Top 5 Keys	Starters	First Substitutions

Man Offense	Zone Offense	Defense	BLOB	SLOB

Line Ups					
Scoring	Go Big	Go Small	Defensive	Pressing	End of Game

Other Notes

Post Game Reflection

Positives	Executed Well	Areas to Improve
Game Highlight	Player Experience	Plan for Improvement

Other Notes:

Date: Opponent: Location

Top 5 Keys	Starters	First Substitutions

Man Offense	Zone Offense	Defense	BLOB	SLOB

Line Ups					
Scoring	Go Big	Go Small	Defensive	Pressing	End of Game

Other Notes

Post Game Reflection

Positives	Executed Well	Areas to Improve
Game Highlight	Player Experience	Plan for Improvement

Other Notes:

Date: Opponent: Location

Top 5 Keys	Starters	First Substitutions

Man Offense	Zone Offense	Defense	BLOB	SLOB

Line Ups

Scoring	Go Big	Go Small	Defensive	Pressing	End of Game

Other Notes

Post Game Reflection

Positives	Executed Well	Areas to Improve
Game Highlight	Player Experience	Plan for Improvement

Other Notes:

Date: Opponent: Location

Top 5 Keys	Starters	First Substitutions

Man Offense	Zone Offense	Defense	BLOB	SLOB

| Line Ups ||||||
Scoring	Go Big	Go Small	Defensive	Pressing	End of Game

Other Notes

Post Game Reflection

Positives	Executed Well	Areas to Improve
Game Highlight	Player Experience	Plan for Improvement

Other Notes:

Date:					Opponent:					Location

Top 5 Keys	Starters	First Substitutions

Man Offense	Zone Offense	Defense	BLOB	SLOB

Line Ups					
Scoring	Go Big	Go Small	Defensive	Pressing	End of Game

Other Notes

Post Game Reflection

Positives	Executed Well	Areas to Improve
Game Highlight	Player Experience	Plan for Improvement

Other Notes:

Date: Opponent: Location

Top 5 Keys	Starters	First Substitutions

Man Offense	Zone Offense	Defense	BLOB	SLOB

Line Ups					
Scoring	Go Big	Go Small	Defensive	Pressing	End of Game

Other Notes

120 | Game Plans

Post Game Reflection

Positives	Executed Well	Areas to Improve
Game Highlight	Player Experience	Plan for Improvement

Other Notes:

Date: Opponent: Location

Top 5 Keys	Starters	First Substitutions

Man Offense	Zone Offense	Defense	BLOB	SLOB

Line Ups					
Scoring	Go Big	Go Small	Defensive	Pressing	End of Game

Other Notes

Post Game Reflection

Positives	Executed Well	Areas to Improve
Game Highlight	Player Experience	Plan for Improvement

Other Notes:

Date: Opponent: Location

Top 5 Keys	Starters	First Substitutions

Man Offense	Zone Offense	Defense	BLOB	SLOB

Line Ups					
Scoring	Go Big	Go Small	Defensive	Pressing	End of Game

Other Notes

Post Game Reflection

Positives	Executed Well	Areas to Improve
Game Highlight	Player Experience	Plan for Improvement

Other Notes:

Date: Opponent: Location

Top 5 Keys	Starters	First Substitutions

Man Offense	Zone Offense	Defense	BLOB	SLOB

Line Ups					
Scoring	Go Big	Go Small	Defensive	Pressing	End of Game

Other Notes

Post Game Reflection

Positives	Executed Well	Areas to Improve
Game Highlight	Player Experience	Plan for Improvement

Other Notes:

Date:	Opponent:	Location

Top 5 Keys	Starters	First Substitutions

Man Offense	Zone Offense	Defense	BLOB	SLOB

Line Ups					
Scoring	Go Big	Go Small	Defensive	Pressing	End of Game

Other Notes

Post Game Reflection

Positives	Executed Well	Areas to Improve
Game Highlight	Player Experience	Plan for Improvement

Other Notes:

Date: Opponent: Location

Top 5 Keys	Starters	First Substitutions

Man Offense	Zone Offense	Defense	BLOB	SLOB

Line Ups					
Scoring	Go Big	Go Small	Defensive	Pressing	End of Game

Other Notes

Post Game Reflection

Positives	Executed Well	Areas to Improve
Game Highlight	Player Experience	Plan for Improvement

Other Notes:

Date: Opponent: Location

Top 5 Keys	Starters	First Substitutions

Man Offense	Zone Offense	Defense	BLOB	SLOB

Line Ups					
Scoring	Go Big	Go Small	Defensive	Pressing	End of Game

Other Notes

Post Game Reflection

Positives	Executed Well	Areas to Improve
Game Highlight	Player Experience	Plan for Improvement

Other Notes:

Date:　　　　　　　　　　　　　　Opponent:　　　　　　　　　　　　　　　　　　　　　Location

Top 5 Keys	Starters	First Substitutions

Man Offense	Zone Offense	Defense	BLOB	SLOB

Line Ups					
Scoring	Go Big	Go Small	Defensive	Pressing	End of Game

Other Notes

Post Game Reflection

Positives	Executed Well	Areas to Improve
Game Highlight	Player Experience	Plan for Improvement

Other Notes:

Date: Opponent: Location

Top 5 Keys	Starters	First Substitutions

Man Offense	Zone Offense	Defense	BLOB	SLOB

Line Ups					
Scoring	Go Big	Go Small	Defensive	Pressing	End of Game

Other Notes

Post Game Reflection

Positives	Executed Well	Areas to Improve
Game Highlight	Player Experience	Plan for Improvement

Other Notes:

Date: Opponent: Location

Top 5 Keys	Starters	First Substitutions

Man Offense	Zone Offense	Defense	BLOB	SLOB

Line Ups						
Scoring	Go Big	Go Small	Defensive	Pressing	End of Game

Other Notes

Post Game Reflection

Positives	Executed Well	Areas to Improve
Game Highlight	Player Experience	Plan for Improvement

Other Notes:

Date: Opponent: Location

Top 5 Keys	Starters	First Substitutions

Man Offense	Zone Offense	Defense	BLOB	SLOB

Line Ups						
Scoring	Go Big	Go Small	Defensive	Pressing	End of Game

Other Notes

Post Game Reflection

Positives	Executed Well	Areas to Improve
Game Highlight	Player Experience	Plan for Improvement

Other Notes:

Date: Opponent: Location

Top 5 Keys	Starters	First Substitutions

Man Offense	Zone Offense	Defense	BLOB	SLOB

Line Ups					
Scoring	Go Big	Go Small	Defensive	Pressing	End of Game

Other Notes

Post Game Reflection

Positives	Executed Well	Areas to Improve
Game Highlight	Player Experience	Plan for Improvement

Other Notes:

Date: Opponent: Location

Top 5 Keys	Starters	First Substitutions

Man Offense	Zone Offense	Defense	BLOB	SLOB

Line Ups

Scoring	Go Big	Go Small	Defensive	Pressing	End of Game

Other Notes

Post Game Reflection

Positives	Executed Well	Areas to Improve
Game Highlight	Player Experience	Plan for Improvement

Other Notes:

Date:	Opponent:	Location

Top 5 Keys	Starters	First Substitutions

Man Offense	Zone Offense	Defense	BLOB	SLOB

Line Ups					
Scoring	Go Big	Go Small	Defensive	Pressing	End of Game

Other Notes

Post Game Reflection

Positives	Executed Well	Areas to Improve
Game Highlight	Player Experience	Plan for Improvement

Other Notes:

Date: Opponent: Location

Top 5 Keys	Starters	First Substitutions

Man Offense	Zone Offense	Defense	BLOB	SLOB

Line Ups					
Scoring	Go Big	Go Small	Defensive	Pressing	End of Game

Other Notes

148 | Game Plans

Post Game Reflection

Positives	Executed Well	Areas to Improve
Game Highlight	Player Experience	Plan for Improvement

Other Notes:

Date: Opponent: Location

Top 5 Keys	Starters	First Substitutions

Man Offense	Zone Offense	Defense	BLOB	SLOB

Line Ups					
Scoring	Go Big	Go Small	Defensive	Pressing	End of Game

Other Notes

Post Game Reflection

Positives	Executed Well	Areas to Improve
Game Highlight	Player Experience	Plan for Improvement

Other Notes:

Date: Opponent: Location

Top 5 Keys	Starters	First Substitutions

Man Offense	Zone Offense	Defense	BLOB	SLOB

Line Ups					
Scoring	Go Big	Go Small	Defensive	Pressing	End of Game

Other Notes

Post Game Reflection

Positives	Executed Well	Areas to Improve
Game Highlight	Player Experience	Plan for Improvement

Other Notes:

Date: Opponent: Location

Top 5 Keys	Starters	First Substitutions

Man Offense	Zone Offense	Defense	BLOB	SLOB

Line Ups					
Scoring	Go Big	Go Small	Defensive	Pressing	End of Game

Other Notes

Post Game Reflection

Positives	Executed Well	Areas to Improve
Game Highlight	Player Experience	Plan for Improvement

Other Notes:

Date: Opponent: Location

Top 5 Keys	Starters	First Substitutions

Man Offense	Zone Offense	Defense	BLOB	SLOB

Line Ups					
Scoring	Go Big	Go Small	Defensive	Pressing	End of Game

Other Notes

Post Game Reflection

Positives	Executed Well	Areas to Improve
Game Highlight	Player Experience	Plan for Improvement

Other Notes:

Date: Opponent: Location

Top 5 Keys	Starters	First Substitutions

Man Offense	Zone Offense	Defense	BLOB	SLOB

Line Ups					
Scoring	Go Big	Go Small	Defensive	Pressing	End of Game

Other Notes

Post Game Reflection

Positives	Executed Well	Areas to Improve
Game Highlight	Player Experience	Plan for Improvement

Other Notes:

Date: Opponent: Location

Top 5 Keys	Starters	First Substitutions

Man Offense	Zone Offense	Defense	BLOB	SLOB

Line Ups					
Scoring	Go Big	Go Small	Defensive	Pressing	End of Game

Other Notes

160 | Game Plans

Post Game Reflection

Positives	Executed Well	Areas to Improve
Game Highlight	Player Experience	Plan for Improvement

Other Notes:

Date:　　　　　　　　　　　　　Opponent:　　　　　　　　　　　　　　　　　　Location

Top 5 Keys	Starters	First Substitutions

Man Offense	Zone Offense	Defense	BLOB	SLOB

Line Ups					
Scoring	Go Big	Go Small	Defensive	Pressing	End of Game

Other Notes

162 | Game Plans

Post Game Reflection

Positives	Executed Well	Areas to Improve
Game Highlight	Player Experience	Plan for Improvement

Other Notes:

Court Diagrams & Notes | 165

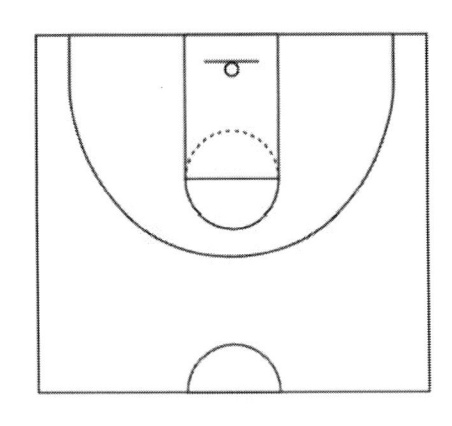

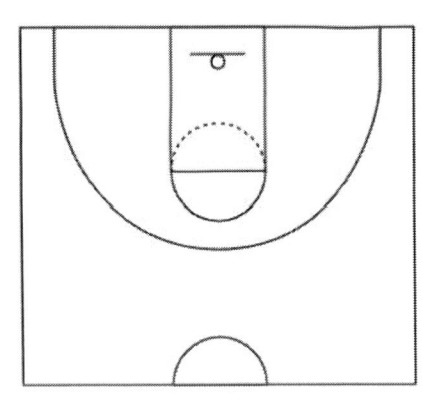

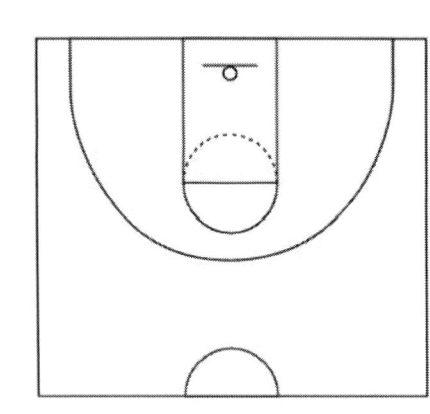

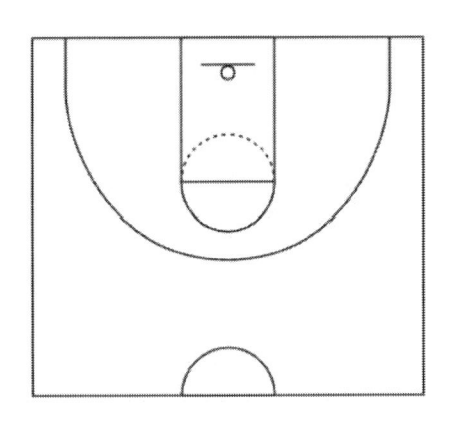

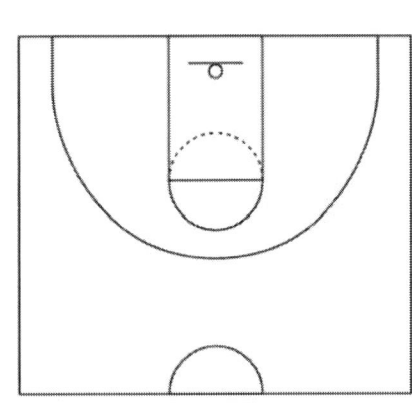

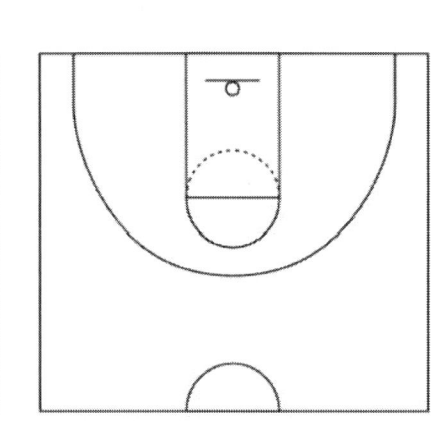

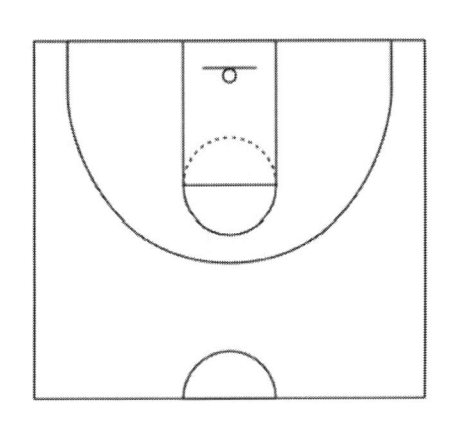

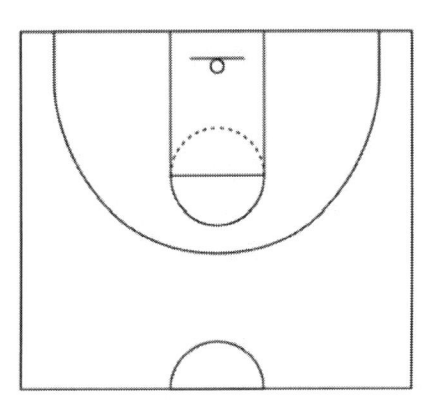

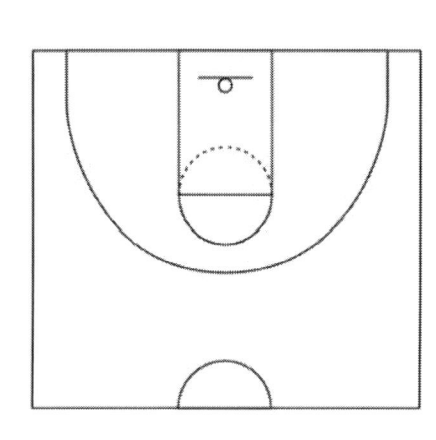

Court Diagrams & Notes | 167

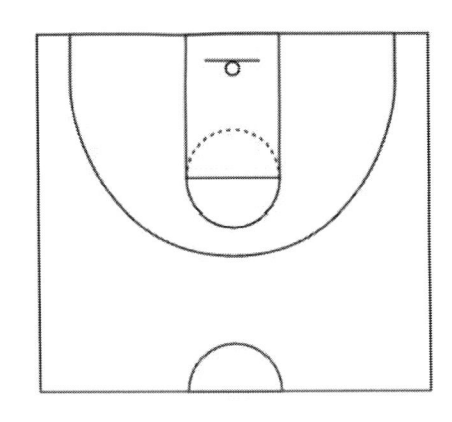

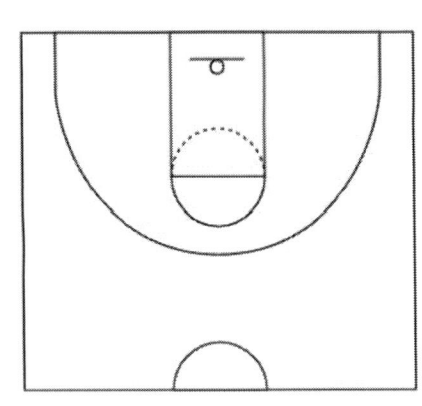

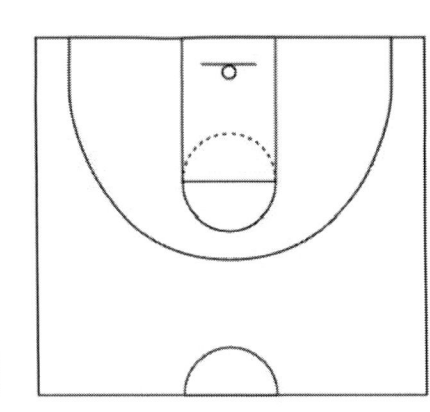

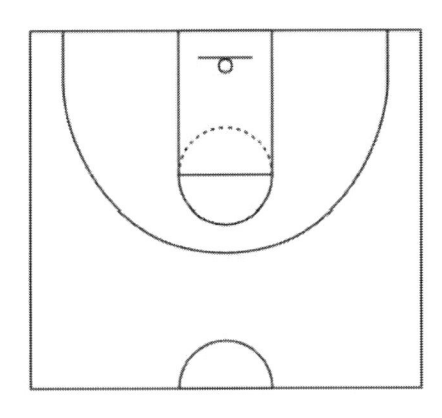

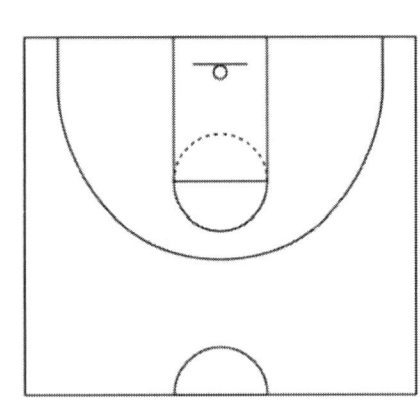

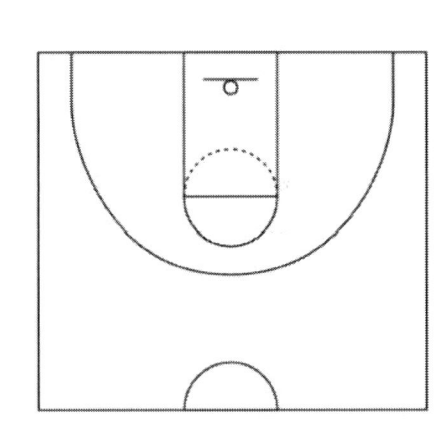

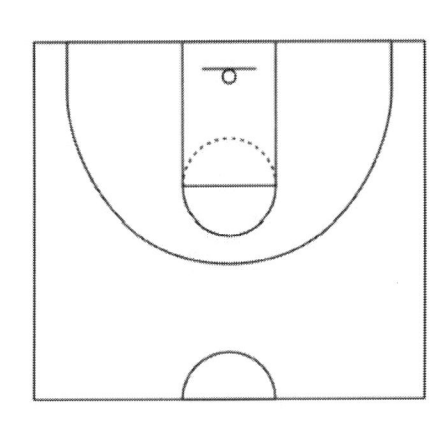

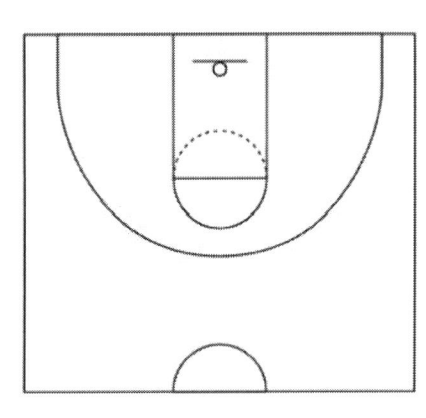

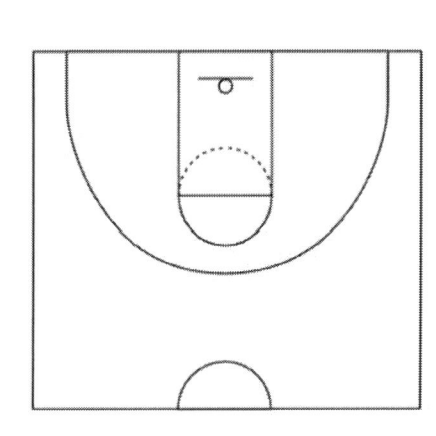

Court Diagrams & Notes | 169

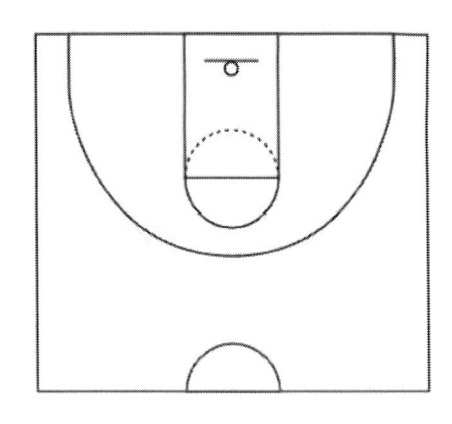

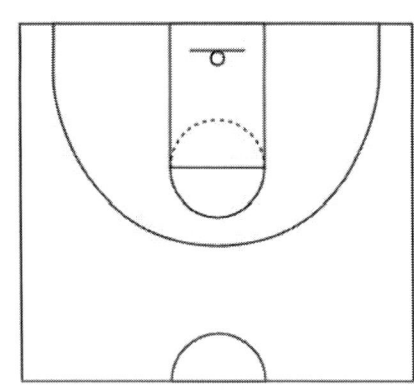

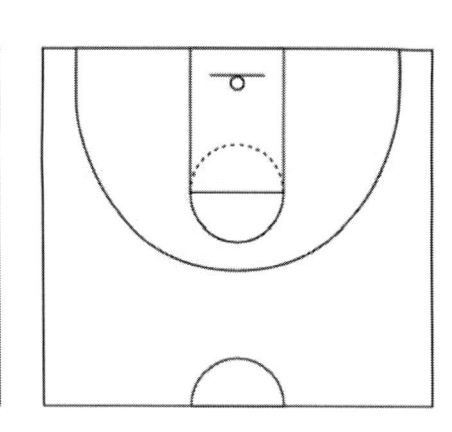

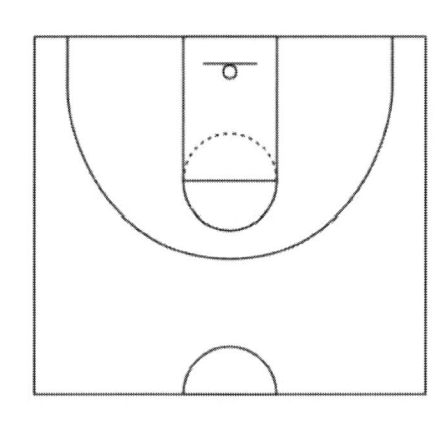

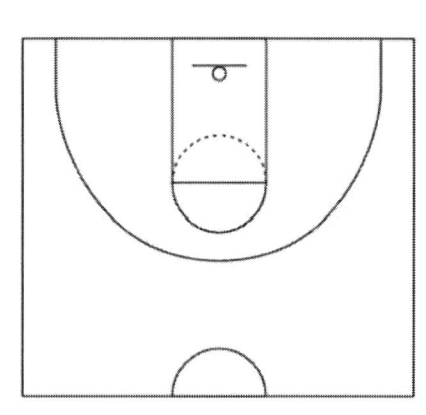

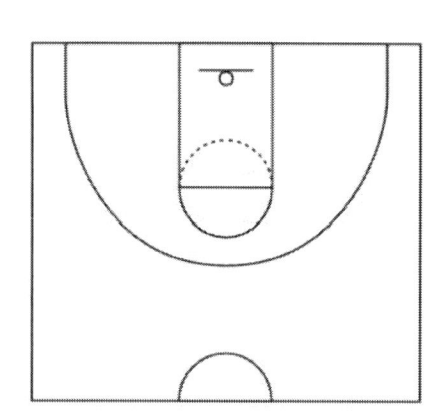

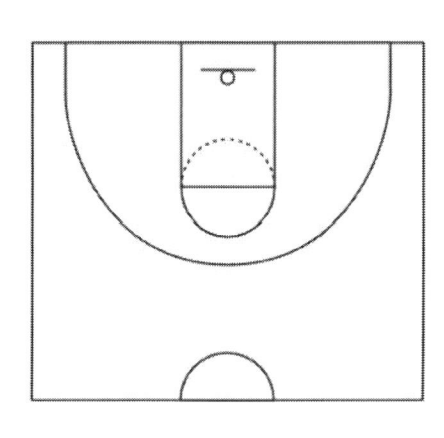

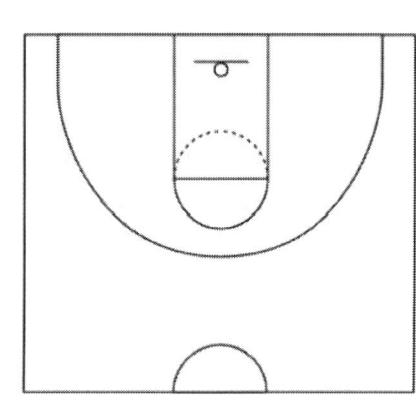

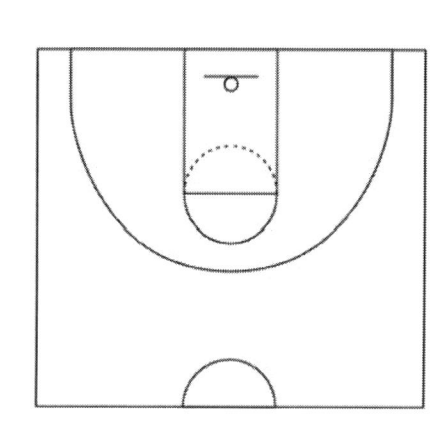

Court Diagrams & Notes | 171

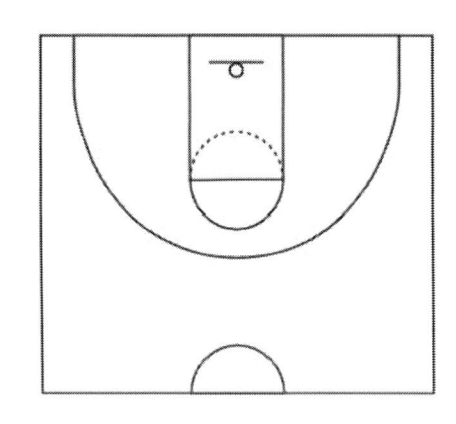

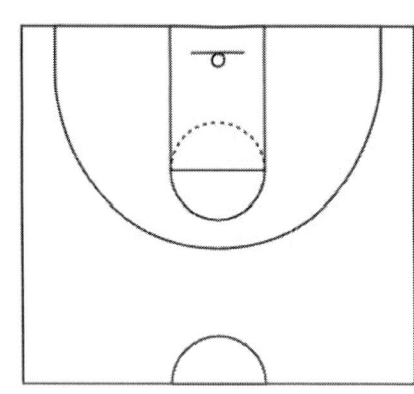

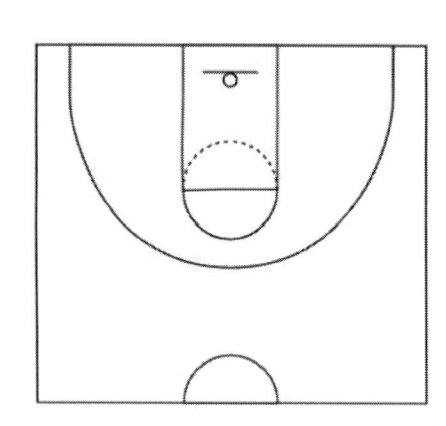

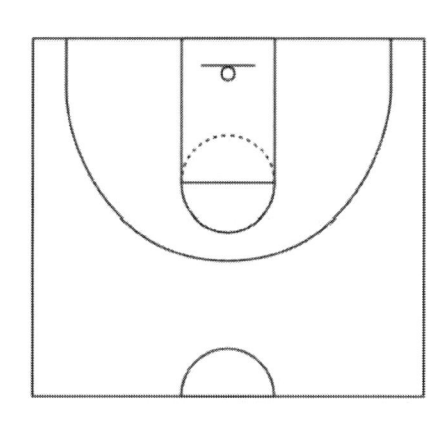

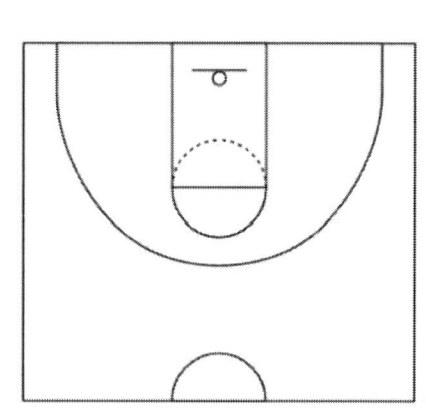

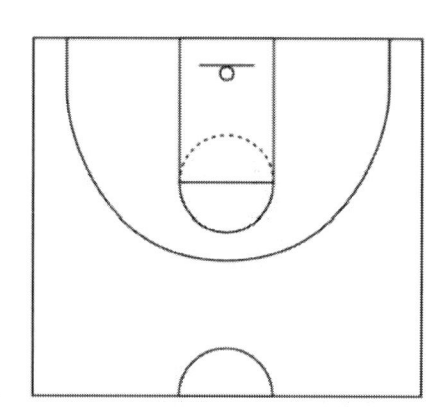

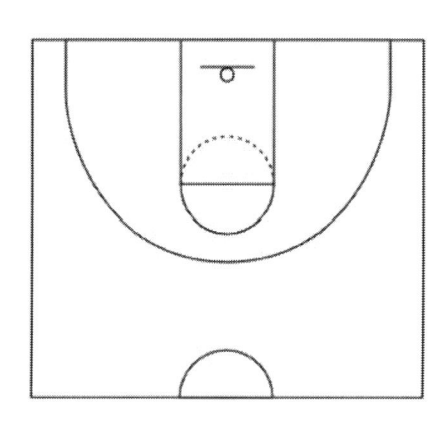

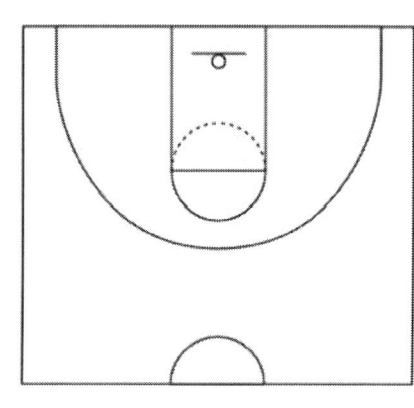

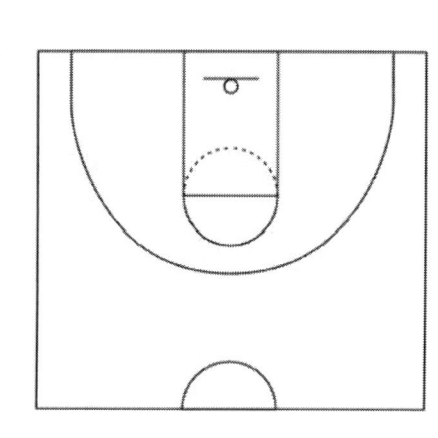

Court Diagrams & Notes | 173

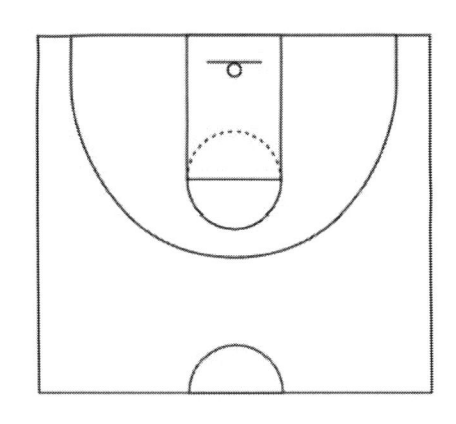

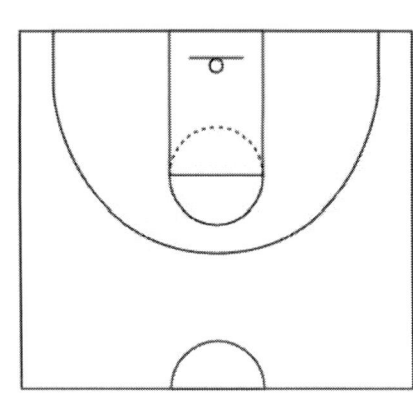

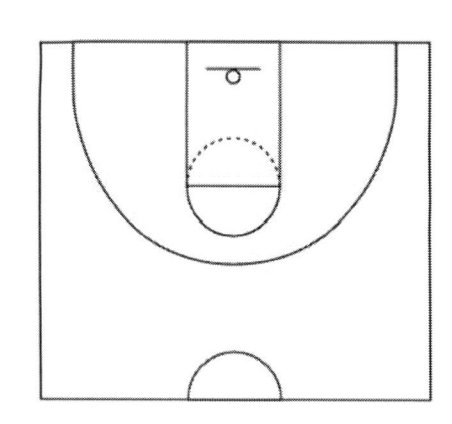

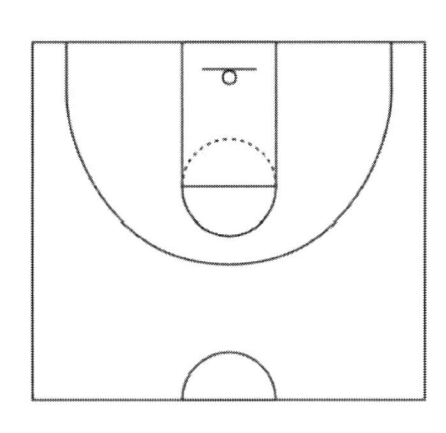

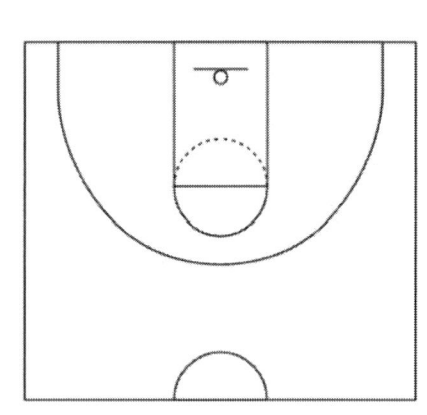

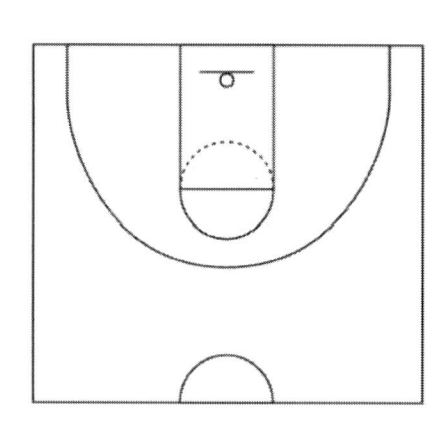

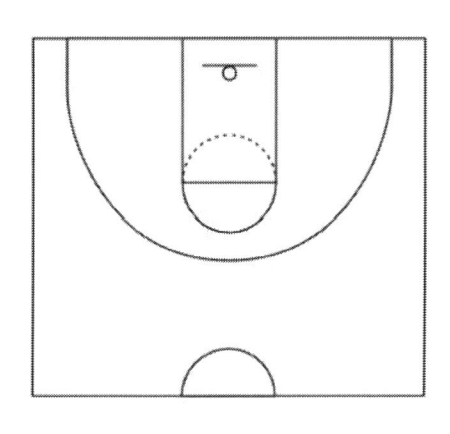

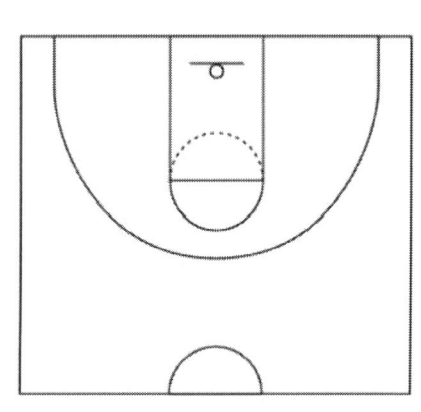

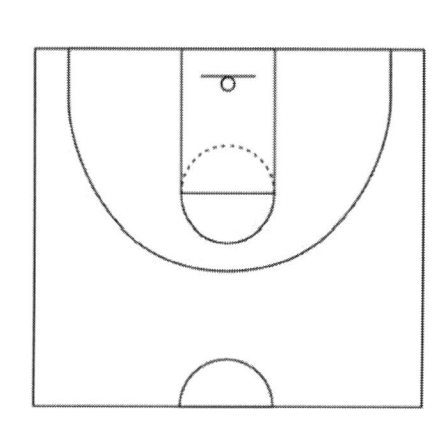

Court Diagrams & Notes | 175

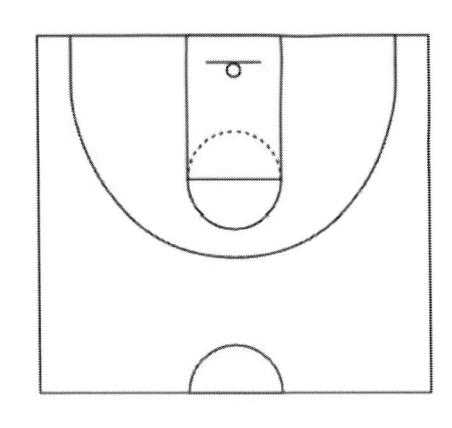

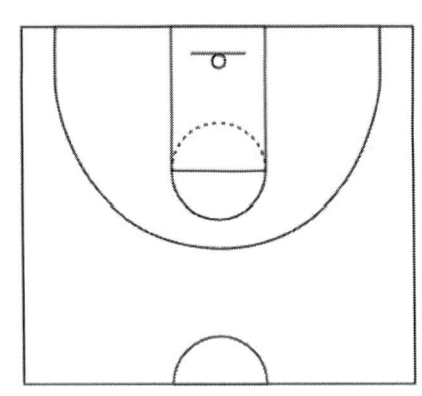

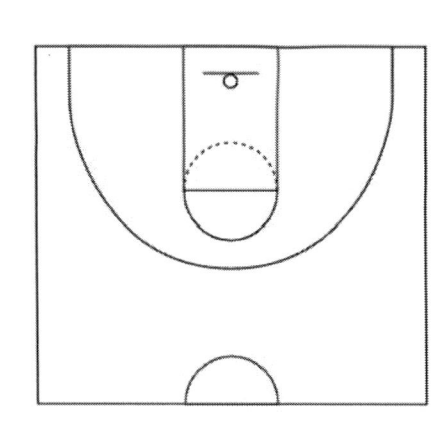

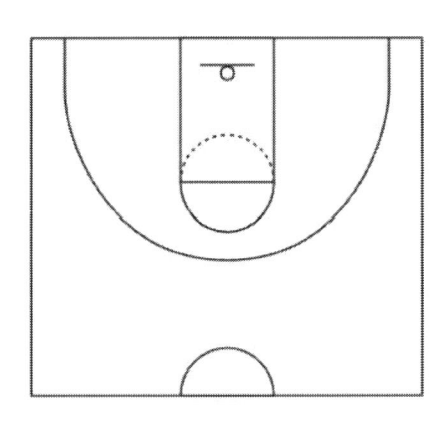

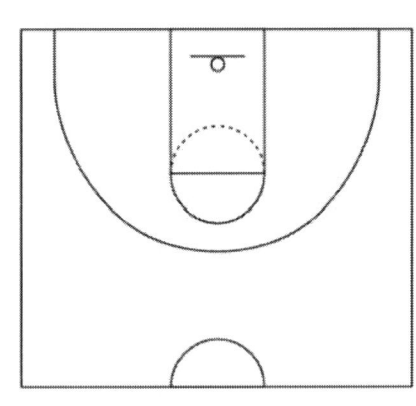

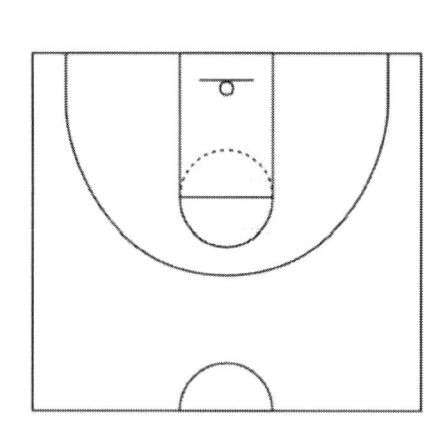

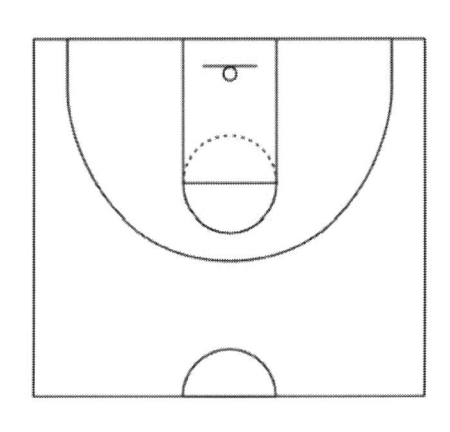

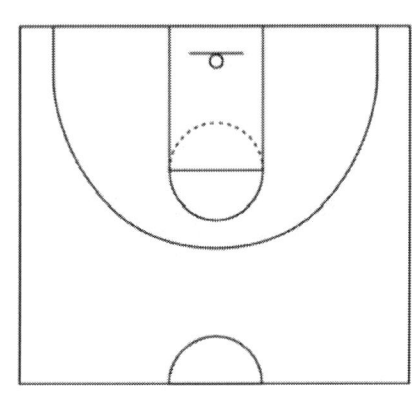

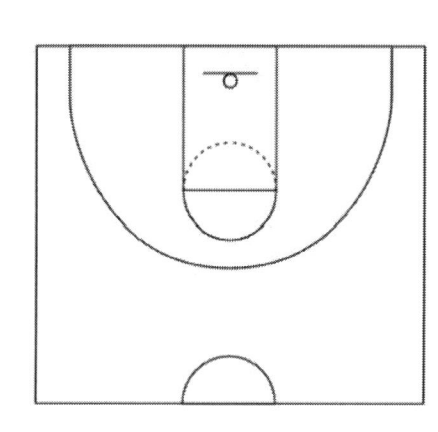

Court Diagrams & Notes | 177

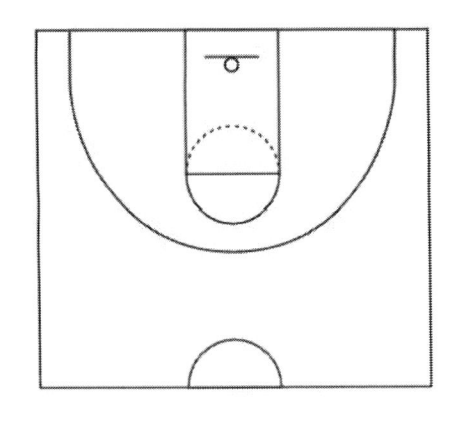

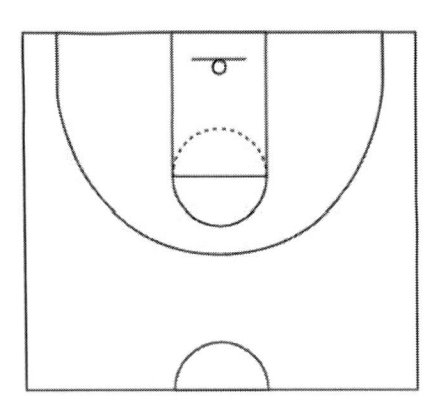

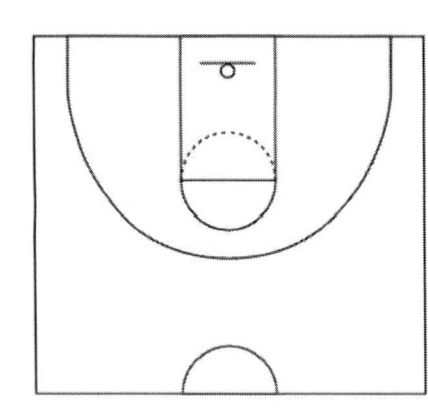

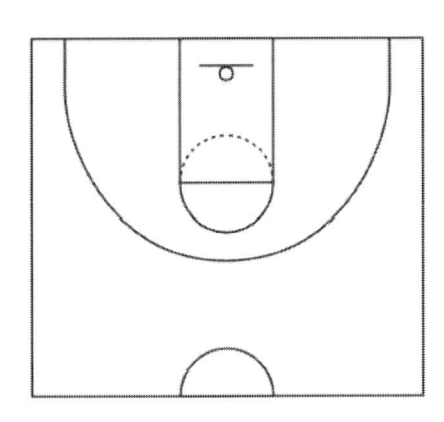

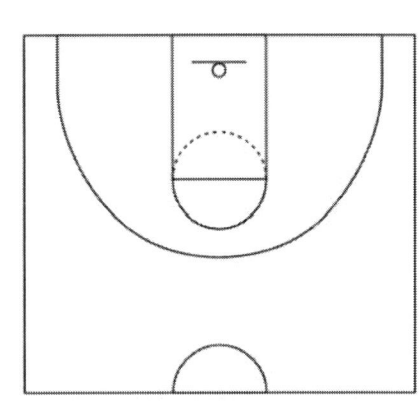

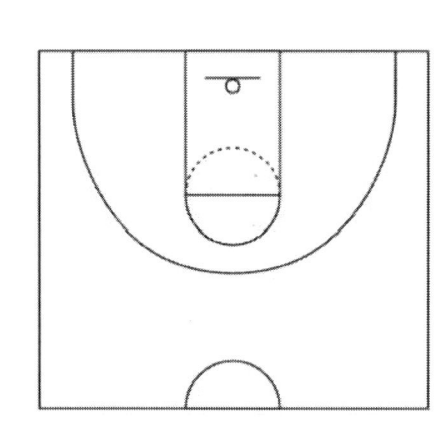

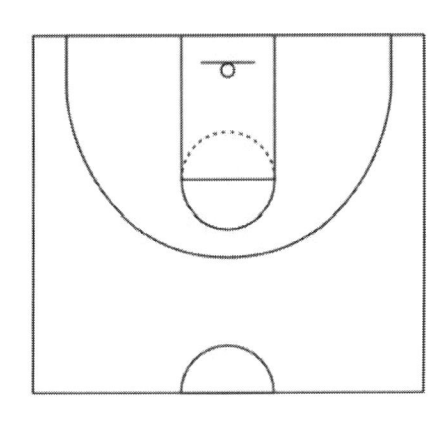

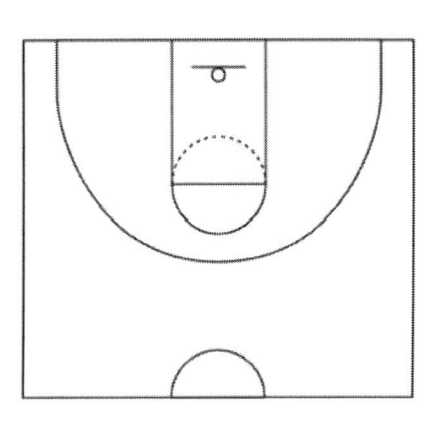

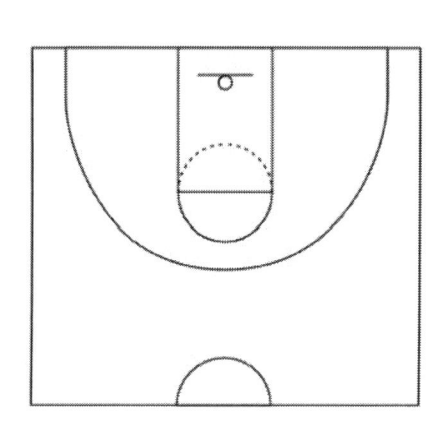

Court Diagrams & Notes | 179

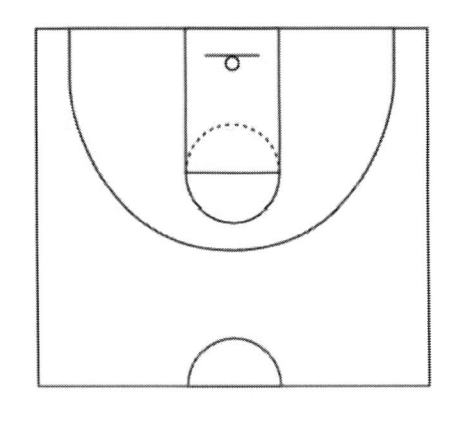

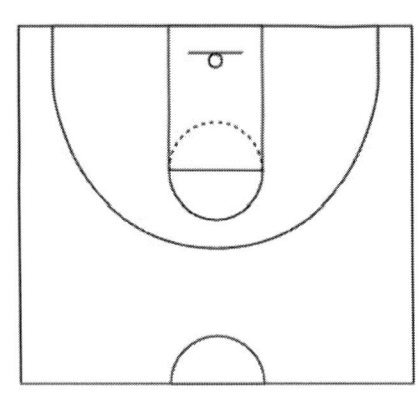

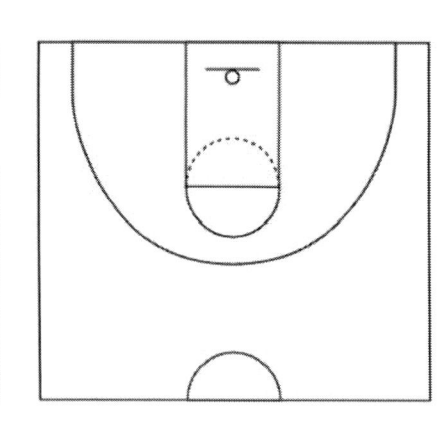

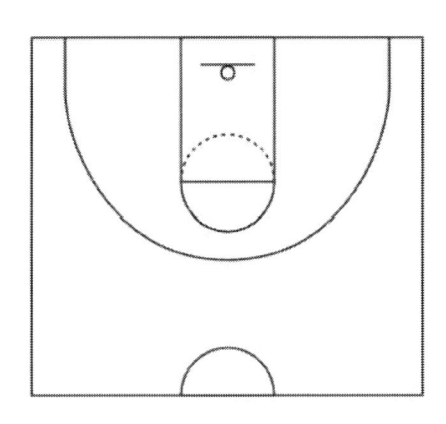

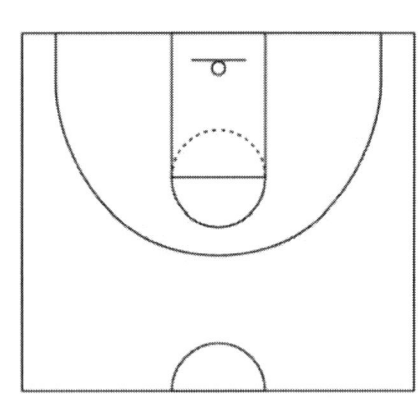

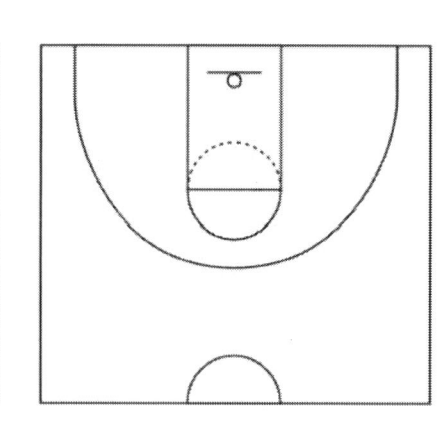

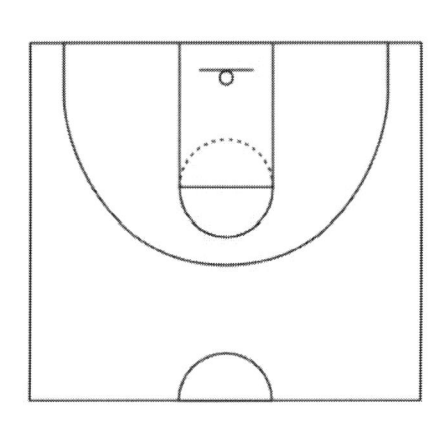

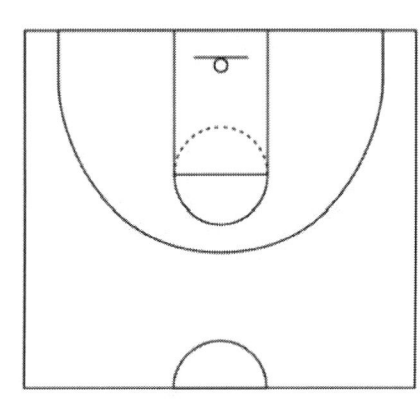

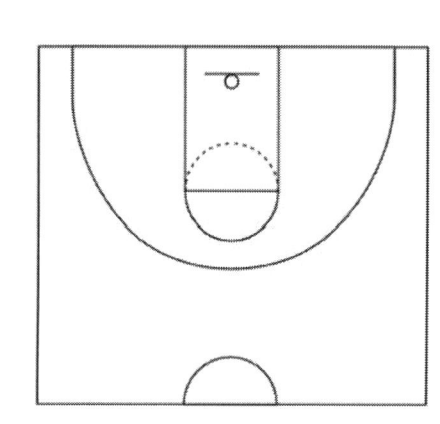

Court Diagrams & Notes | 181

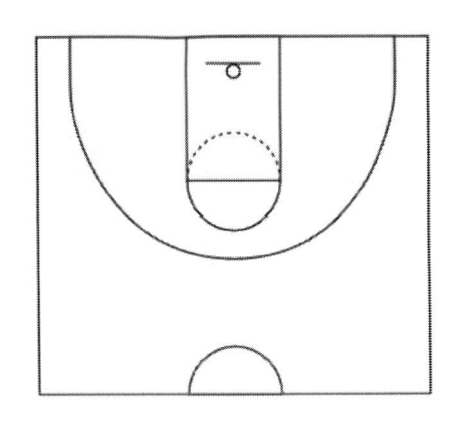

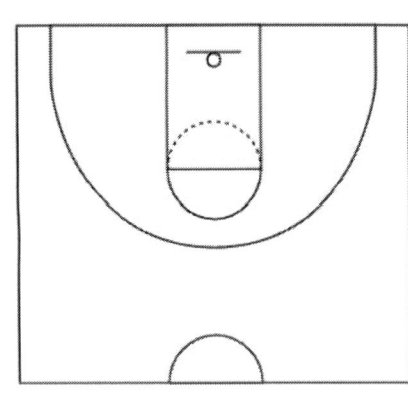

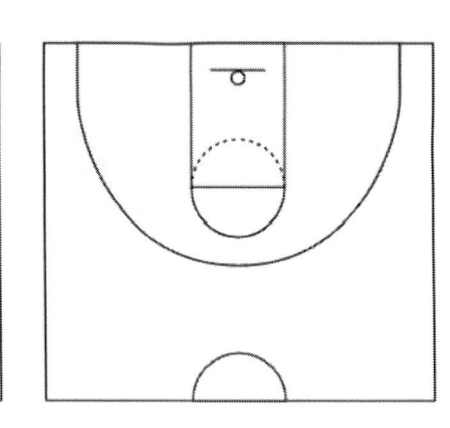

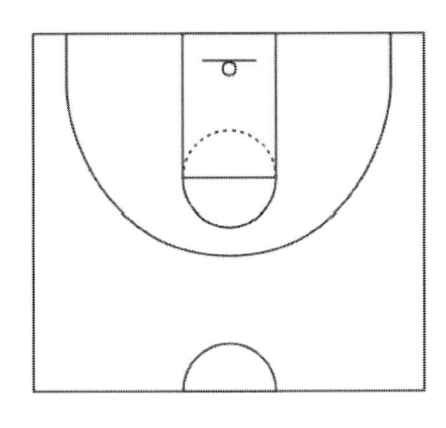

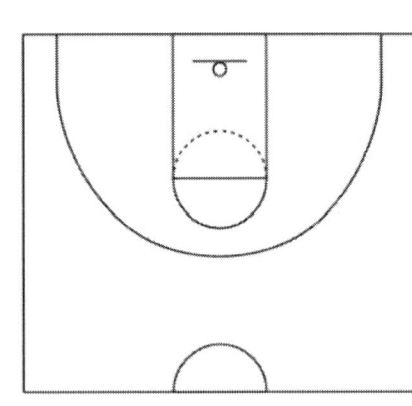

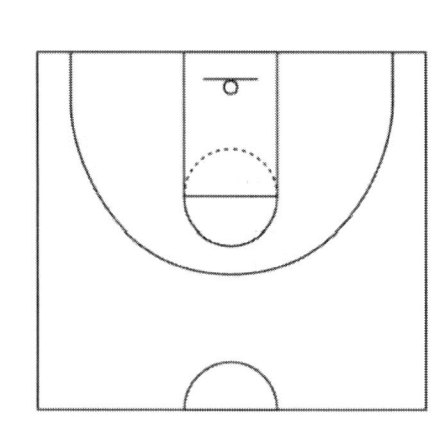

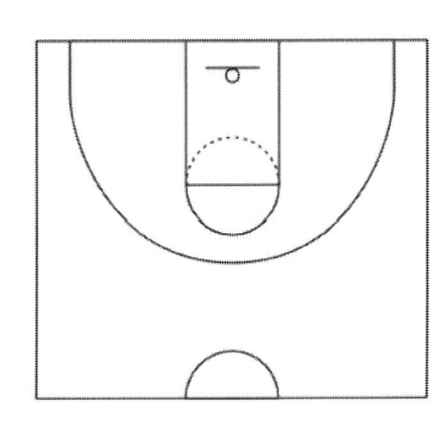

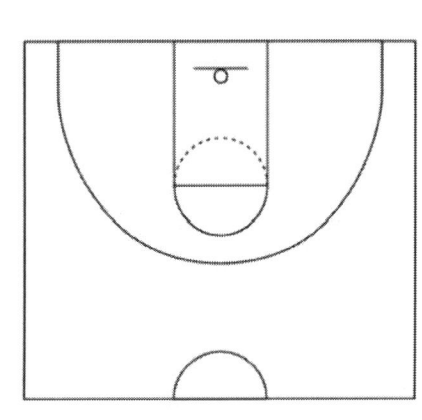

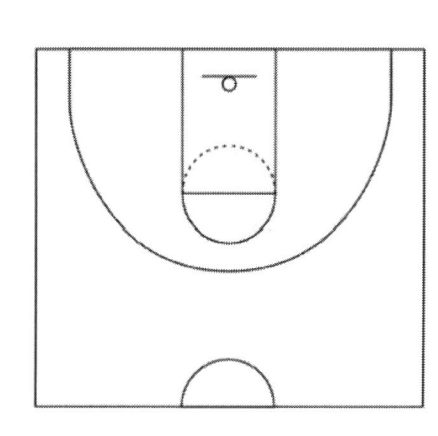

Court Diagrams & Notes | 183

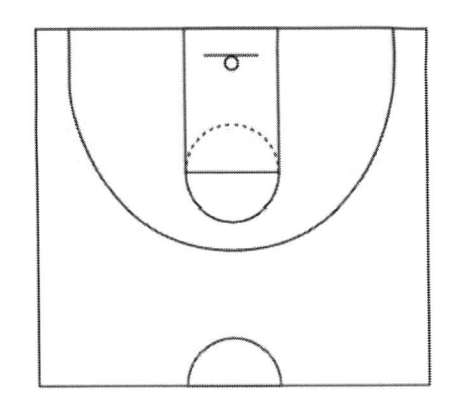

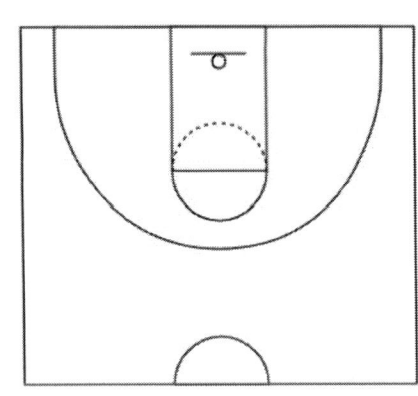

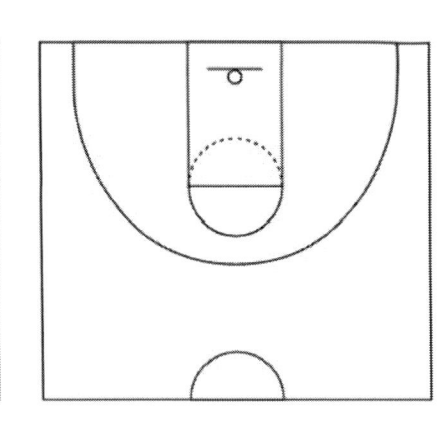

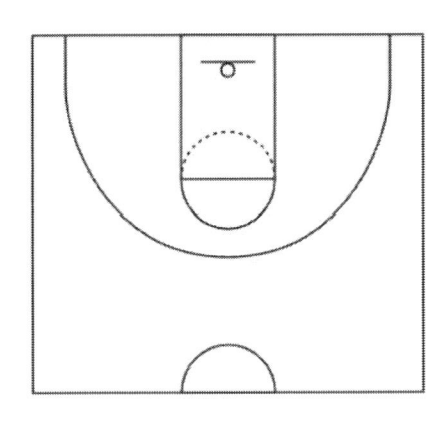

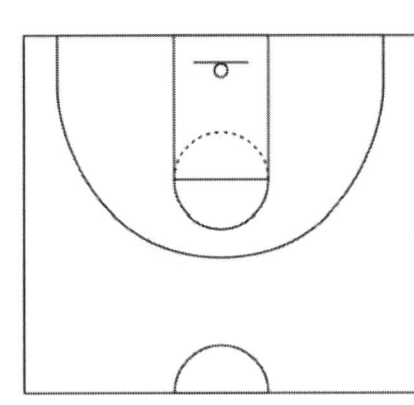

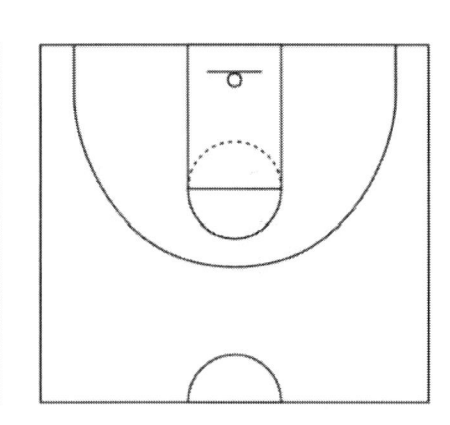

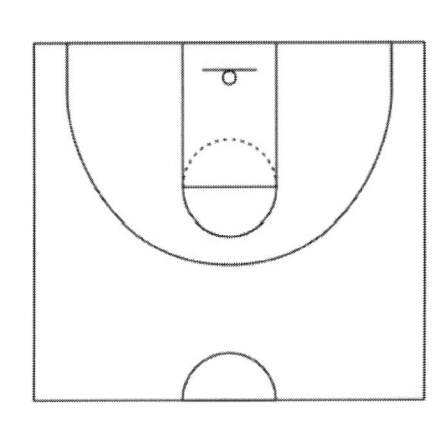

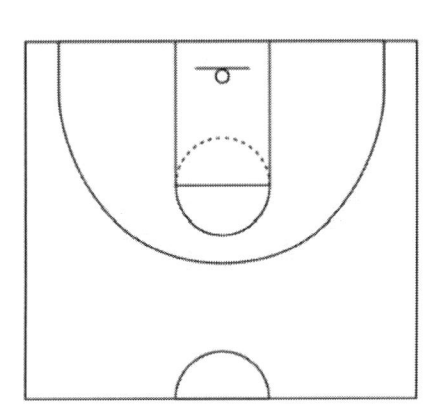

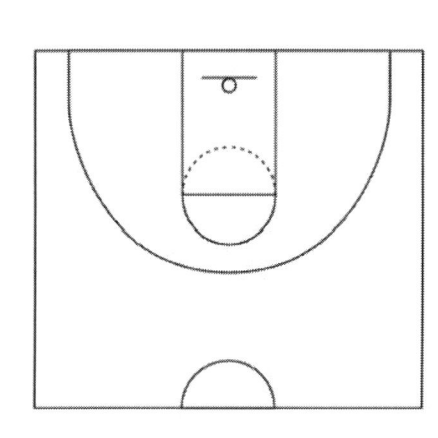

Court Diagrams & Notes | 185

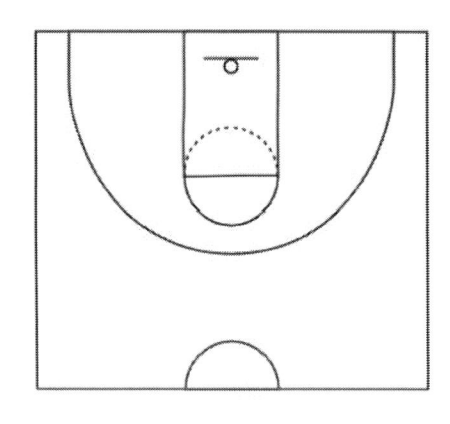

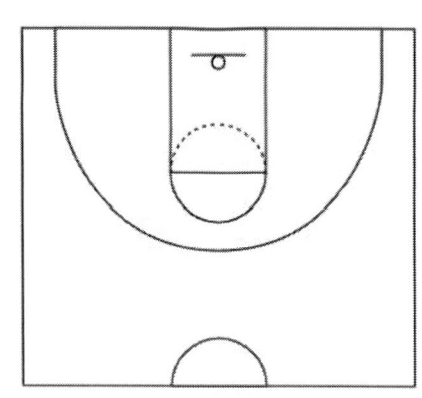

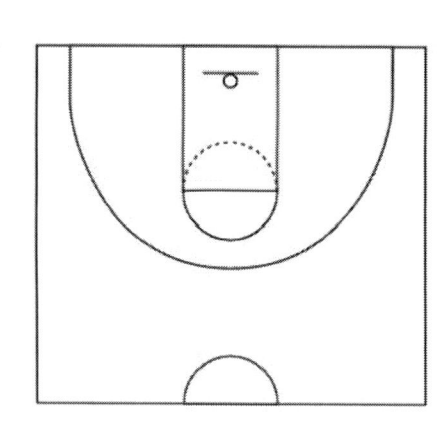

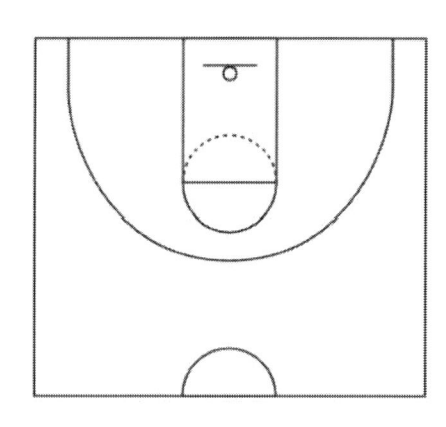

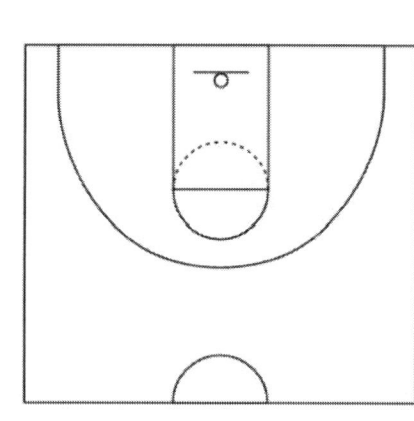

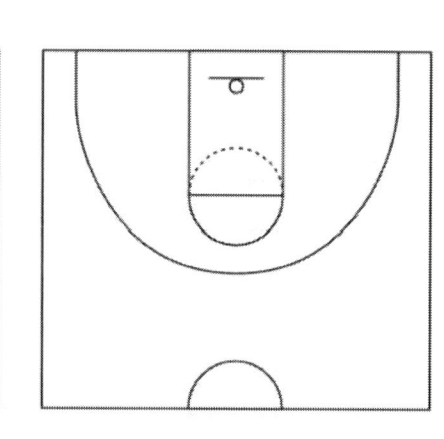

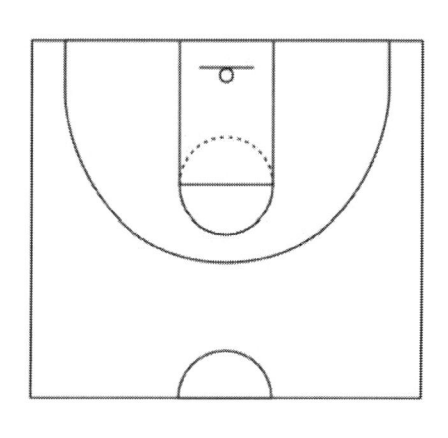

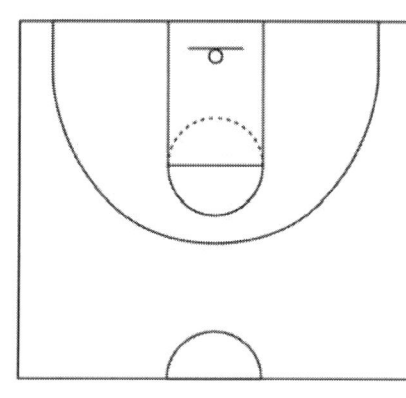

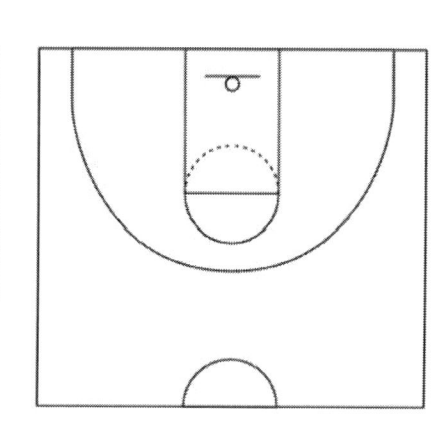

Court Diagrams & Notes | 187

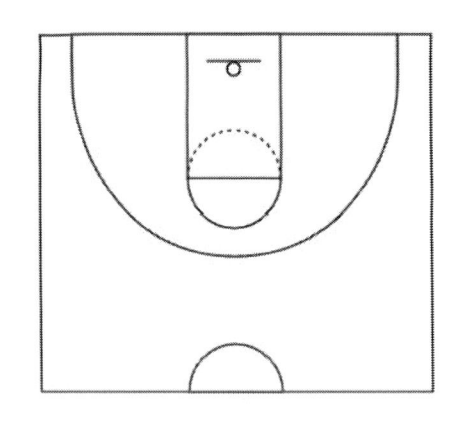

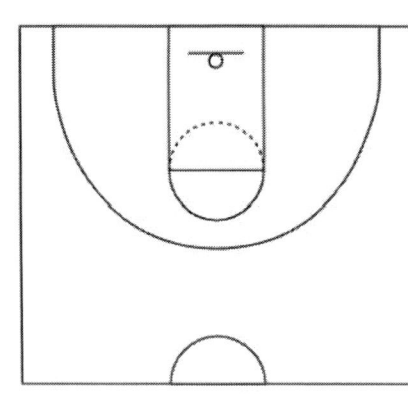

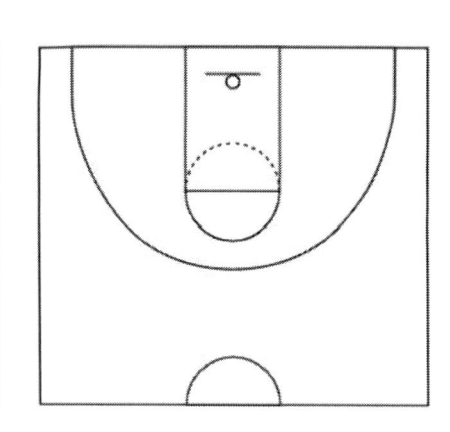

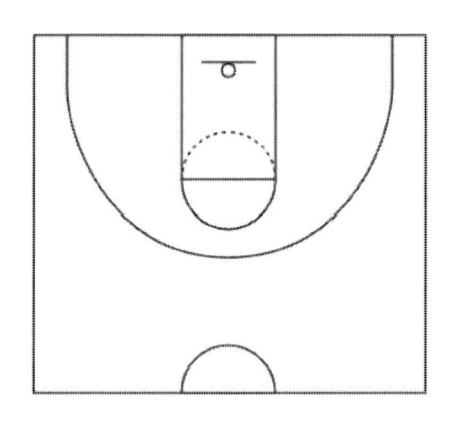

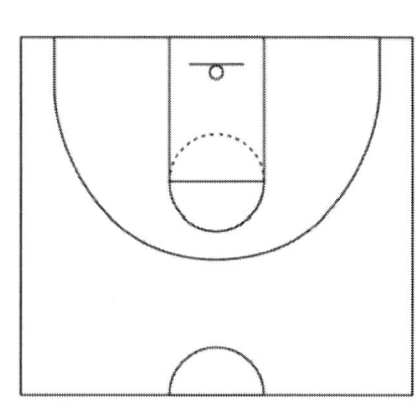

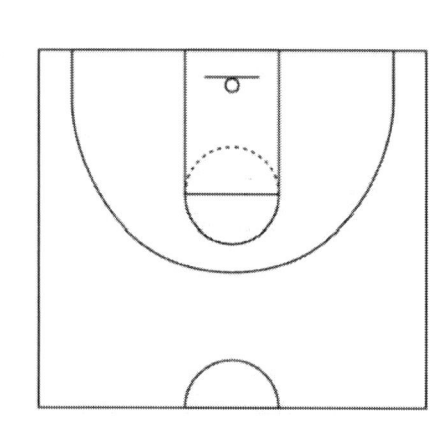

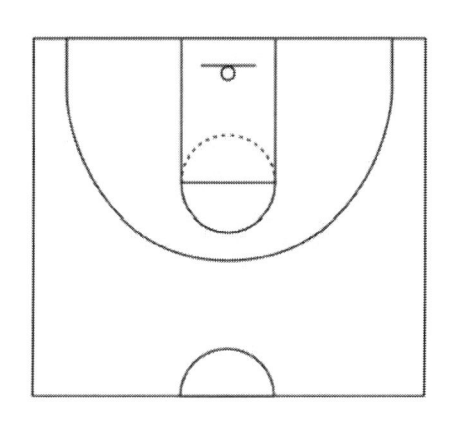

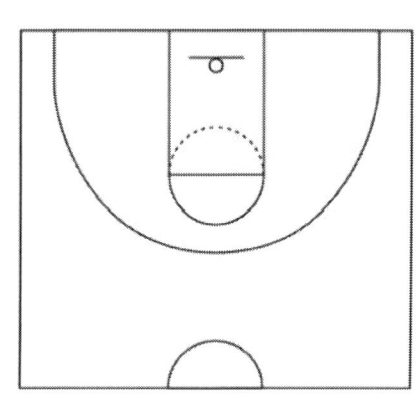

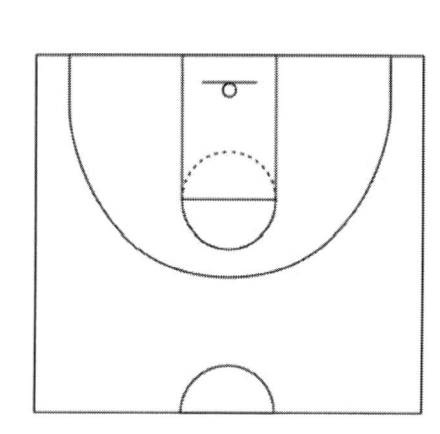

Court Diagrams & Notes

Court Diagrams & Notes | 189

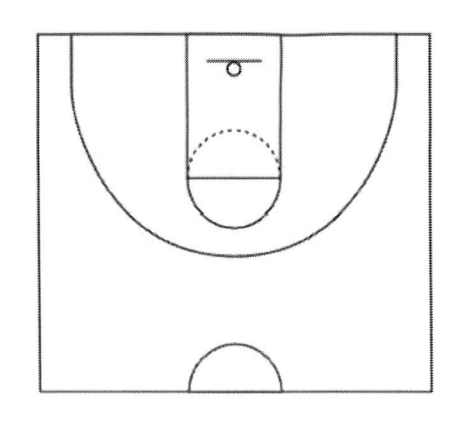

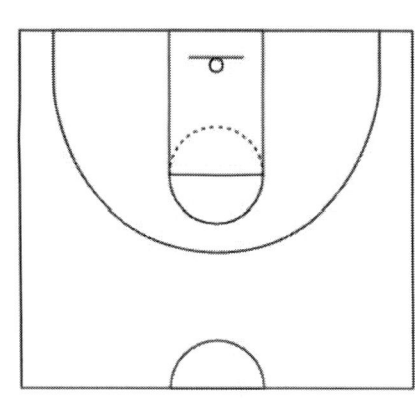

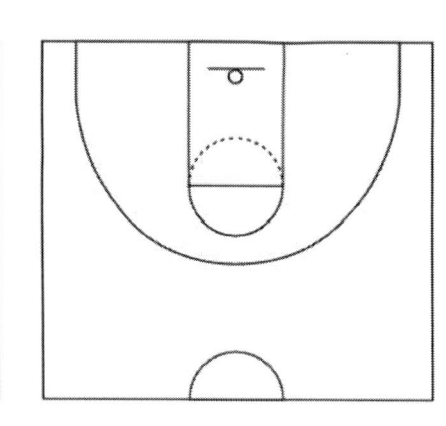

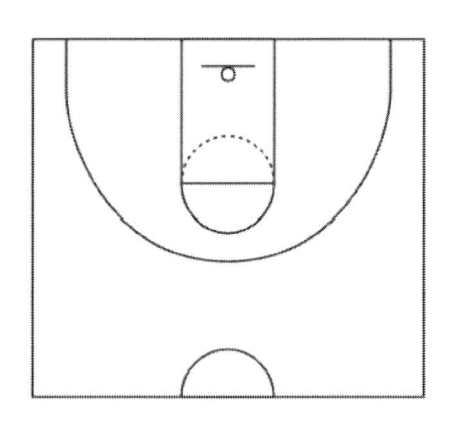

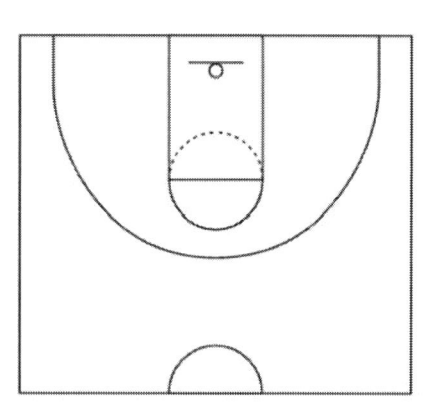

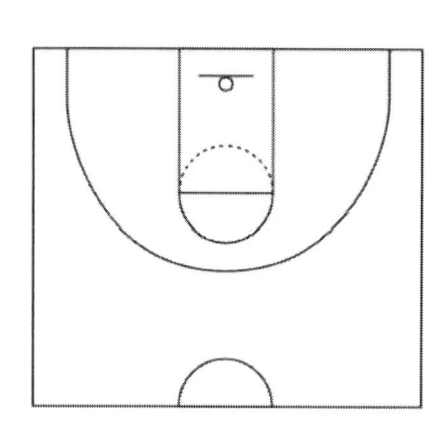

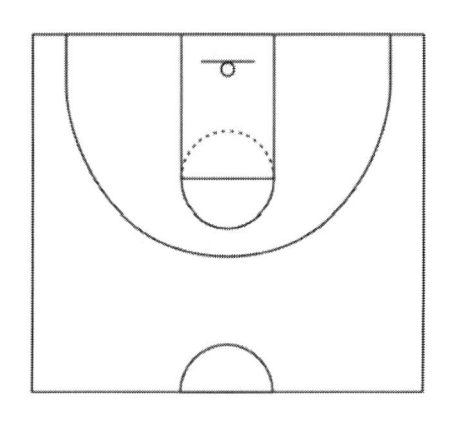

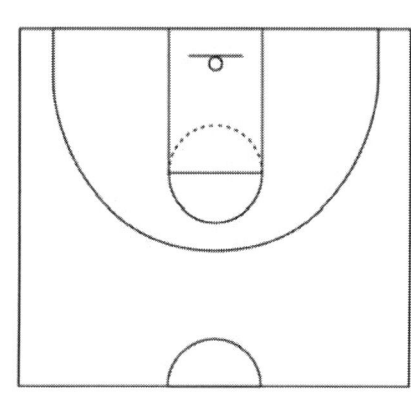

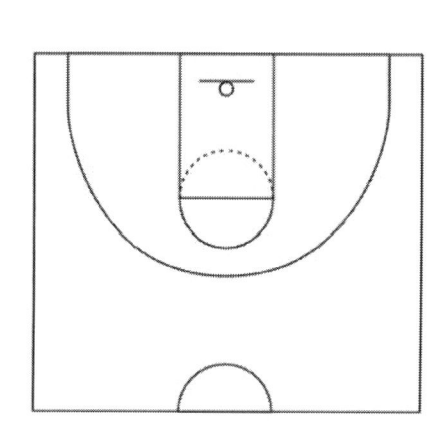

Court Diagrams & Notes | 191

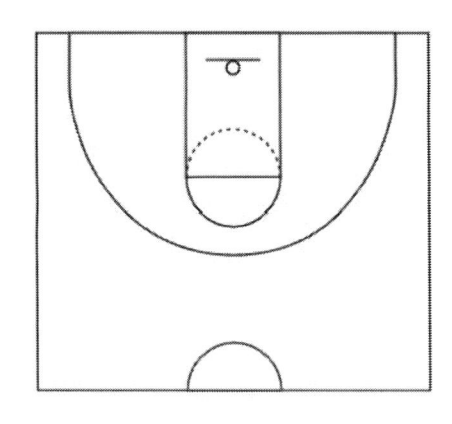

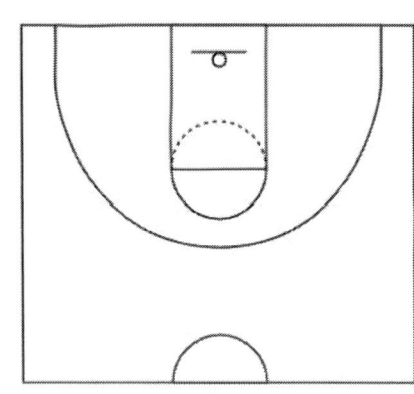

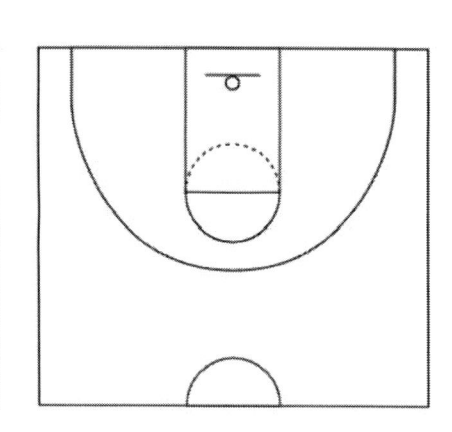

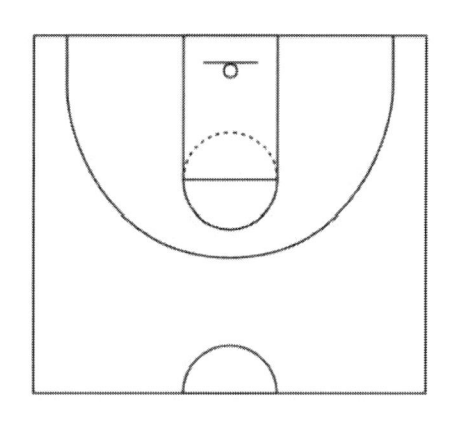

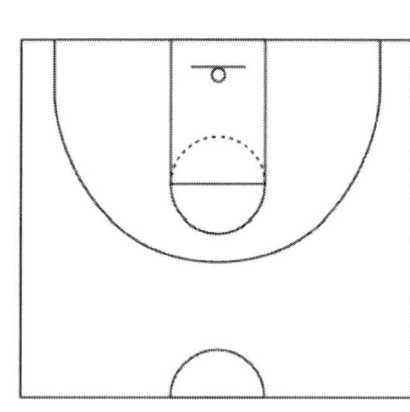

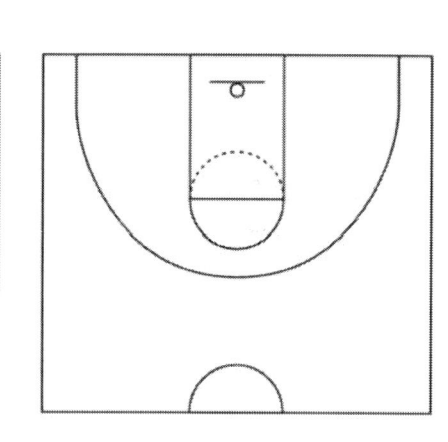

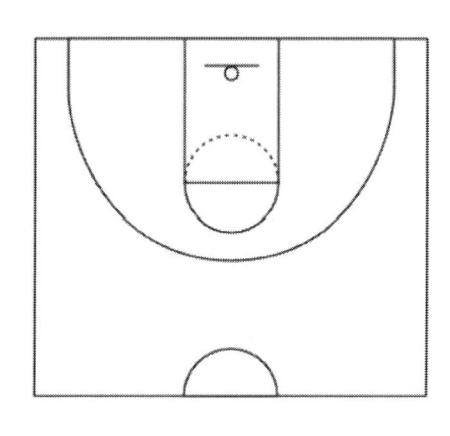

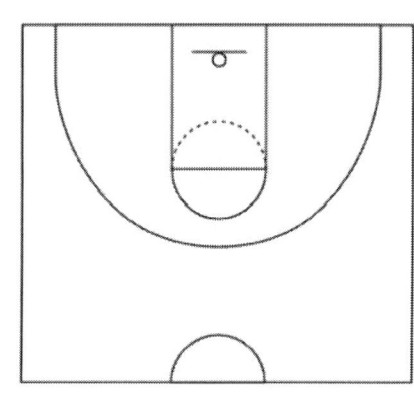

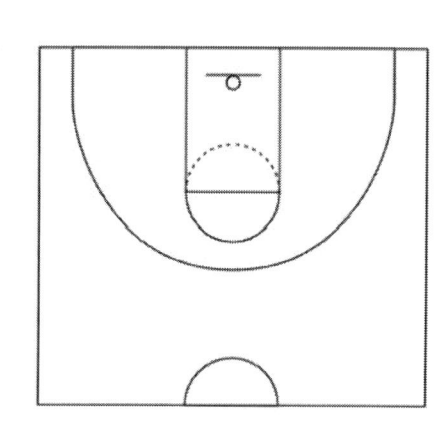

Court Diagrams & Notes | 193

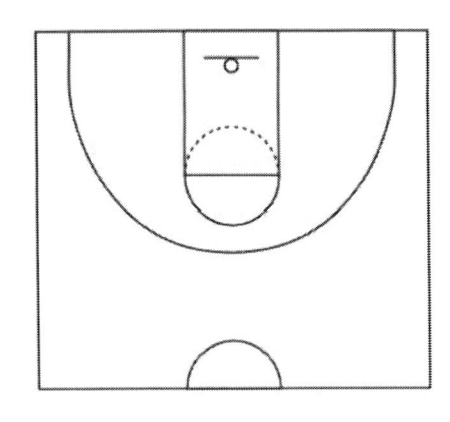

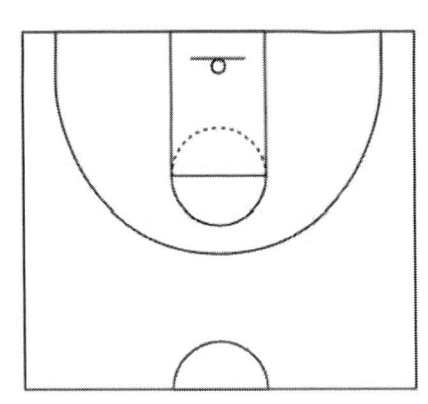

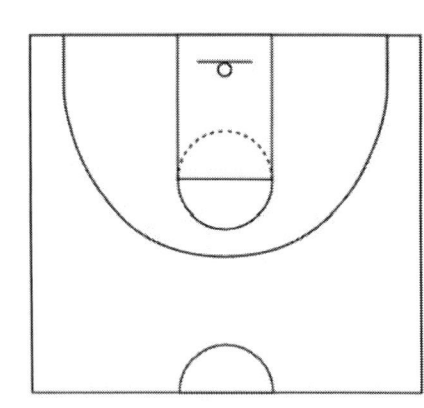

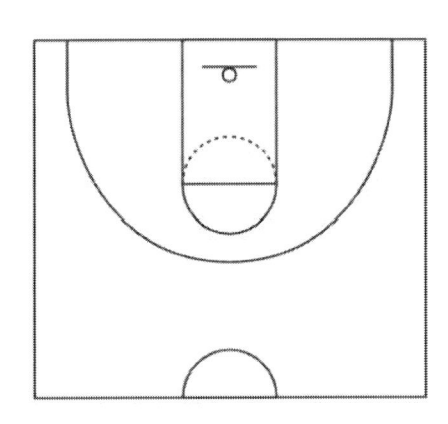

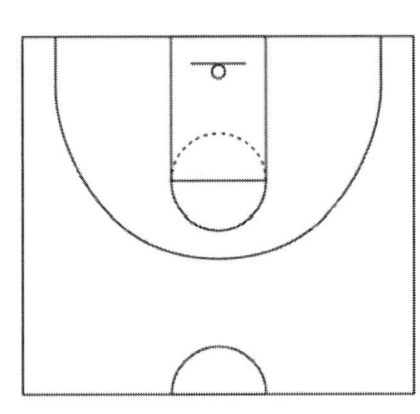

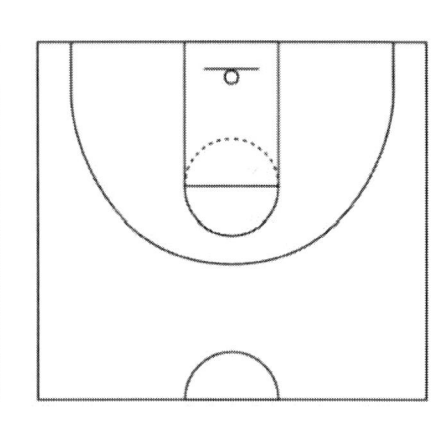

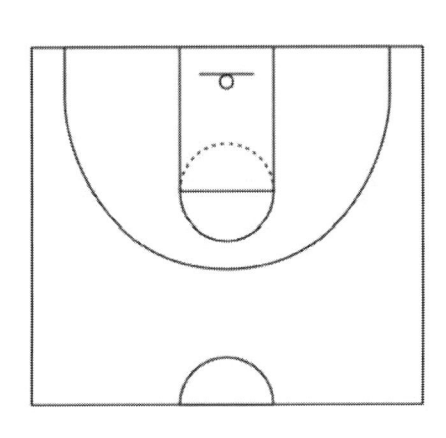

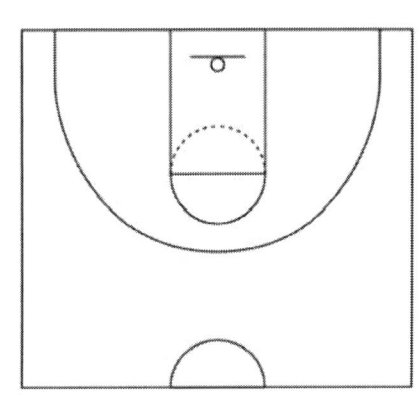

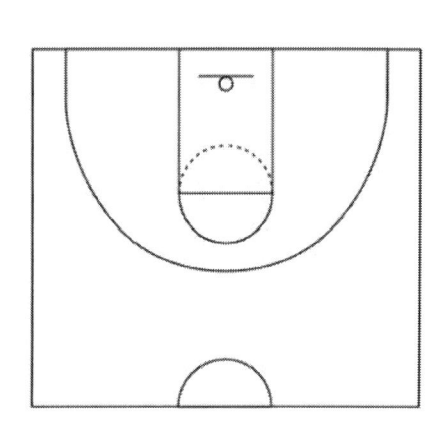

Court Diagrams & Notes | 195

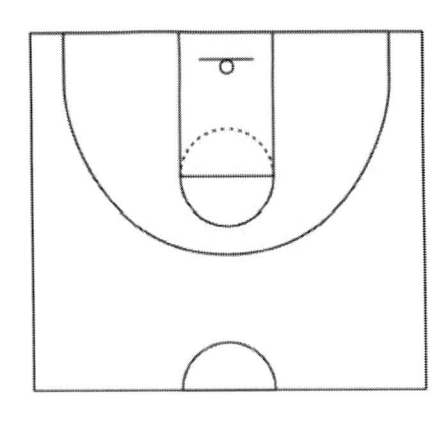

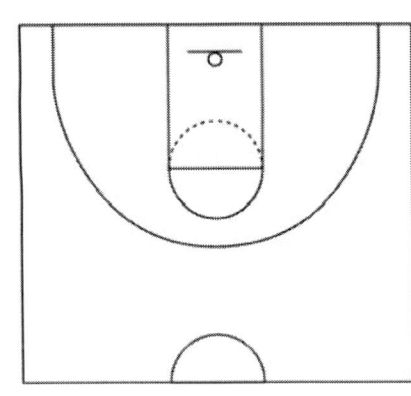

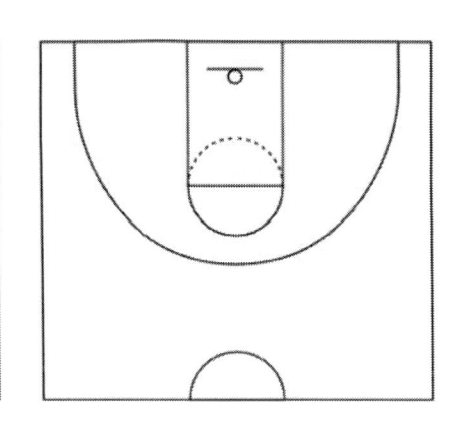

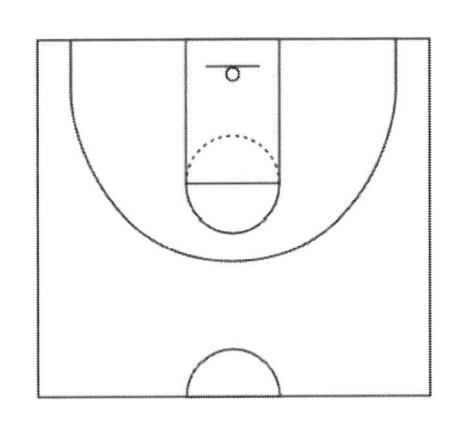

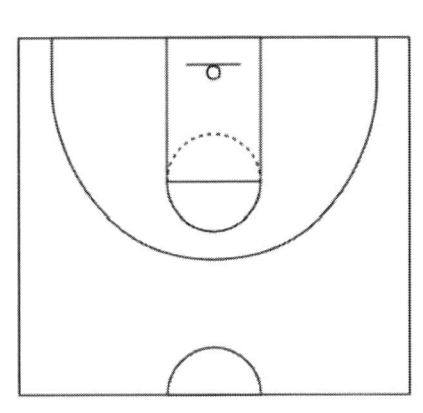

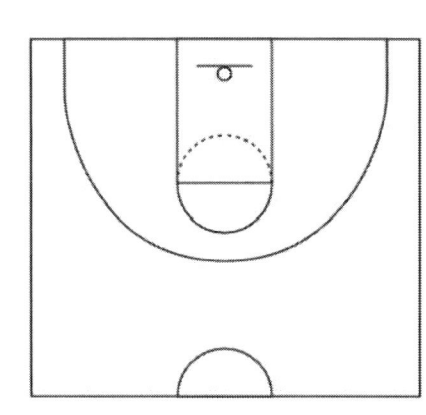

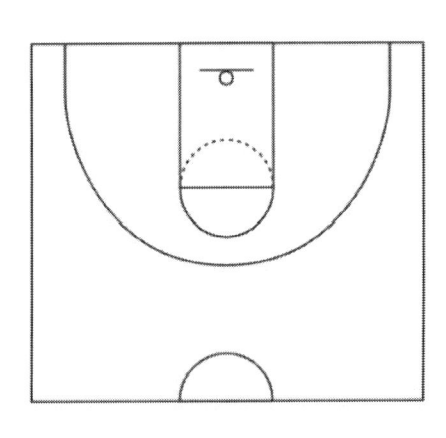

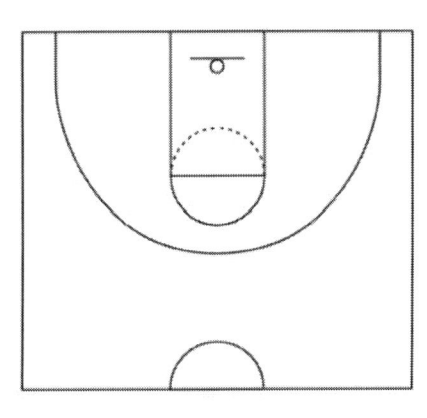

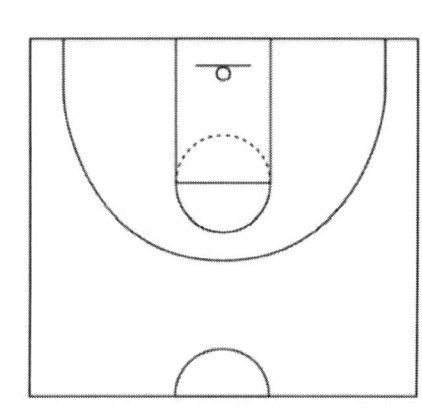

Court Diagrams & Notes | 197

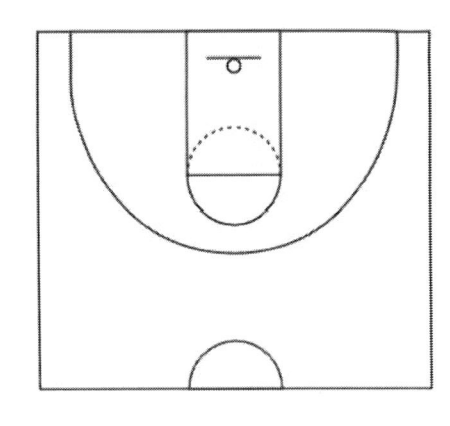

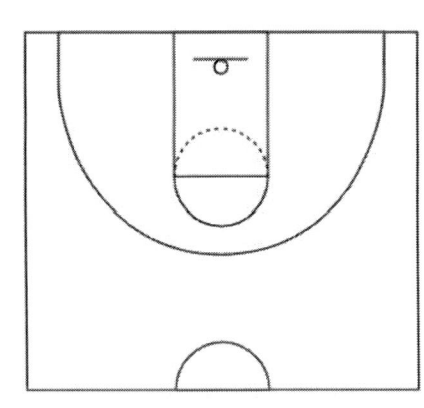

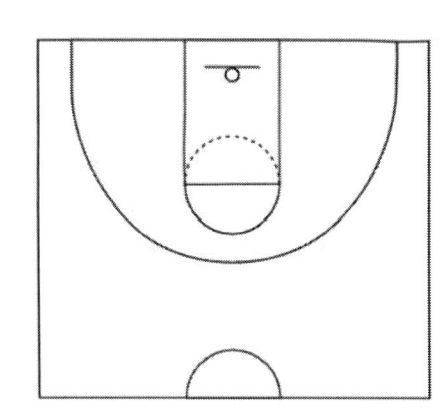

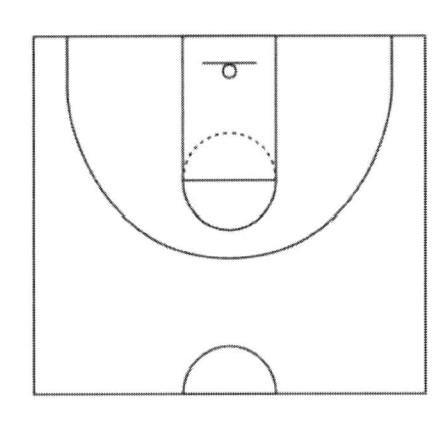

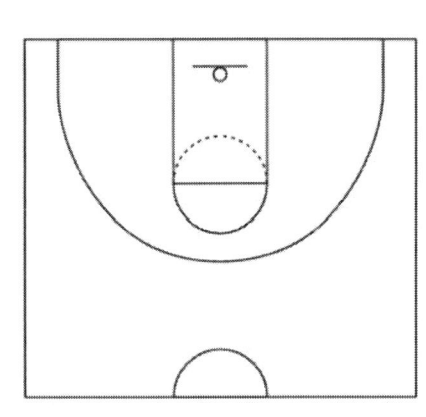

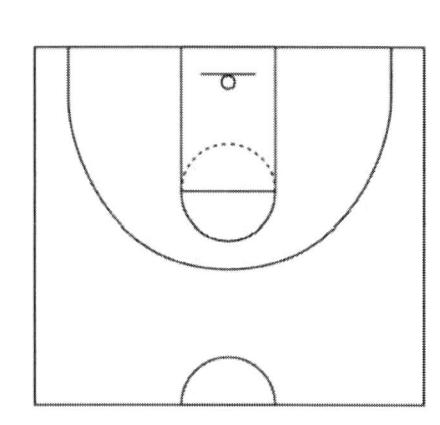

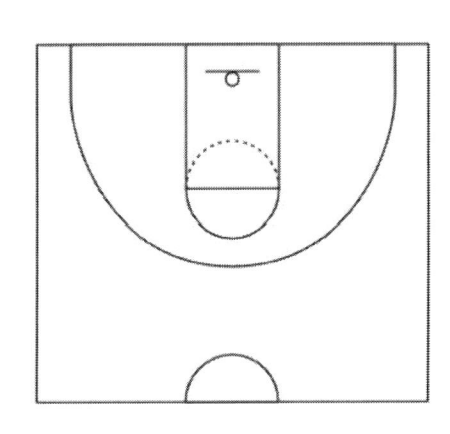

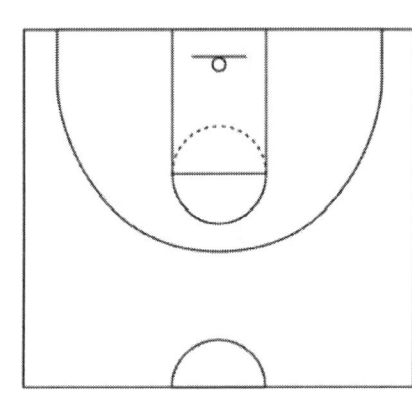

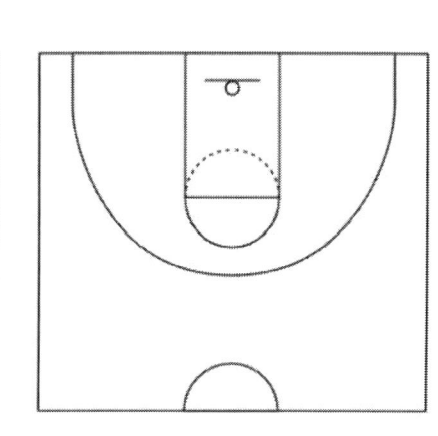

Court Diagrams & Notes | 199

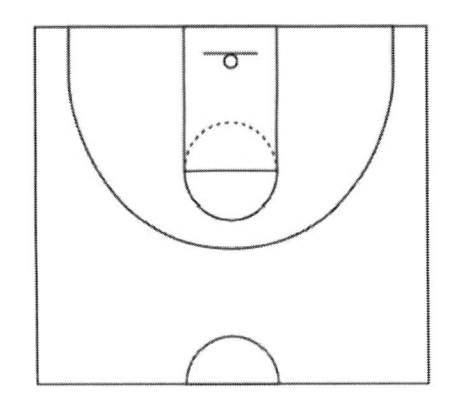

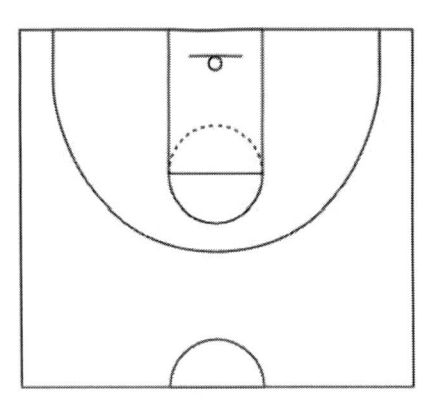

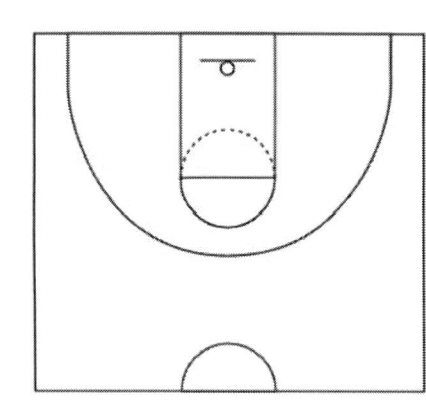

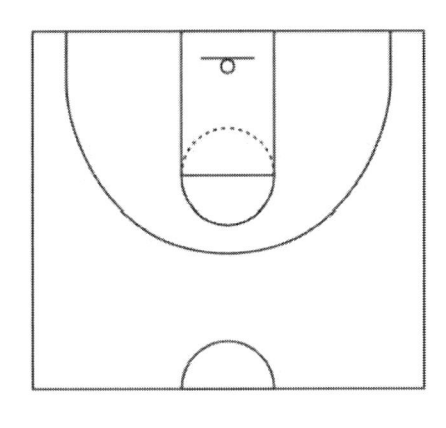

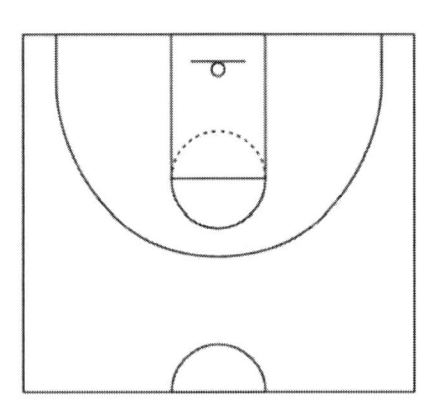

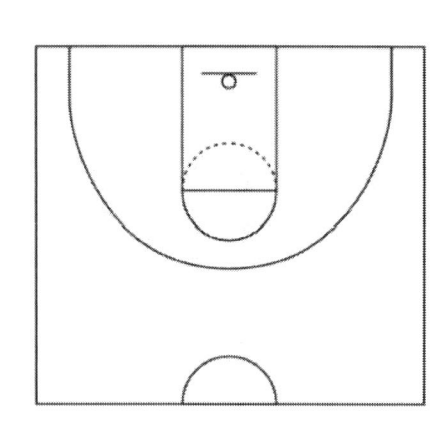

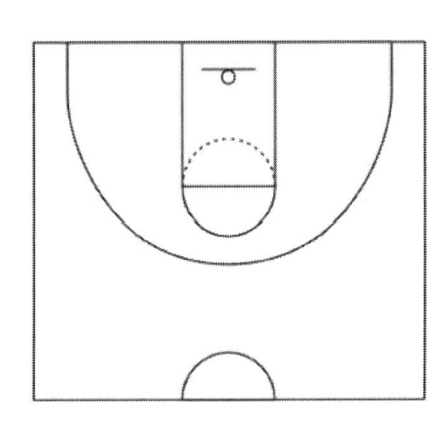

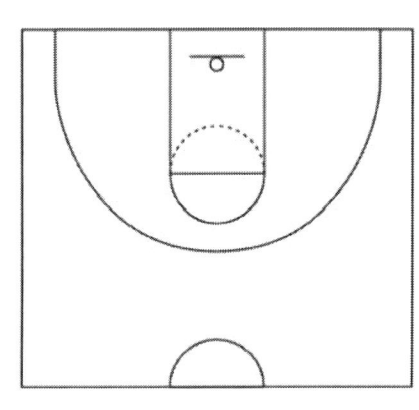

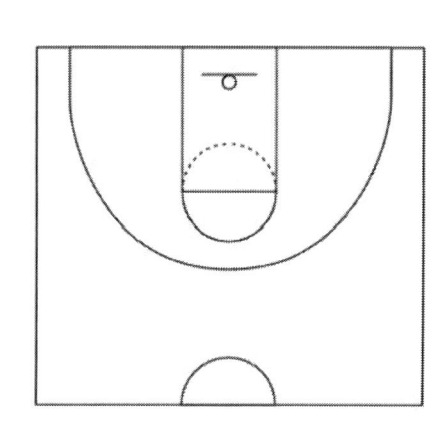

Court Diagrams & Notes | 201

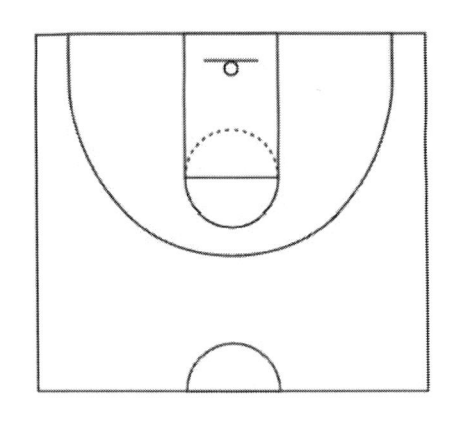

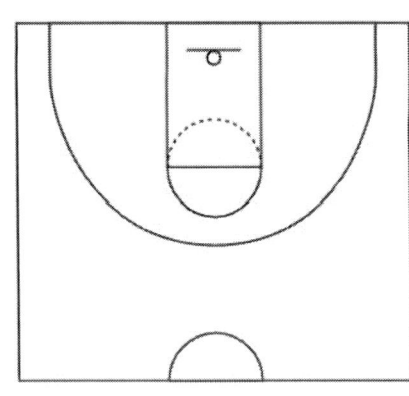

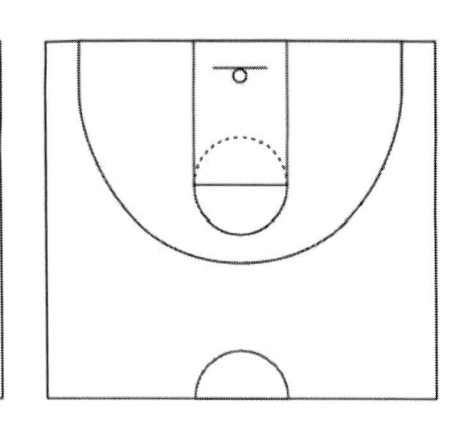

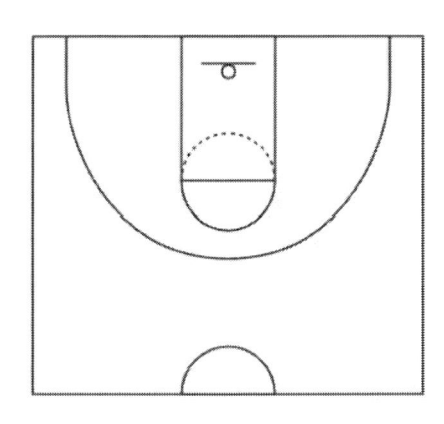

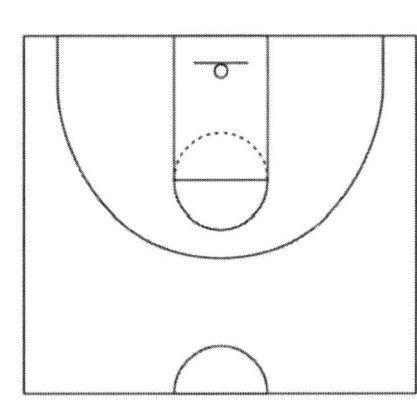

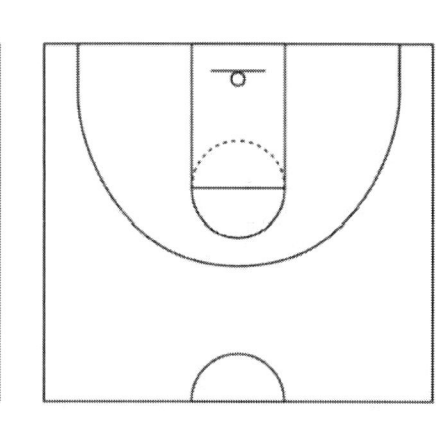

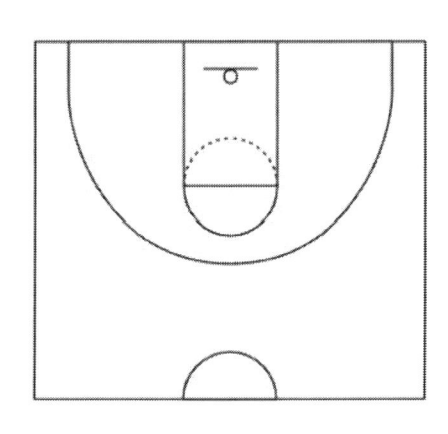

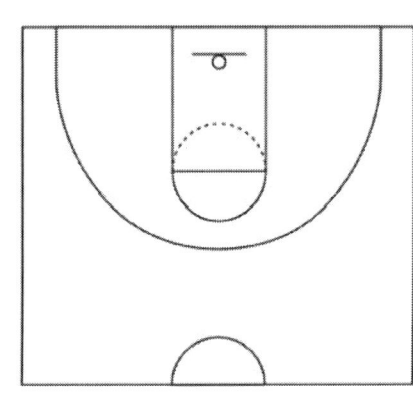

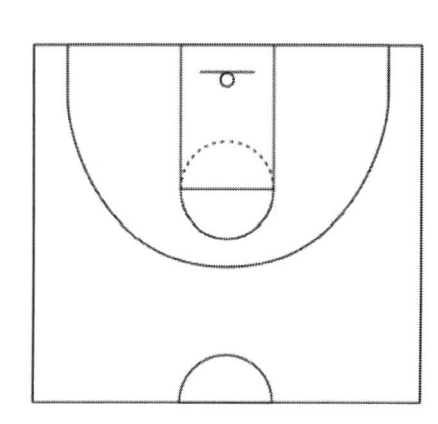

Court Diagrams & Notes | 203

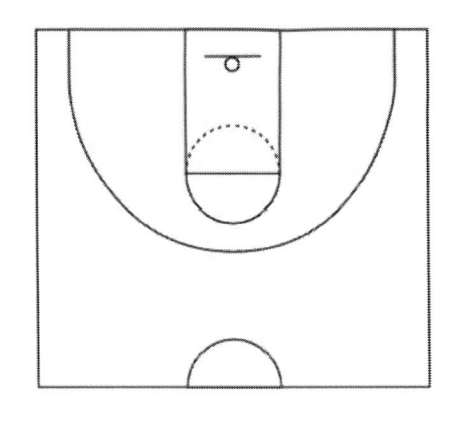

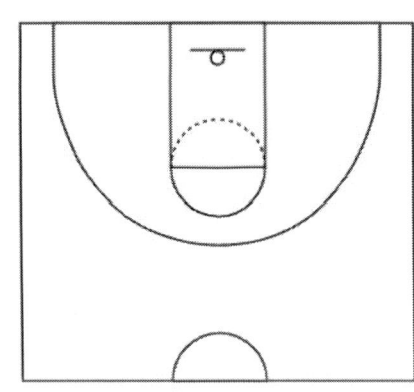

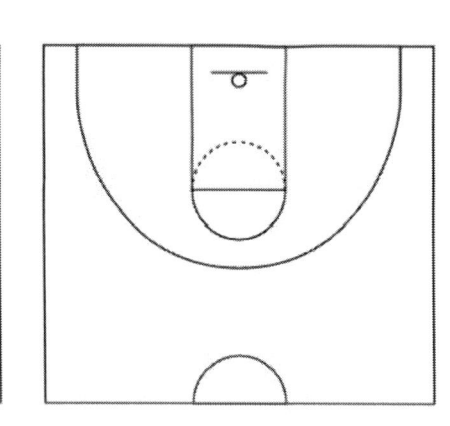

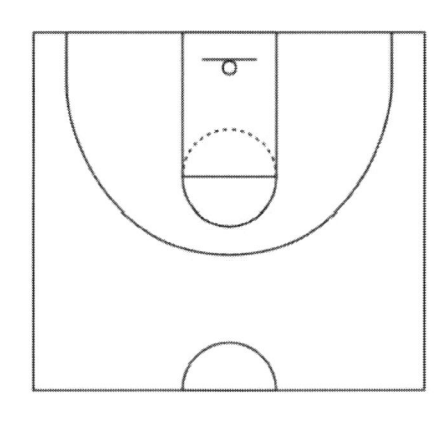

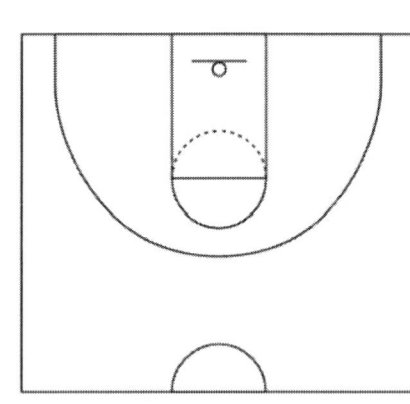

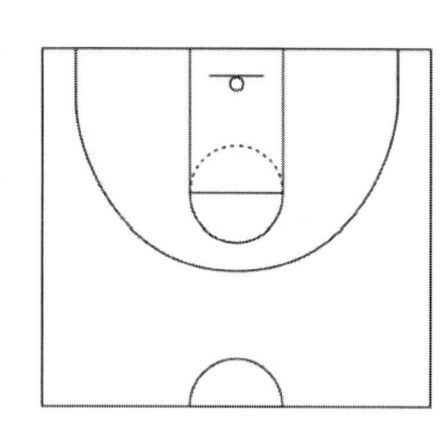

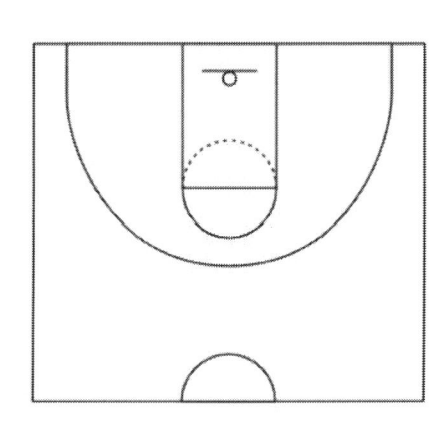

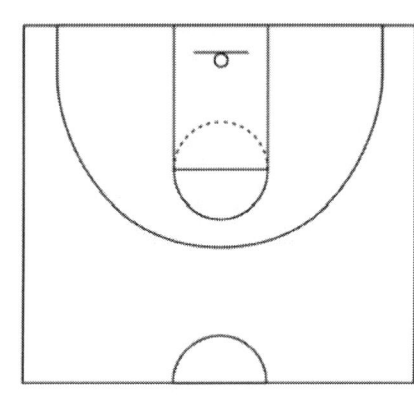

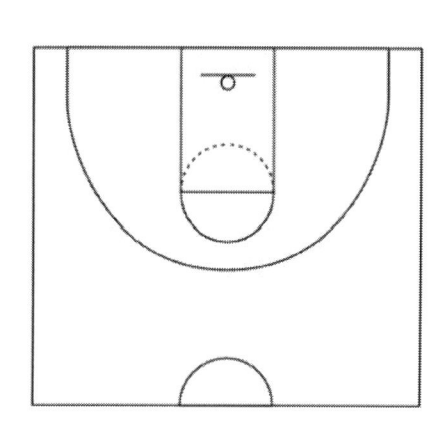

Court Diagrams & Notes | 205

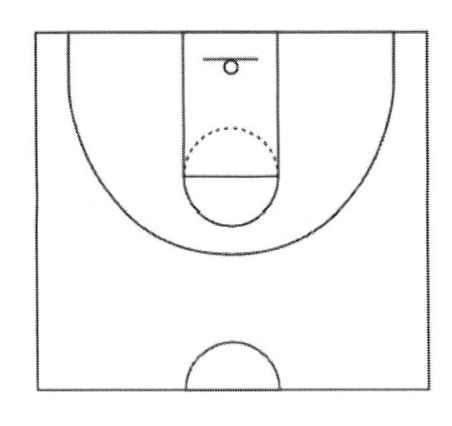

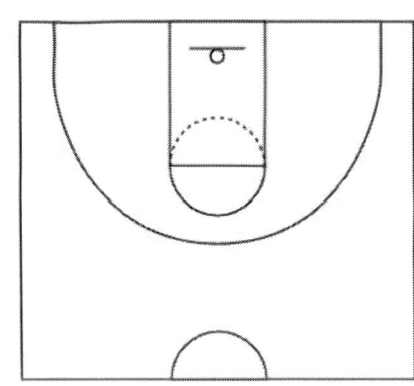

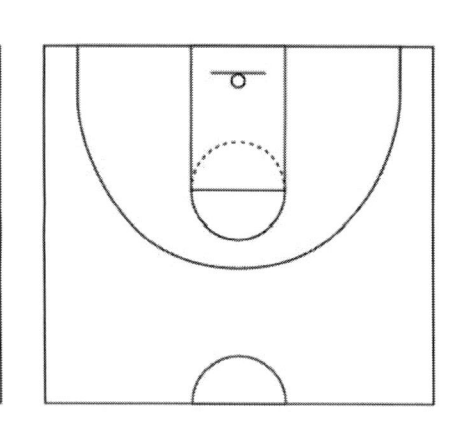

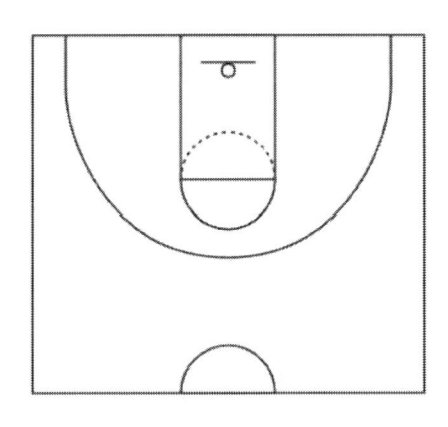

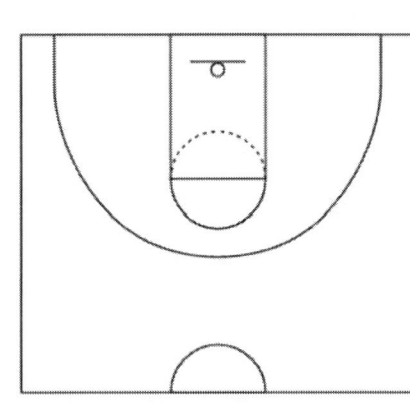

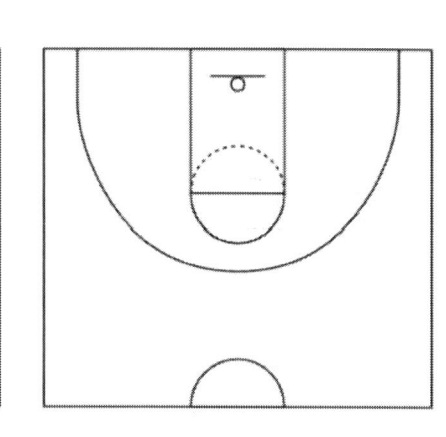

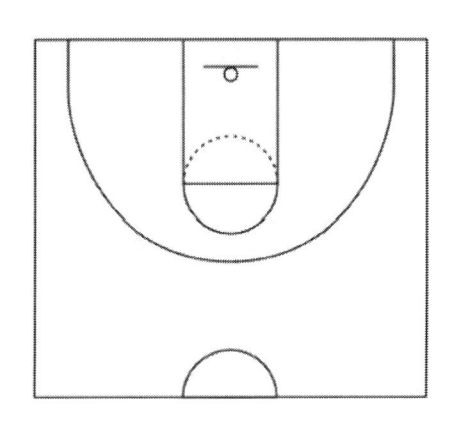

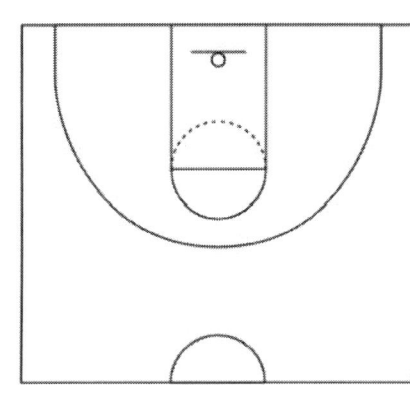

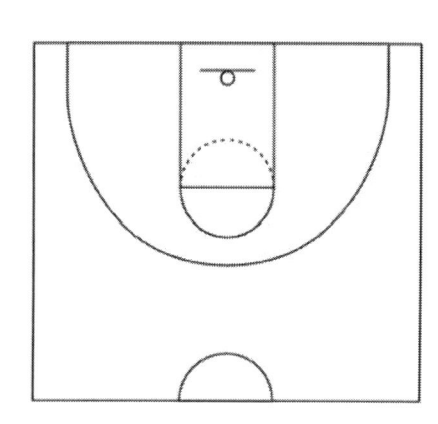

Court Diagrams & Notes | 207

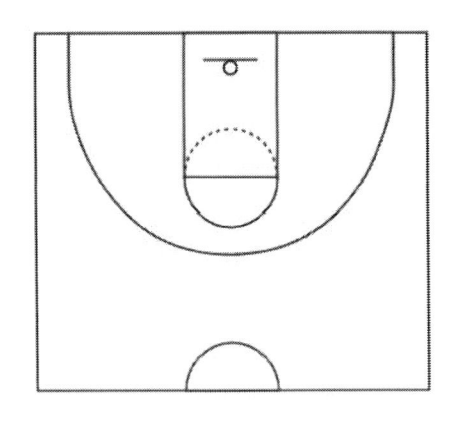

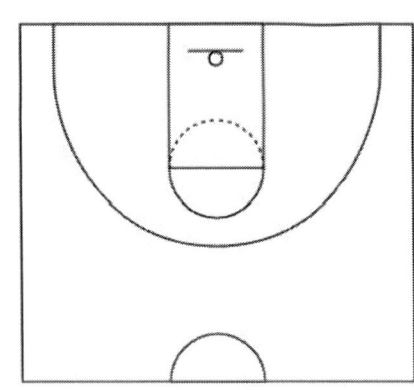

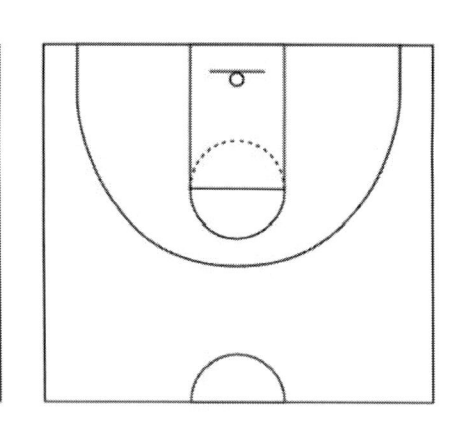

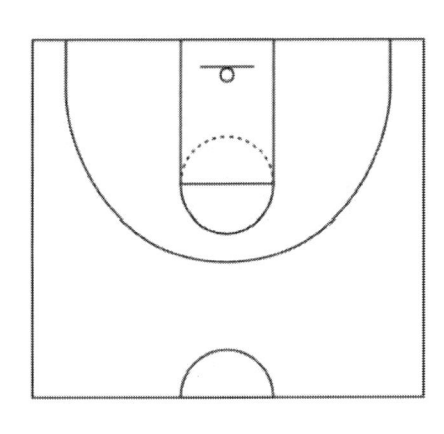

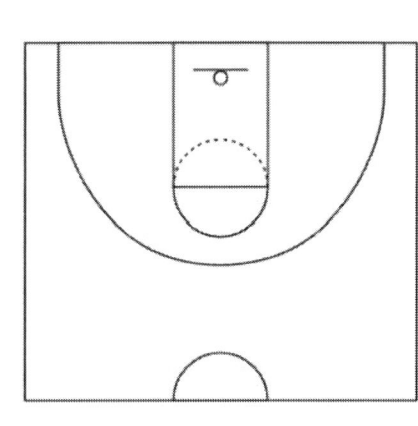

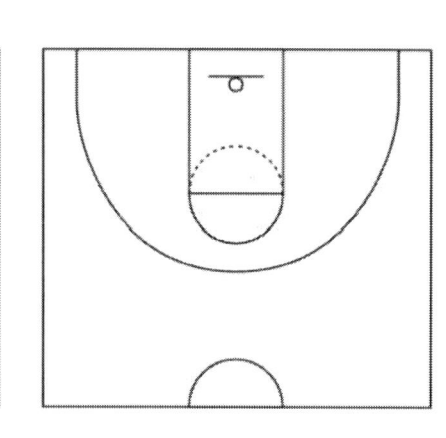

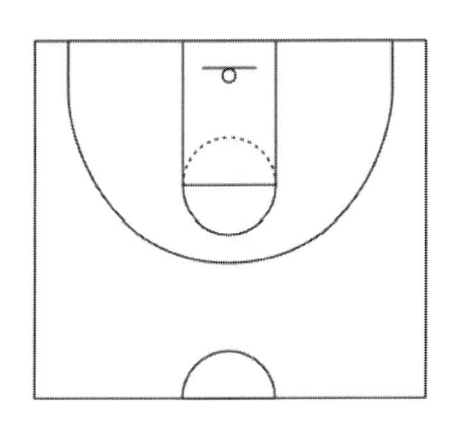

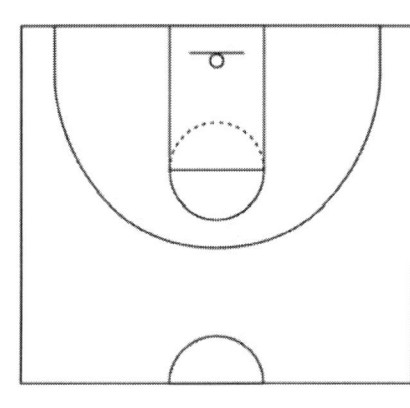

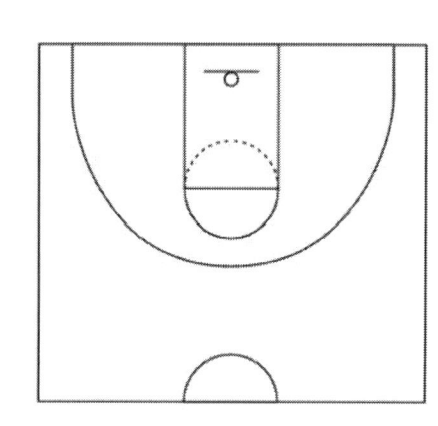

Court Diagrams & Notes | 209

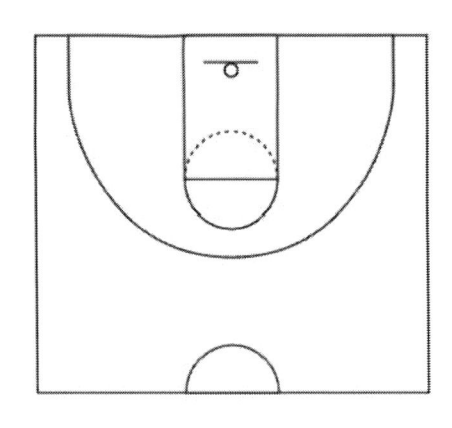

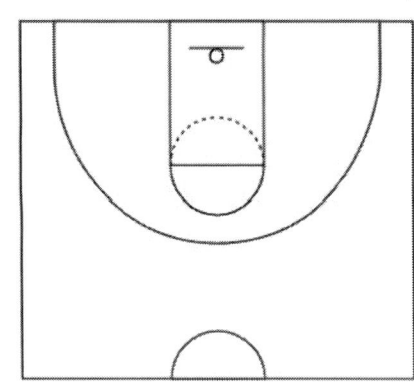

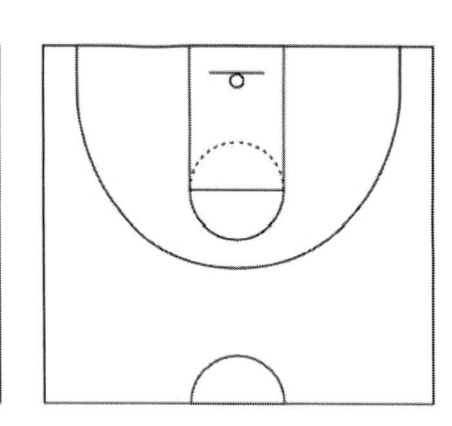

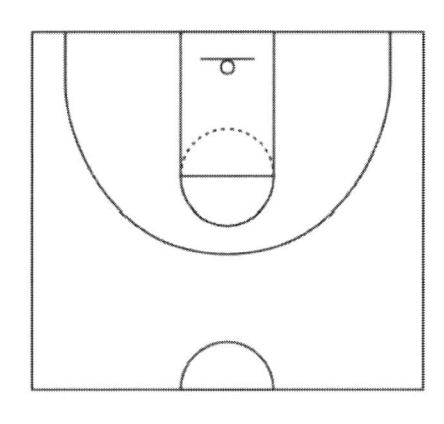

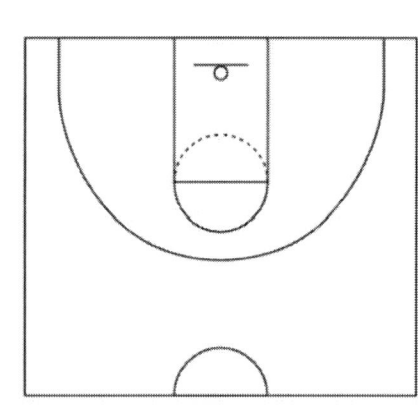

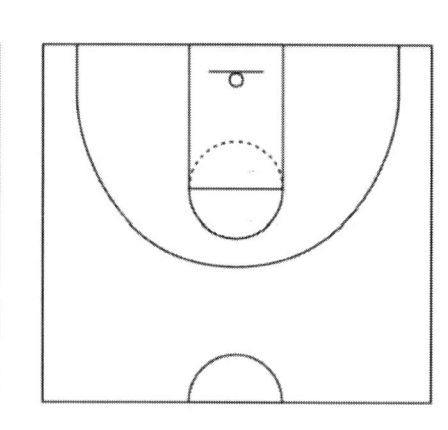

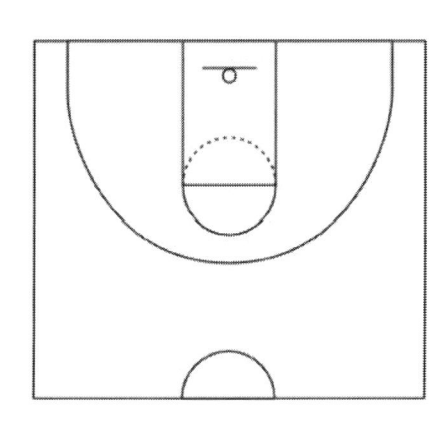

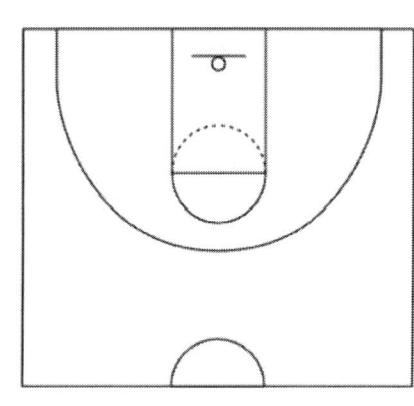

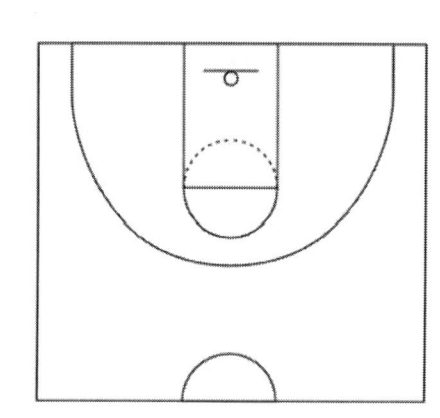

Court Diagrams & Notes | 211

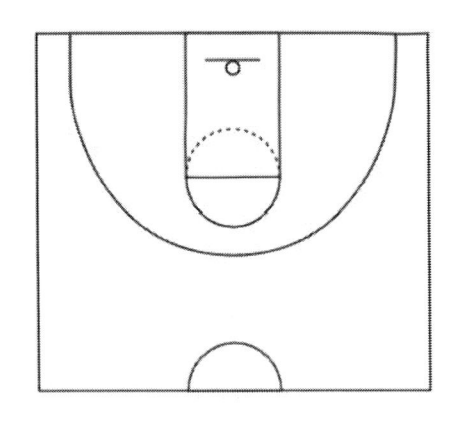

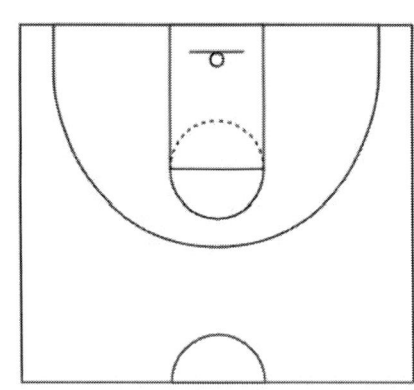

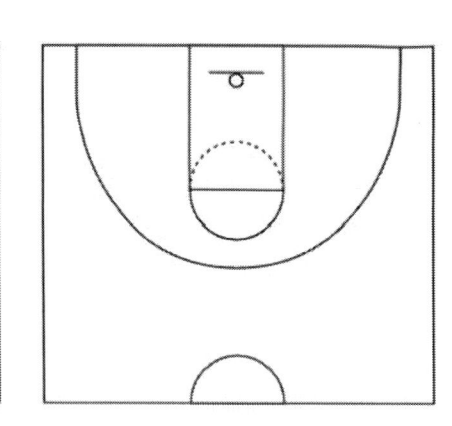

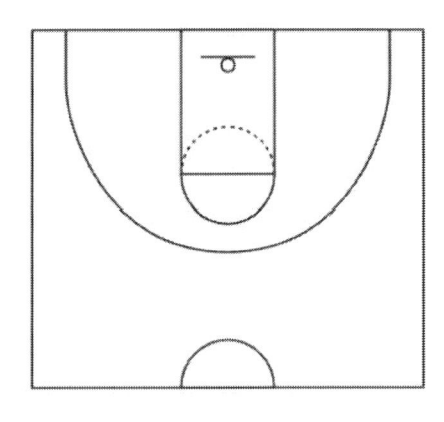

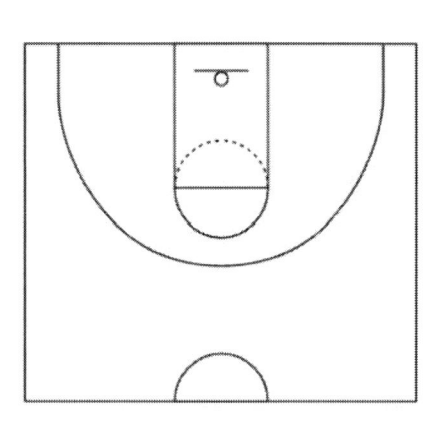

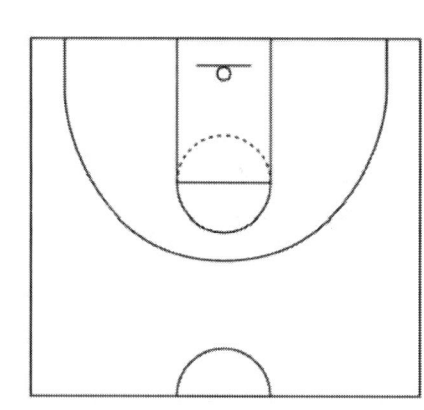

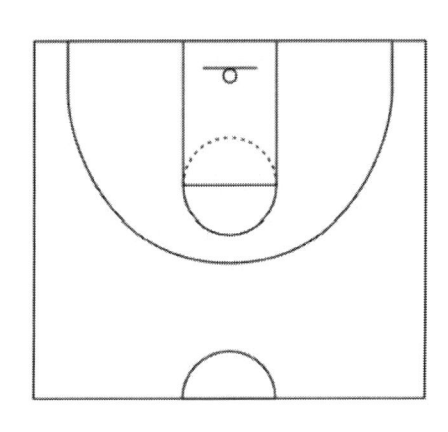

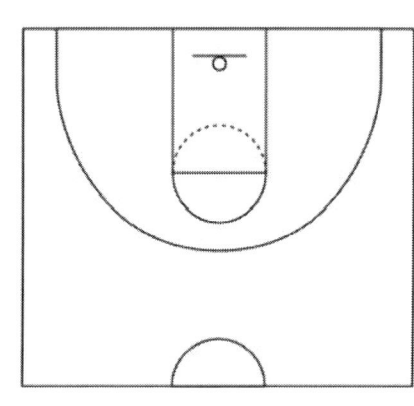

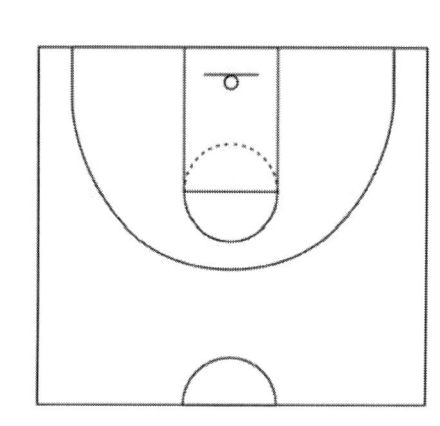

Court Diagrams & Notes | 213

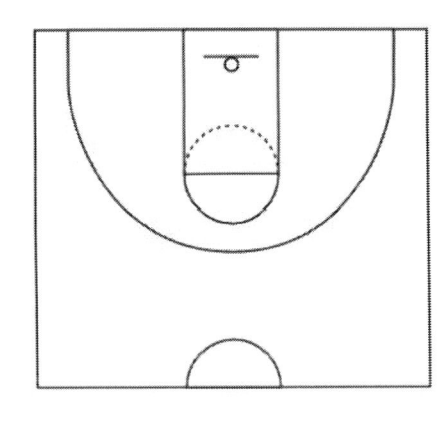

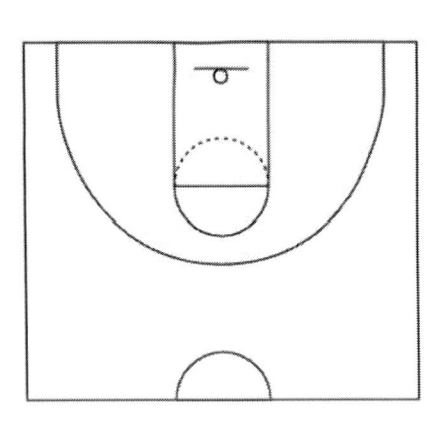

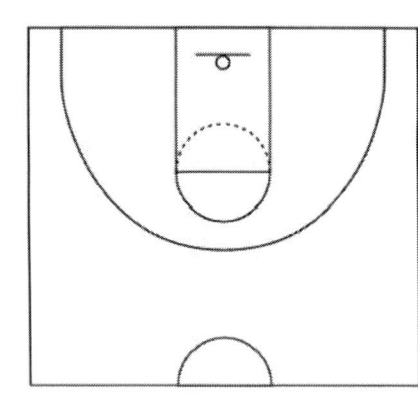

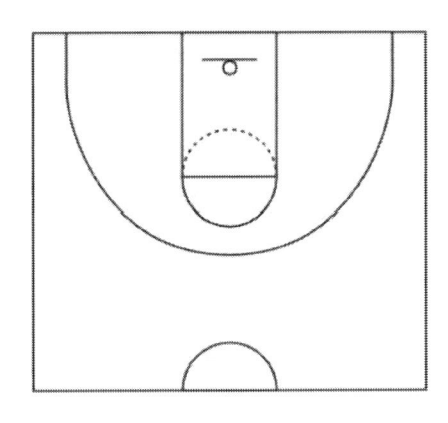

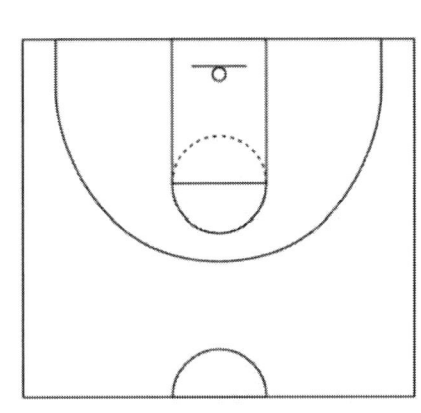

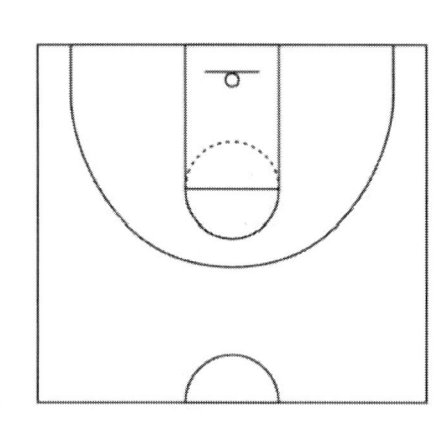

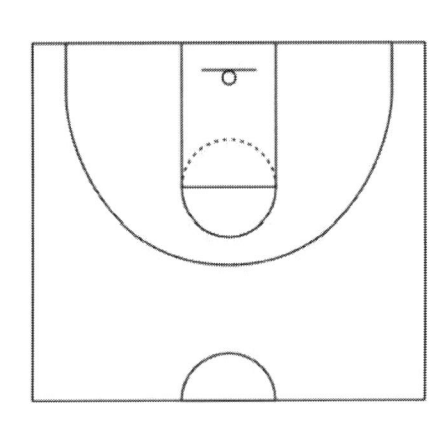

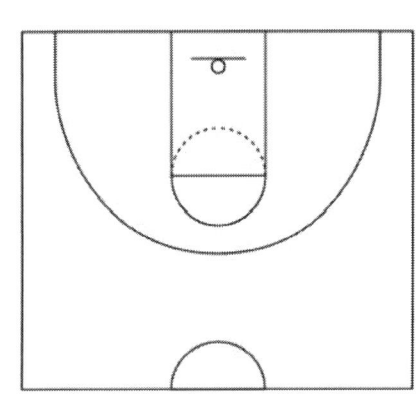

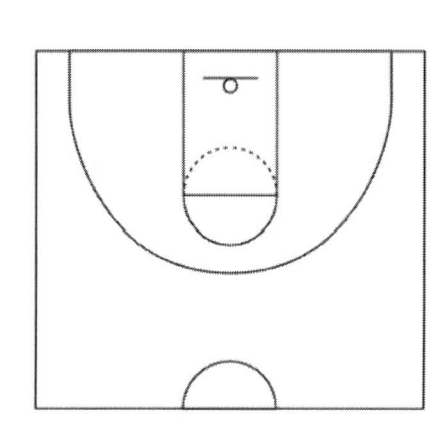

Court Diagrams & Notes | 215

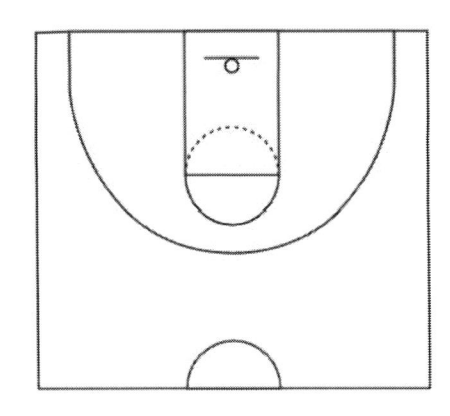

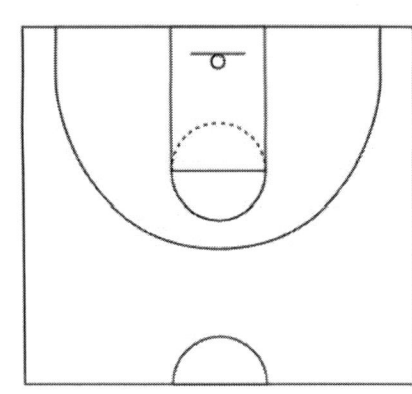

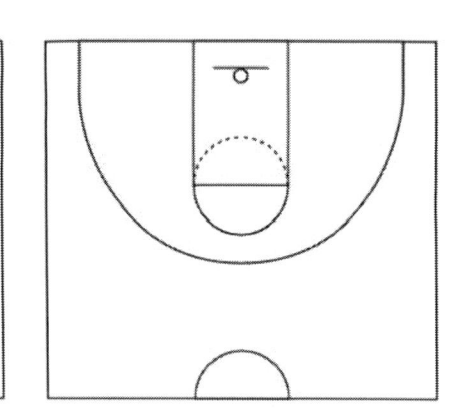

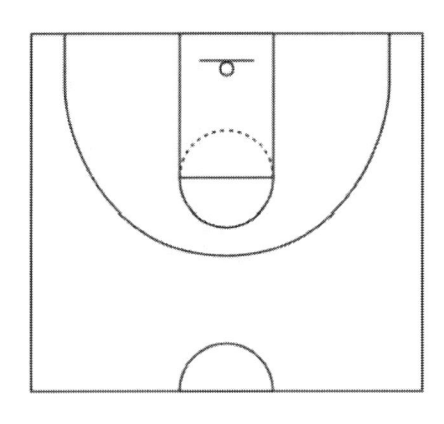

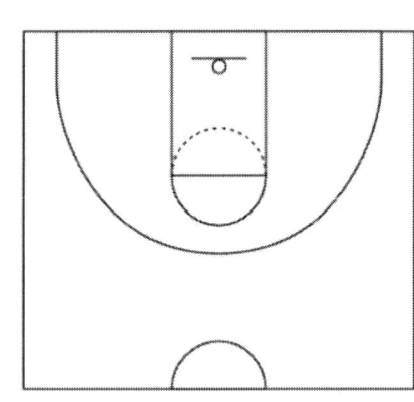

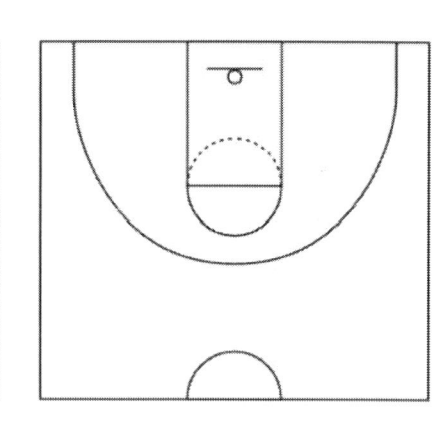

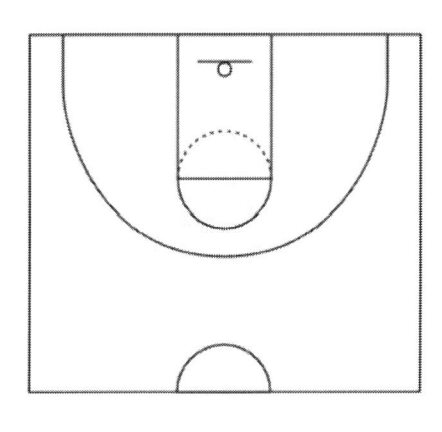

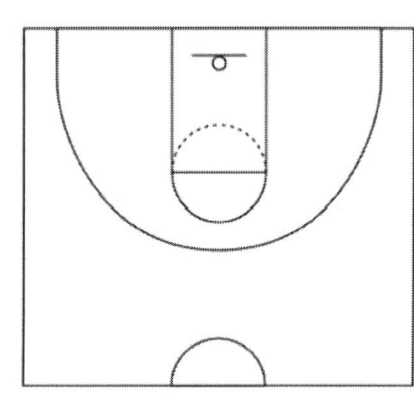

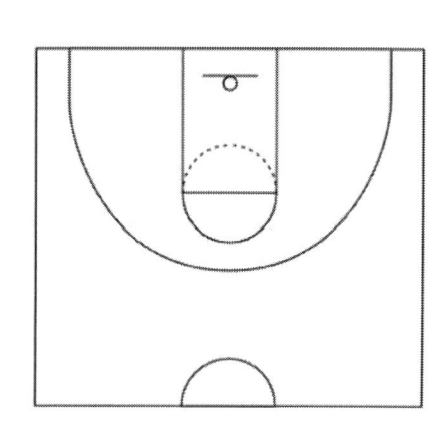

Court Diagrams & Notes | 217

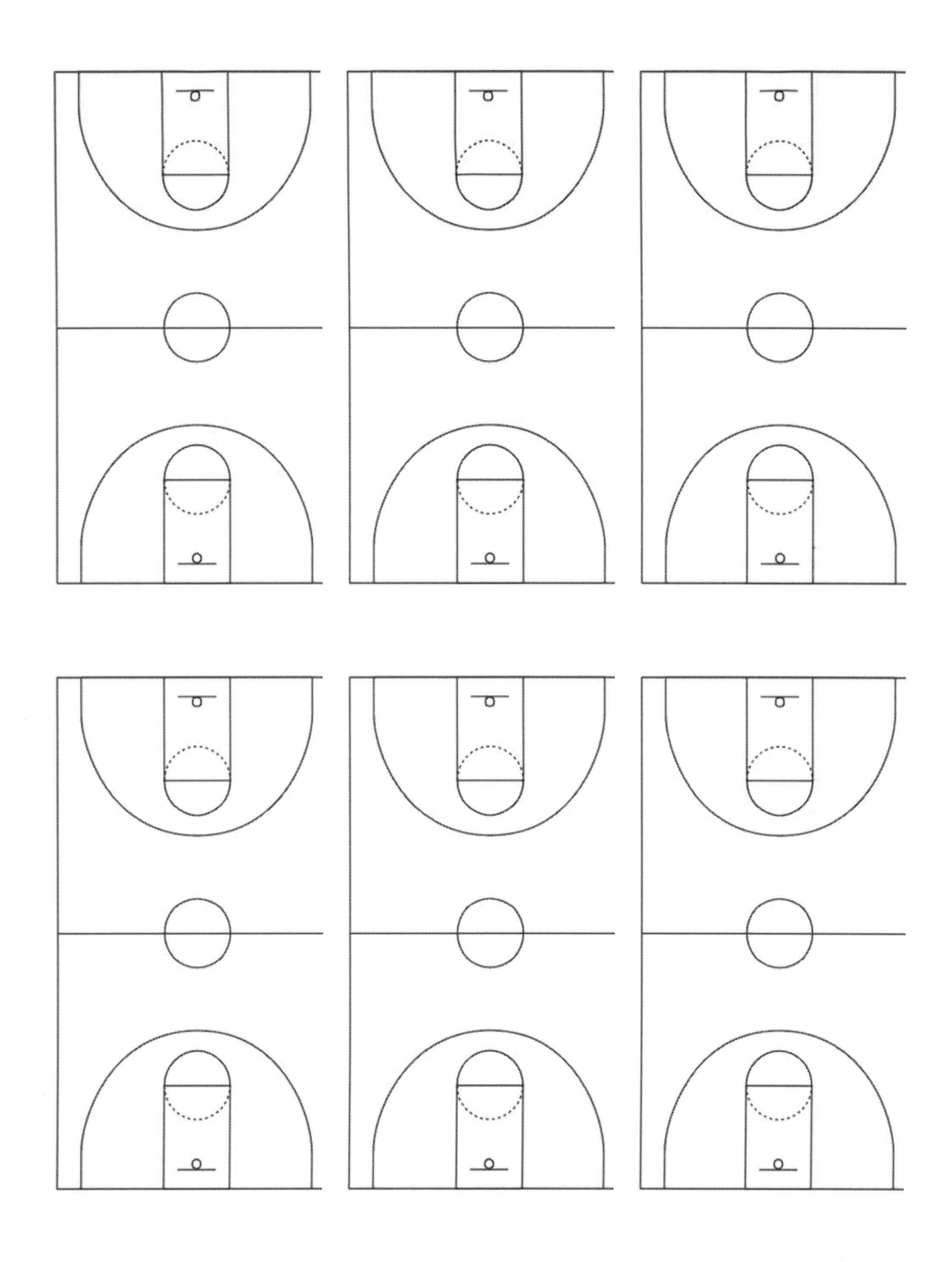

Court Diagrams & Notes | 219

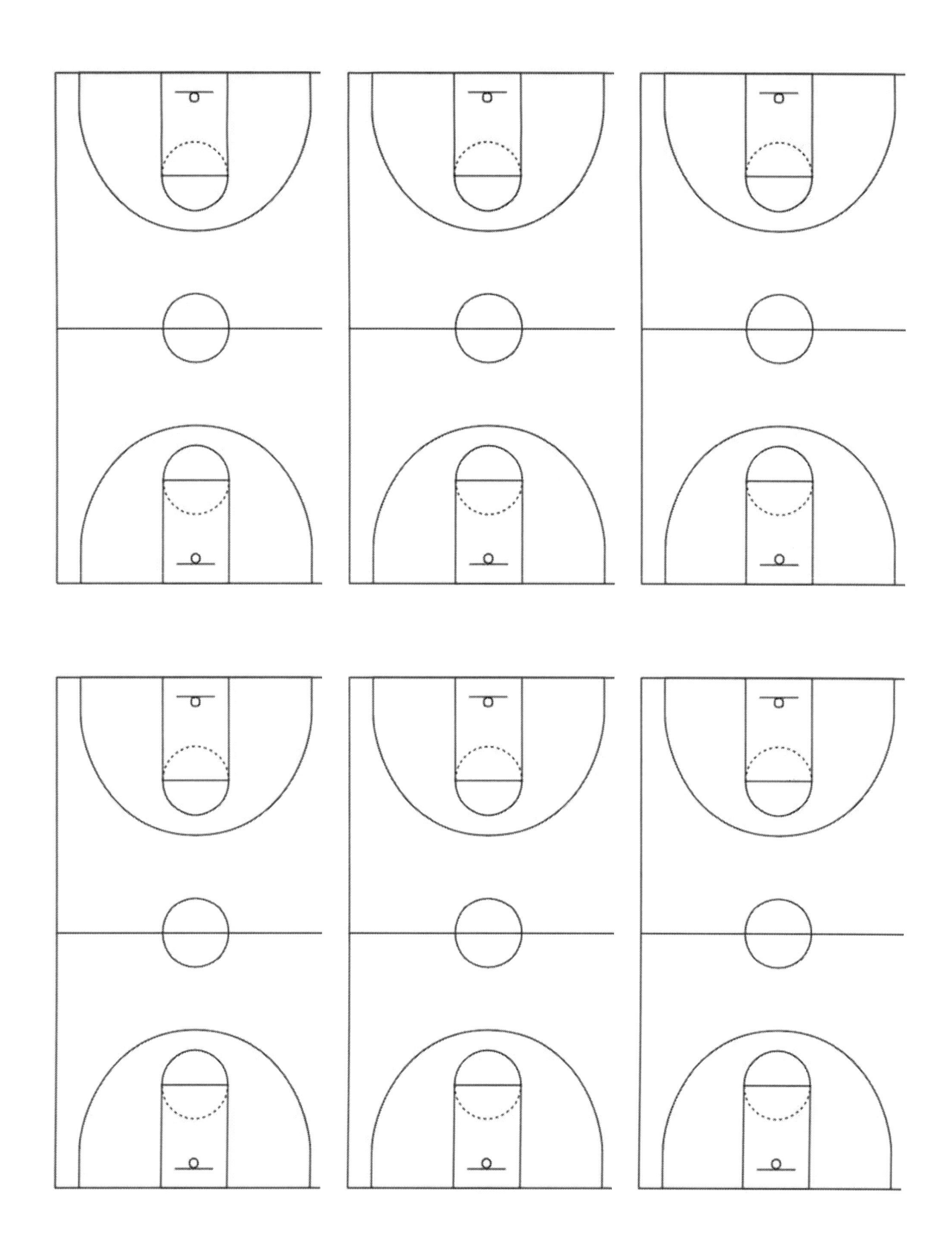

Court Diagrams & Notes | 221

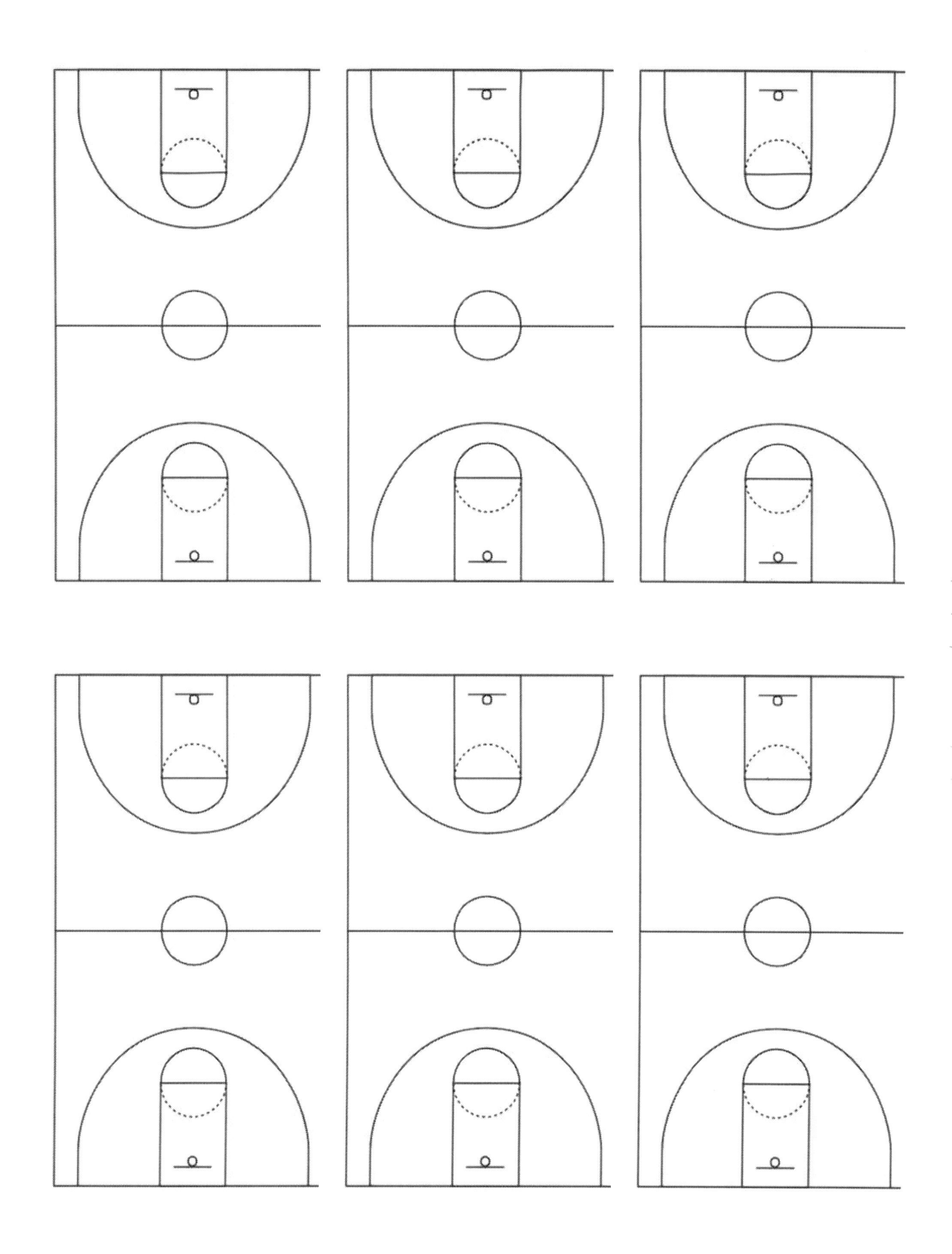

Court Diagrams & Notes | 223

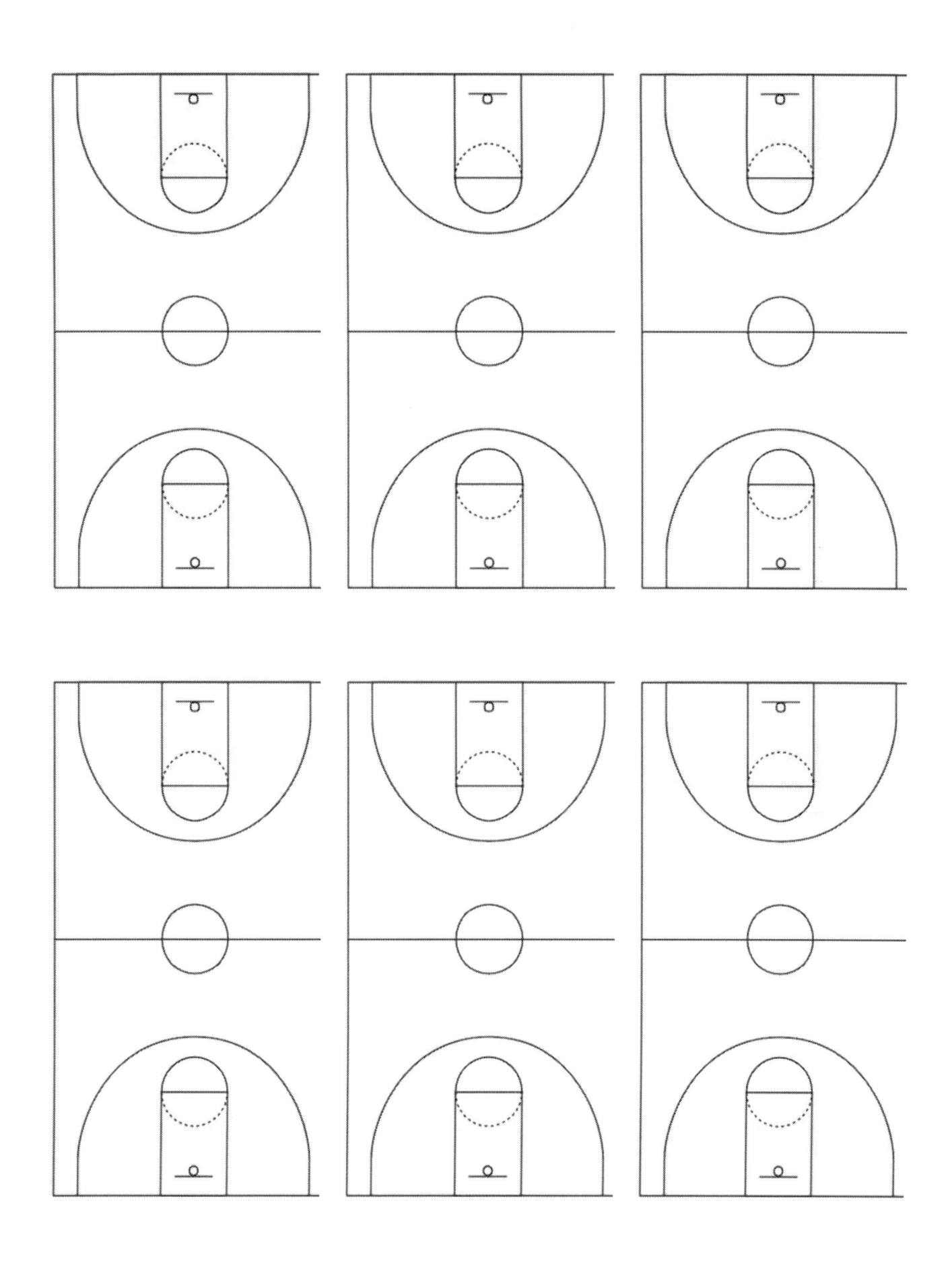

Court Diagrams & Notes | 225

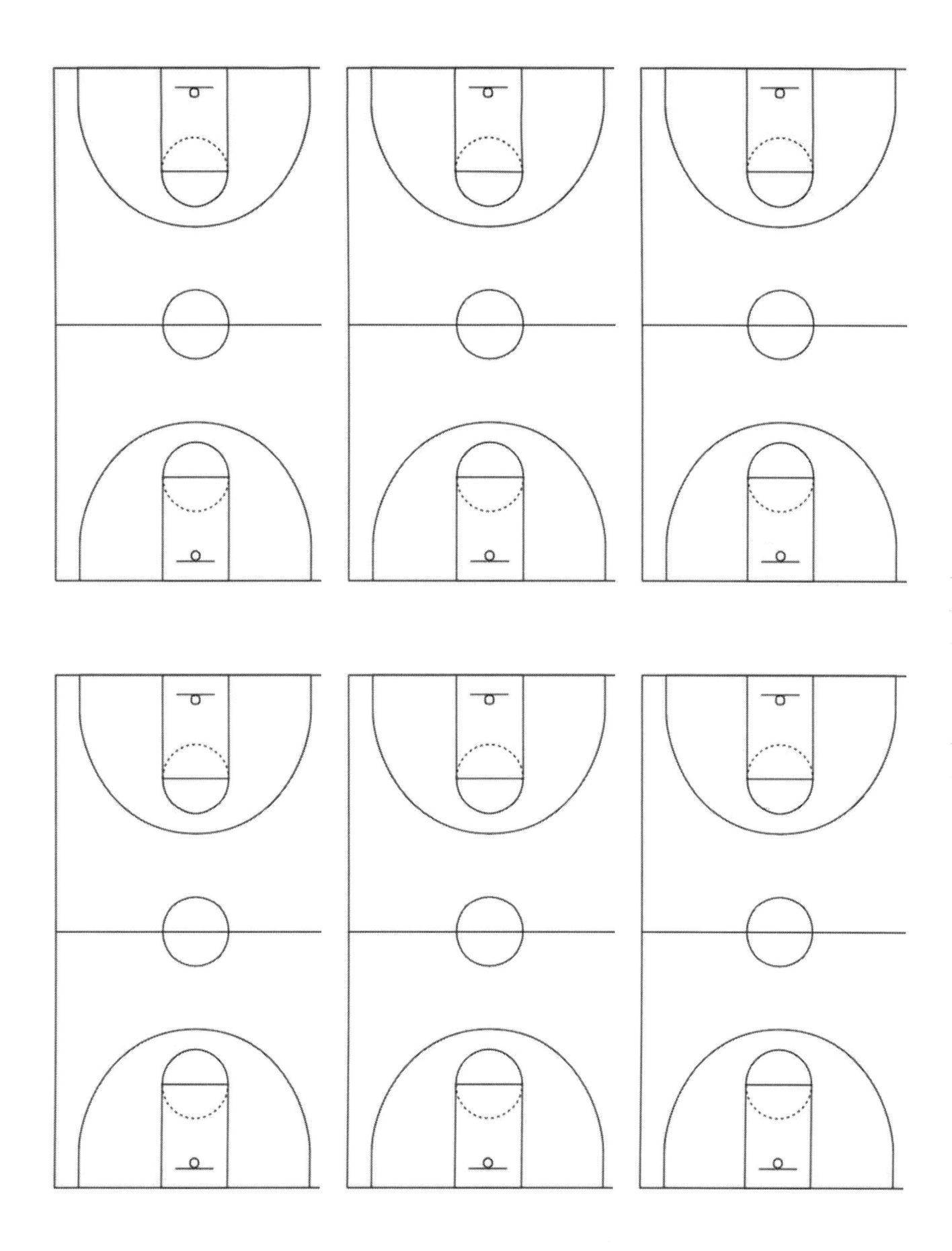

Court Diagrams & Notes | 227

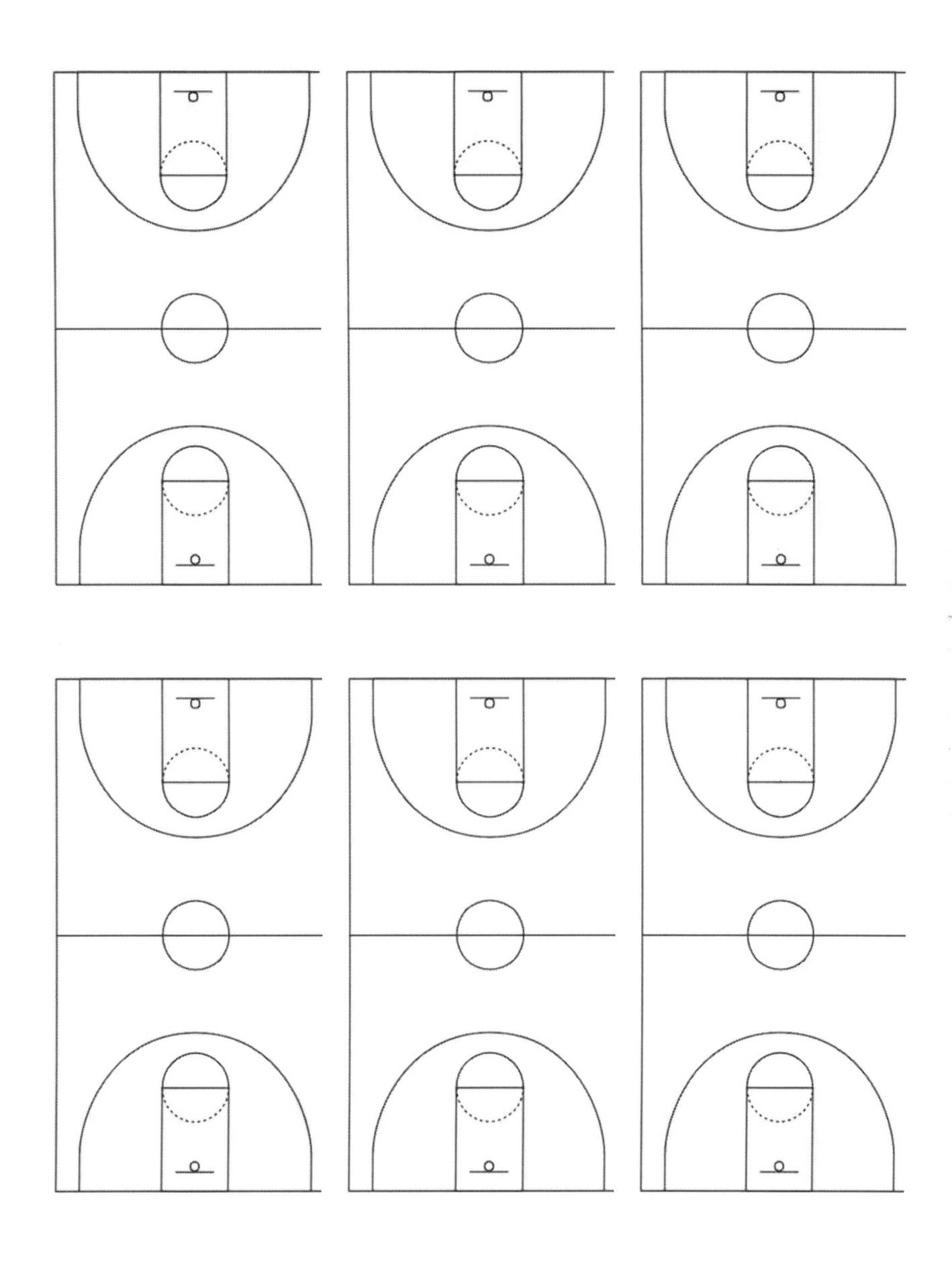

Court Diagrams & Notes | 229

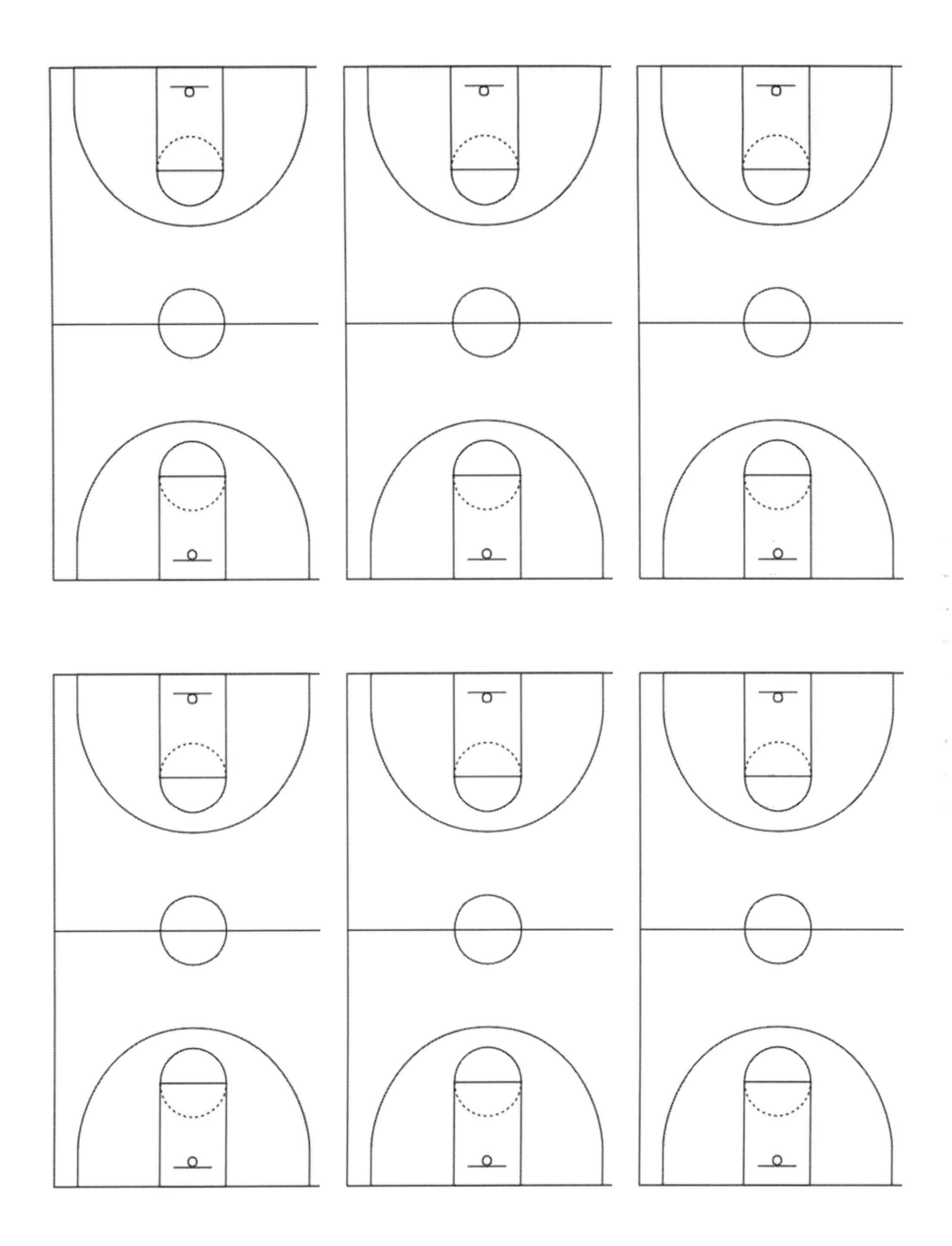

Court Diagrams & Notes | 231

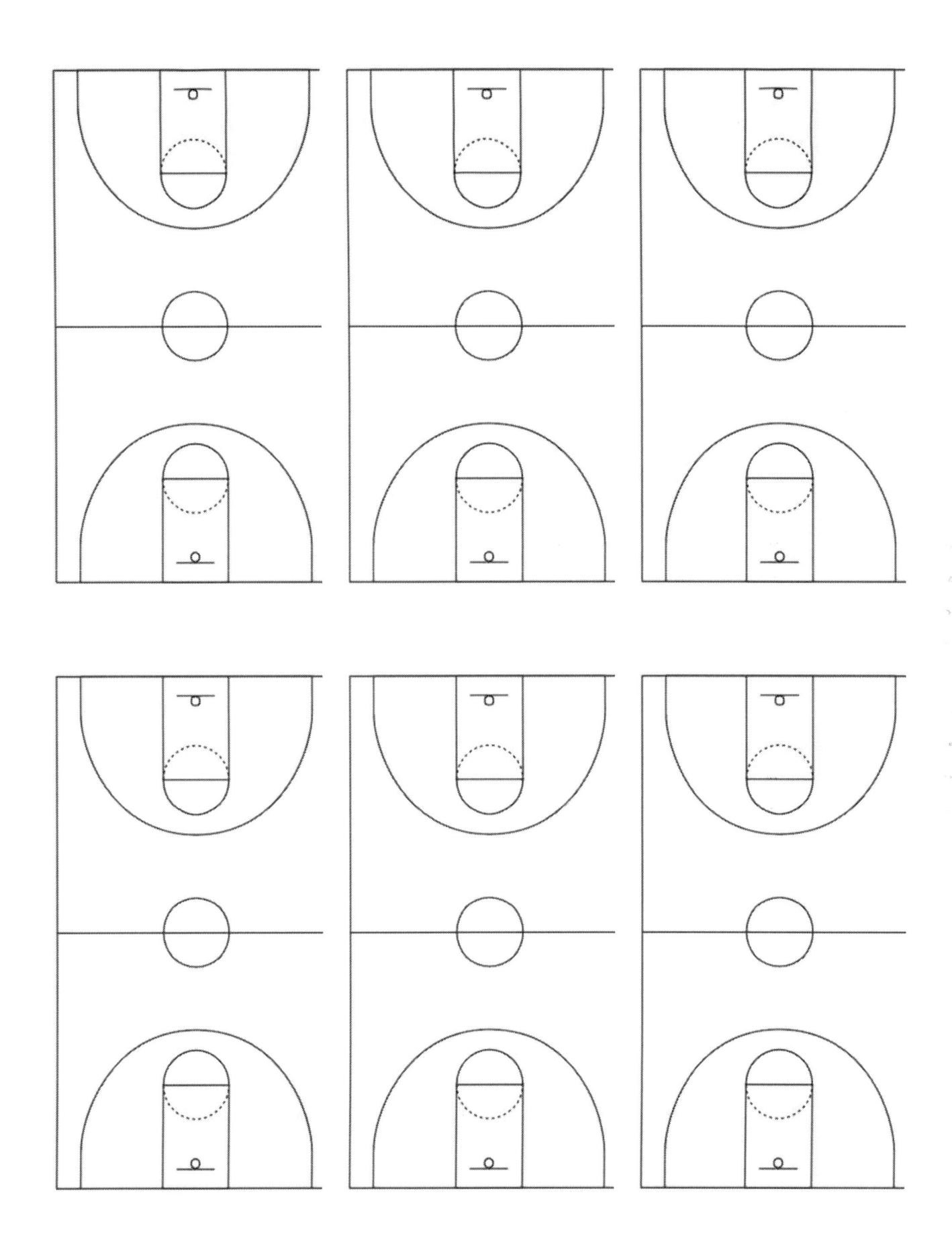

Court Diagrams & Notes | 233

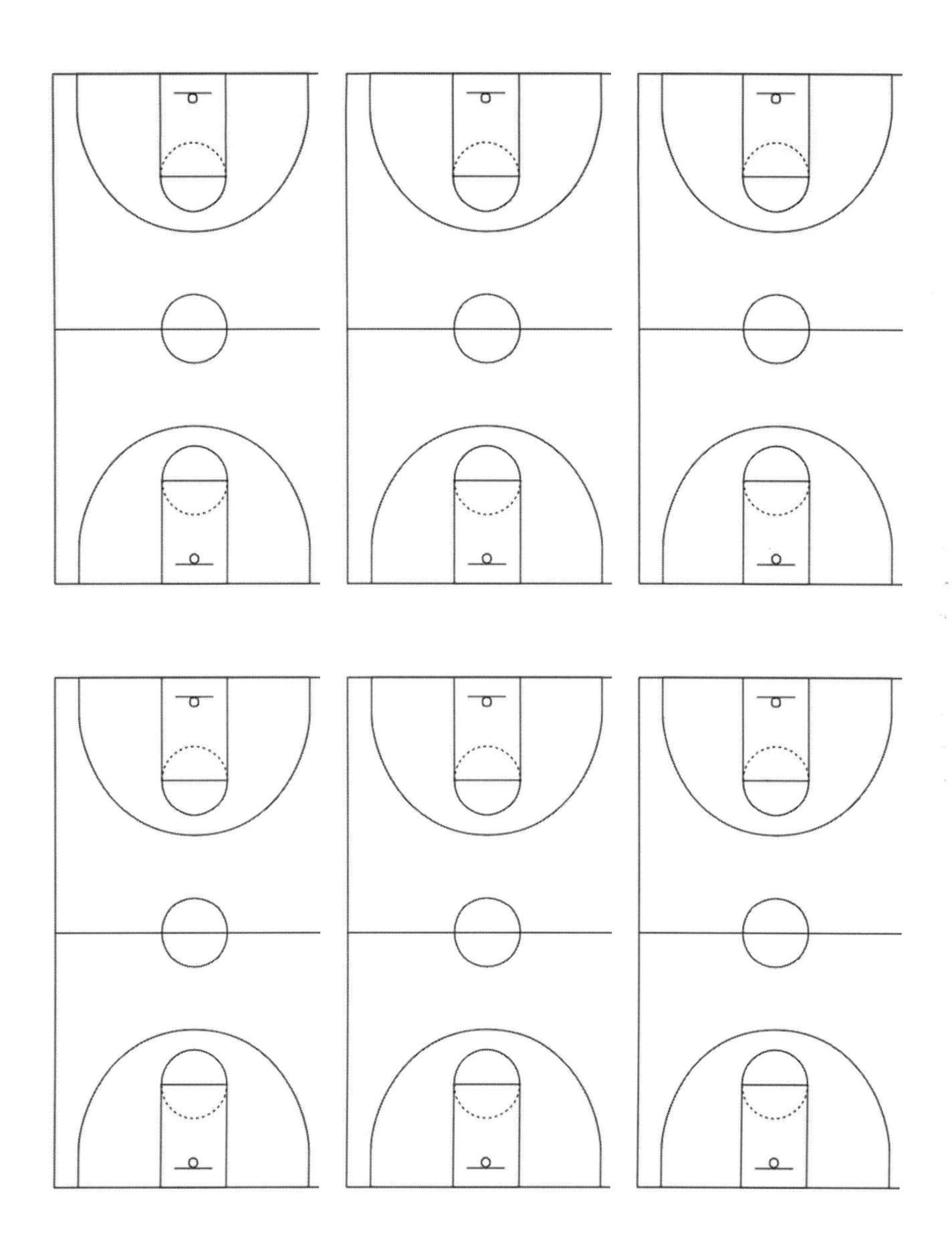

Court Diagrams & Notes | 235

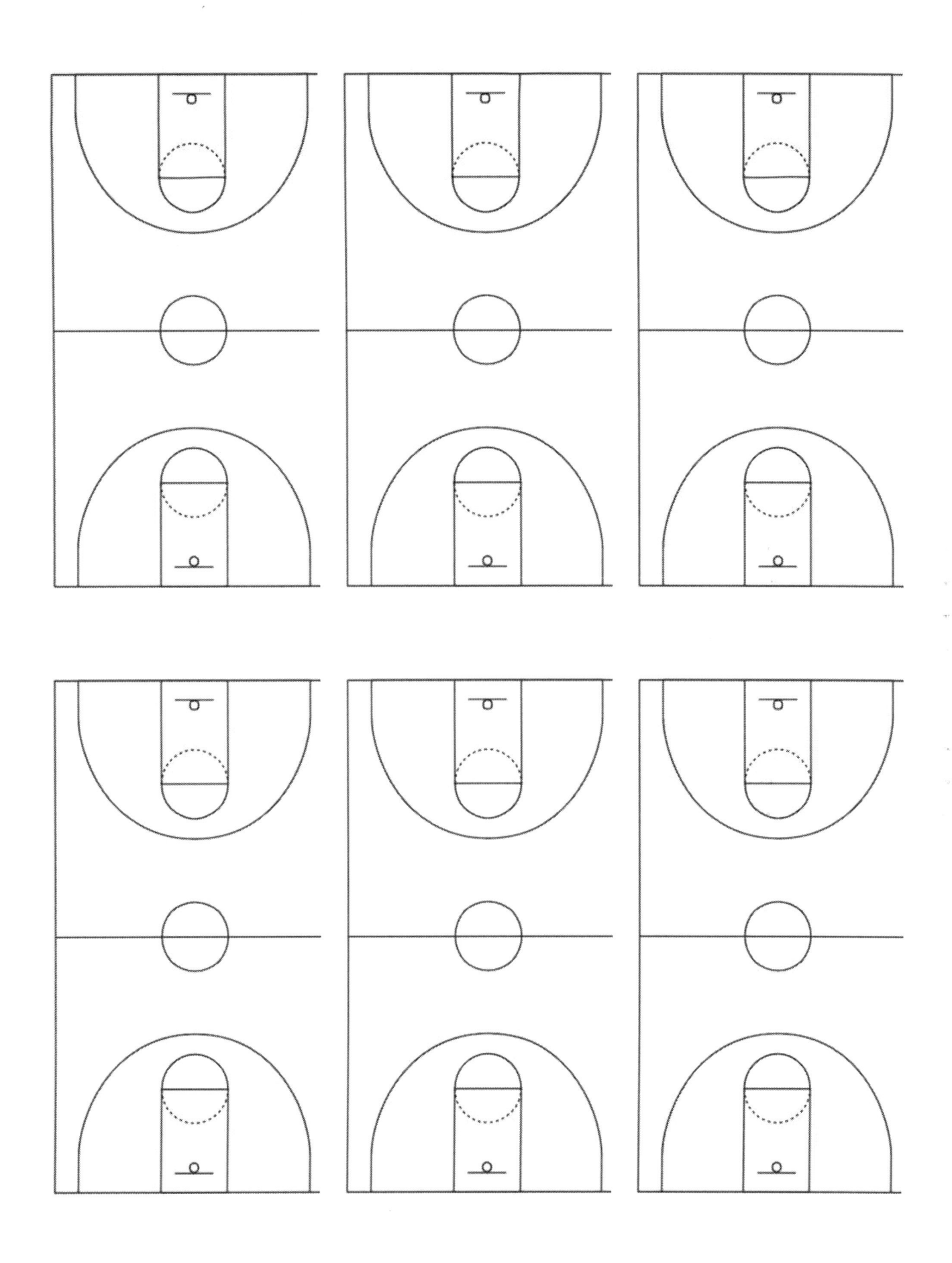

Court Diagrams & Notes | 237

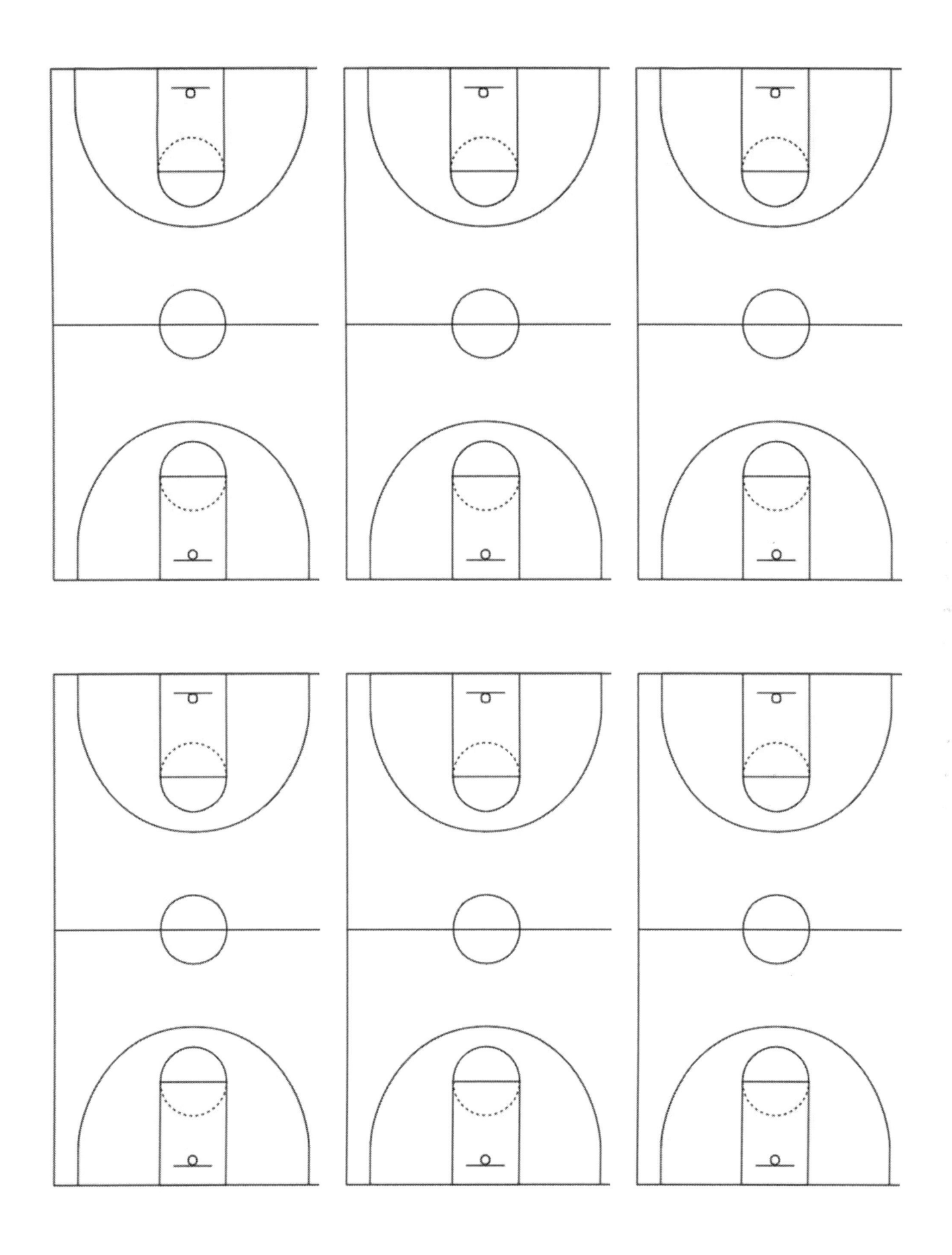

Court Diagrams & Notes | 239

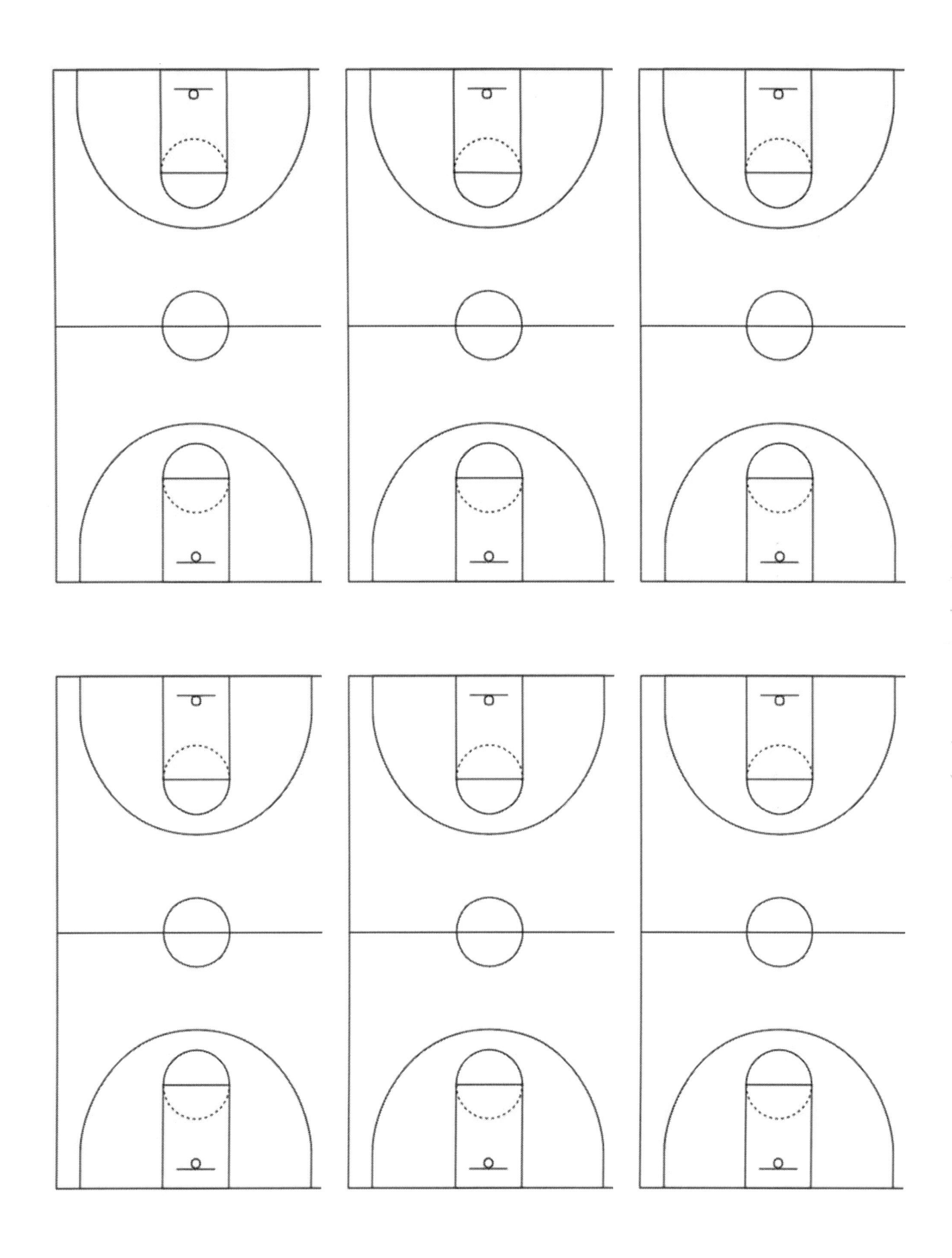

Court Diagrams & Notes | 241

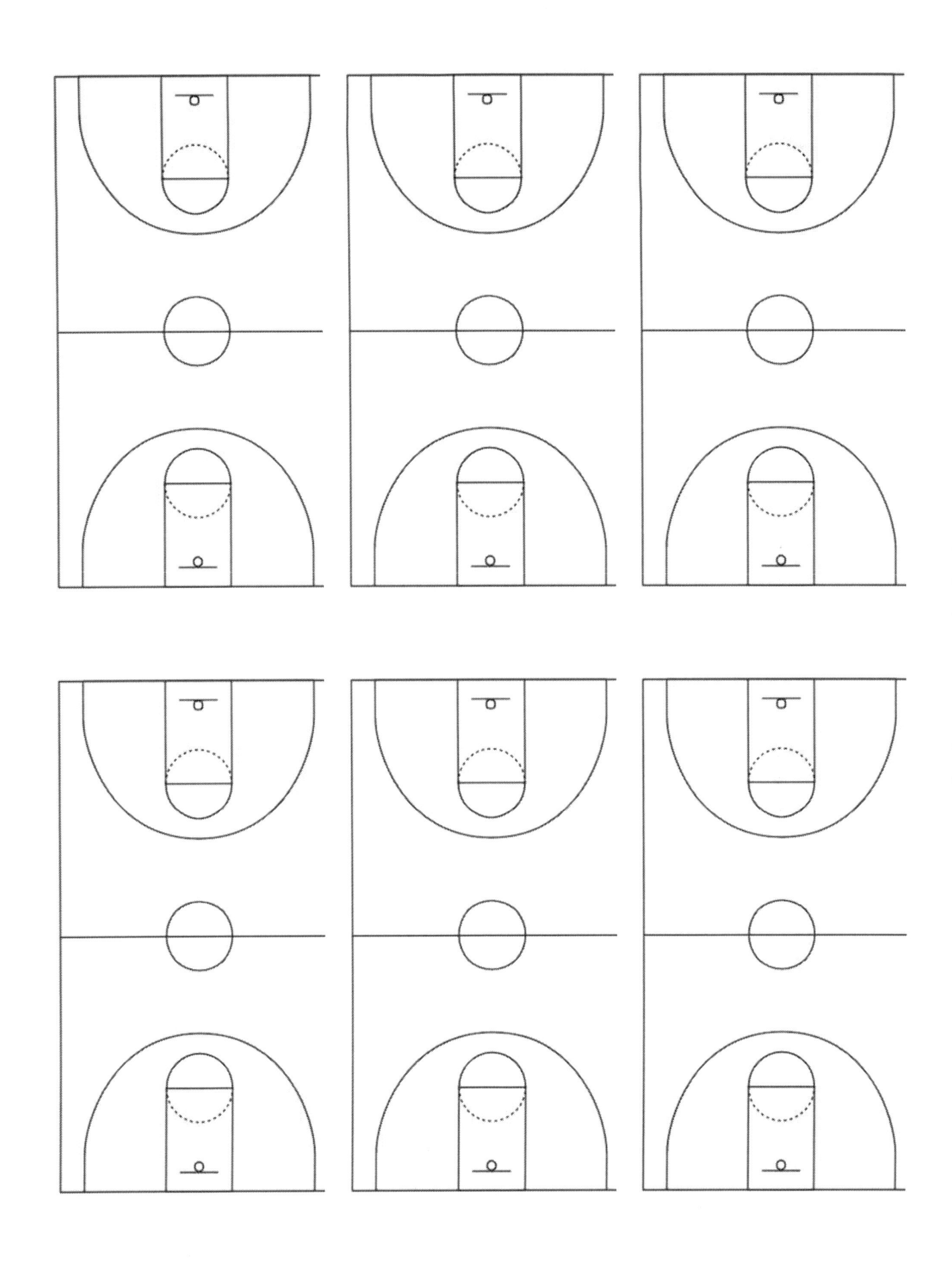

Made in the USA
Las Vegas, NV
31 August 2021